BIG PHIL
CAMPION'S
REAL WORLD
SAS
SURVIVAL
GUIDE

BIG PHIL CAMPION'S
REAL WORLD
SAS
SURVIVAL
GUIDE

ANY THREAT • ANY SITUATION • SORTED!

Phil Campion
Julie Davies

Quercus

CONTENTS

Introduction 8

1 KING OF YOUR CASTLE 12

▸ Burglars and unwanted visitors: what to do and what not to do 14
▸ Forensic-style tactics: what to do if you suspect that you've been burgled 20
▸ Security: locks, alarms, lights and cameras 22
▸ The garden and yard: how to keep thieves out 25
▸ Fire in the home: how to survive a disaster 27

2 CUTTING ABOUT 30

▸ On foot: how to handle gangs, muggings and aggressive dogs 32
▸ By car: how to avoid theft, carjacking and road rage 39
▸ By motorbike or bicycle: how to gear up and stay safe 45

▸ Public transport: how to stay safe on buses, tubes and trains 47
▸ Hitchhiking: travelling safely for free 48
▸ Urban chaos: what to do if you're caught up in a robbery, shooting or riot 51

3 THE SOCIAL SCENE 56

▸ Drink and drugs: drunks, overdoses and how to stay out of trouble 58
▸ Drink spiking: avoidance tactics 63
▸ Date rape: precautions and escaping from dodgy situations 65
▸ Spotting trouble: reading nightspots like an SAS trooper and how to stay safe 68
▸ Kebab shop trouble: avoiding flashpoints and getting home in one piece 71

▸ Eating is cheating: how to drink right through the night and survive 72

▸ Keeping a lookout: the buddy system and shark watch for nights out 73

4 THE CYBER SCENE 76

▸ Social networks: the promises, pitfalls and dangers 78

▸ Hooking up: online friends and relationships – how to do it safely 80

▸ Internet security: safeguarding your identity online 84

▸ Shopping, selling and banking online: how to avoid the fraudsters 89

▸ Internet nasties: cyberbullies and trolls – what to do 93

▸ Internet scams: what to look for and how to deal with them 96

5 NATURAL DISASTERS 98

▸ Avalanches: surviving a snow slide and essential equipment 100

▸ Hurricanes and tornadoes: recognizing and surviving storms and twisters 105

▸ Landslides: what to do when the earth moves like water 109

▸ Earthquakes: how to stay alive when the earth starts to shake 110

▸ Tsunamis: beating the killer waves 114

▸ Volcanoes: what to do when one erupts 116

▸ Floods: staying afloat in your home and on the roads 118

▸ The big freeze and the scorching heat: surviving temperature extremes 120

▸ Wild animal attack: what to do when face-to-face with tooth and claw 127

6 MAN-MADE DISASTERS 130

▸ Car crash: drivers, passengers and pedestrians – how to stay alive 132

▸ Sinking ship: when something's wrong – preparation and escape 140

▸ Air disaster: enhancing your chances of survival 143

▶ Train crash: preparation and survival 150
▶ Buildings and bridges: how to stay alive if they collapse 152
▶ Nuclear power station leak: what to do if you're hit by radiation 155

7 AWAY FROM HOME 158

▶ Prevention not cure: extra procedures to adhere to while abroad 160
▶ Scams and street robberies: prevention tactics 165
▶ Getting around abroad: how to avoid road accidents and dodgy journeys 168
▶ Drugs: how to avoid becoming an unwitting drug mule 171
▶ Kidnap: how to avoid being snatched and what to do if you're abducted 174
▶ Murder: how to holiday safely in dangerous destinations 177
▶ Piracy: precautions and what to do if you're attacked 180
▶ War zone: caught up in conflict and crossfire, the dos and don'ts 181

8 SURVIVING GWOT 188

▶ Terrorist attacks: staying alert and recognizing suspicious activity 190
▶ Bombing and suicide operations: spotting the bad guys and aiding your survival 192
▶ Dirty bombs: signs to look out for and action you can take 196
▶ Death in the air: what to do in the event of a chemical or biological attack 198
▶ Hijacked: tactics for an aeroplane hi-jacking 200
▶ Siege: hostage situations, escape and evasion, and special forces rescue 206
▶ Special-Forces rescue: what to do when the men in black come to bust you out 212

9 SELF-DEFENCE, SAS STYLE 214

▶ Pull your punches: how to avoid a fight and talk your way out of trouble 216

▸ On the defensive: getting out of trouble, quick and easy 219
▸ Striking back: when there's no way out 226
▸ Getting the f*** out: escape and evasion with the bad guys on your heels 232
▸ Extreme self-defence: improvised weapons 234

10 THE BARE ESSENTIALS 238

▸ How to save a life: symptoms and treatment for life and death conditions 240
▸ Medical emergencies: practical solutions, any time, any place 247
▸ Improvisation: using everyday household items to fix your body 254

11 BIG PHIL'S LOCKER 256

▸ The emergency survival kit: what to include in a grab-and-run situation at home 258
▸ The car survival kit: what to take in case you get stranded on the road 261
▸ The travel survival kit: the essentials in case things go wrong 264
▸ Survival choices: essential kit and improvisations 267

12 OLD SKILLS REVISITED 276

▸ Shelter and fire: the essentials for survival 278
▸ Water collection: means and methods 284
▸ Food sourcing: the art of scavenging and survival 286
▸ Navigation: the bare essentials 290
▸ Signalling and search- and-rescue: how to alert others to your whereabouts 293

Appendix 296
Index 298

INTRODUCTION

Today's world is a tough, mean place where learning to build elaborate fish traps or being able to identify a hundred different types of fungi won't help you survive the minefield of modern life, with all its dangers. You don't need to be in Timbuktu for some aggro: today's challenges linger on our own doorstep where anyone unlucky enough to be in the wrong place at the wrong time can find themselves facing street crime, natural disasters, travel nightmares or terror attacks. Even though you may be somewhere considered the safest place on the planet, it can go off like Chinese New Year at a moment's notice.

This modern world calls for a new type of survival: one that blends traditional self-sufficiency with the skills born out of our twenty-four seven interconnected lifestyles. Smartphones, Facebook and Twitter allow us to stay connected anyplace, anytime, sharing knowledge with a vast community across the world. Combine this with the skills of old, and a new set of tools has been unleashed, to aid our survival in times of trouble.

Over the years, since starting life as a streetwise little shit in kids' homes, I've served as an elite soldier in the SAS and worked as a private military operator. In that time, I've travelled the entire planet to some of the world's most dangerous places, learning to think on my feet and adapt to whatever circumstances come my way. When you're faced with a madman and a gun, or an aeroplane that's about to crash, your ability to use what's around you as a weapon or a defence can often mean the difference between life and death for you and your loved ones.

Survival in the twenty-first century is all about using your head, adapting to the situation at hand, utilizing everything that's available around you – including the latest technology – and, occasionally, throwing in the odd left-field idea. It's about staying one step ahead of the rest and always being prepared for the unexpected. And, it's about knowing what to do when it turns noisy – when you're in deep trouble and your back is up against the wall. This is the time when you lead, follow or get out of the way. In essence, this book is about learning and applying those rules for living.

Over twelve chapters, I address the kind of everyday problems we could all face at home, work or on holiday. Offering up some simple but effective solutions, it's aimed at helping us protect all that we cherish most. The average survival manuals are great if you want to hike through the Yellowstone National Park or spend a week in the jungles of Brazil. But learning to identify which plant may save your life if you happen to be stranded miles from civilization is hardly practical or useful to most people's lives.

For the modern-day man or woman trying to negotiate their way through life, either abroad or nearer home, what's needed is a set of skills based in the real world that you and I inhabit, where threats such as muggings, burglaries, snow storms and holiday disasters are all too familiar. These are the kinds of incidents that we think will never happen to us – until they do. How many people have found themselves wishing they knew what to do when their child is choking on a peanut, or regretting not taking the time to learn a little self-defence when they're cornered on a deserted street? Rarely do you hear what precautions you should take or what preparations you should make, and yet survival relies on these measures. As I was taught in the army: 'proper planning and preparation prevents piss-poor performance', and it's this strategy that can help you stay alive.

I hope you have fun with this book, and I hope that it will stir within you the primal instinct for survival. At the very least, it should show you how to look at the world with fresh eyes, and equip you with the skills needed to defend yourself in any circumstance. By combining the basic skills of old with today's modern innovations, I want to share with you a very new type of survival.

Phil Campion

EX D SQUADRON 22 SAS, JUNE 2014

1 KING OF YOUR CASTLE

THE ENGLISHMAN'S HOME IS HIS CASTLE, AND ANY INTRUSION IS AS WELCOME AS A FART IN A PHONE BOX. HERE'S HOW TO DEFEND WHAT IS YOURS.

YOUR HOME AND HOW TO MAKE IT SAFER

Burglars and unwanted visitors: what to do and what not to do

Forensic-style tactics: what to do if you suspect that you've been burgled

Security: locks, alarms, lights and cameras

The garden and yard: how to keep thieves out

Fire in the home: how to survive disaster

YOU'RE FAST ASLEEP and enjoying the best dream in ages when suddenly you find yourself awakened with a jolt. It's the dead of night, but you're sure you just heard a noise. Your wife/husband is next to you and as per normal she/he's snoring. You're about to reach over and shake them when you hear the noise again and this time you recognize the creak of the stairs. You glance at the crack beneath the door – you can't see any shadows lurking outside, but the creaking is getting louder and nearer to your bedroom door. You've got an intruder – possibly a burglar – in your home. Do you reach for your mobile phone and call 999? Go out and tackle them man to man or confront them with a weapon of sorts? You'd like to think you'll be as cool as a penguin's pecker, but you're actually shaking like a dog taking a dump. Now, what do you do?

BIG PHIL'S ADVICE: Never put yourself in harm's way. Create a barrier between you and the intruder: lock your bedroom door or place a chair under the handle before raising the alarm. Alternatively, feign sleep. Only if the intruder is about to make physical contact should you go on the attack.

Every 40 seconds someone's home is burgled in Britain. It's one of those crimes that can leave you feeling angry, violated and frightened. Every one of us has the right to feel safe in our homes, protected from the world of intruders and thieves, but it's down to us to ensure that our properties are up to the job of keeping undesirables out and our loved ones safe indoors.

Technology has brought us a huge array of security gadgets designed to deter even the most determined of burglars, but the real key to managing and averting this sort of crisis is to utilize common sense precautions.

In this section, I'd like to show you how some simple safety measures can help you navigate your way around any number of emergencies and disasters. Follow my tips and you can make your home safer than Superman's pants.

BURGLARS AND UNWANTED VISITORS: WHAT TO DO AND WHAT NOT TO DO

Arriving back to a ransacked home is an experience we all dread. Wondering whether your prized possessions – often those with more sentiment than value – are gone forever is a stress we can all do without, not to mention the mess left behind. I have witnessed some proper hovels in my time, but nothing compares to a burglar's looting.

I was burgled once just before Christmas. Although I wasn't there at the time, I could tell from the moment I put my key in the door that something was wrong – I couldn't unlock the door. The burglars had broken in through the back and had dead-locked the front door in case they were rumbled.

Real burglars are opportunists who'll look for an easy way in. Forget the artful cat burglars of the movies or the geezer with a striped top, mask and a bag labelled SWAG – modern burglars are

BURGLAR PET HATES

- ▶ **A pebble or gravel driveway** or gravel around the back doors – no chance of a silent approach.
- ▶ **Dogs,** especially visible ones.
- ▶ **Anti-climbing paint** on drainpipes, walls and balconies.
- ▶ **CCTV cameras,** dummy or real.
- ▶ **Motion-sensor** lighting.

WHEN A BURGLAR STRIKES:

32%	30%	23%	20%	10%
of burglaries take place in the evening	over the weekend	at night	in the afternoon	in the morning

only interested in a trouble-free break-in. It's your job to make it as hard as possible for any unwanted intruder to gain access. Ensure your property is the one that the 'scrap metal guy' doesn't return to – this time to rob you.

Burglars will invariably recce a potential target, looking for telltale signs that the owners are away or that there's something valuable to steal. Be aware of anyone who visits your house that you don't know and only let them see what you want to and no more. Unfortunately, anyone can be a suspect: bin men, postmen, paper boys, delivery men, workmen (and their female counterparts), canvassers, fast-food couriers, even your children's friends. This was how my house got burgled – my son told his mates we were going away.

Post or junk mail sticking out of letter boxes, even a milk bottle left outside for more than a day or two is a dead giveaway of your absence. Keep valuable possessions hidden from the outside world. Showing off your brand-new sixty-inch widescreen television and being flasher than a rat with a gold tooth to the neighbours might boost your ego, but you may as well stick up a sign to every thief in town saying 'please rob me'. In fact, leave the door open; it will save paying for a window.

Graffiti or a strange symbol in the street outside your house may not be the work of vandals, but part of a burglar's code to tip off other criminals that your house has something worth stealing. An 'X' means that your home is a good target and a sign to you to move any temptations out of view.

Curtain twitching SAS style

Having a good nosey can help you stay one step ahead of burlgars and bored teenagers intent on vandalism. Just remember: it's good form to be observant; poor form to be discovered. Here are some simple precautions to avoid any unpleasant reprisals.

Choose the most unlikely window to engage in your spy fest. I would sooner use the cat flap than be seen. It may reduce your field of view, but it will lessen your chance of compromise.

Never profile yourself. Make sure the the lights are off and always view some distance back from the curtain. Don't wear bright coloured clothes: aim to blend into your surroundings.

Net curtains offer the perfect cover. Your view may be slightly diminished, but your prescence will be obscured.

Keep noise and movement to a minimum. Talking or dashing from room to room will act as a red alert to any burglar.

The rogue trader and distraction burglar

Crafty and well practised, these individuals are masters of manipulation and will use every trick in the book to worm their way into your house. If you can, before opening any door, check who it is and look for a recognizable vehicle. Stay alert and don't fall for any of their stage-managed performances. They may say they're from your gas or electricity company, pose as a market researcher or a police officer. Some will feign illness and ask for a glass of water, others might even claim that there's an emergency and that they must have access to your property to protect you from harm. Remember: this is all part of their act. Here's how you can spot when someone's trying to pull a fast one, and send them packing.

Keep your door on the chain, or if you don't have one, wedge your foot up against the corner of the door when you open it – this will buy you valuable time if they try and force their way in. If you have a

IF SOMEONE KNOCKS AT YOUR DOOR, ALWAYS BE ON YOUR GUARD

NO MATTER WHO they say they are, keep to the simple rule: trust no f***er (TNF). Don't feel pressured to open the door, and never let someone in your home until you've established exactly who they are and that they're legitimate.

window that overlooks the doorway, have a discreet butcher's before you go to answer the door, and if you're not happy simply ignore them.

Stand firm and always ask to see some form of identity. Check it over carefully and, if you're still doubtful, tell them to wait outside until you check their credentials. Always call the organization yourself directly and don't accept any mobiles or numbers that they try to give you. If you're not happy, call your local police non-emergency number and provide a description of the caller and their vehicle.

Some burglars will brazenly knock on doors to see if anyone is at home and, when answered, use the ruse that they're in the area cleaning gutters. They'll look for the tiniest sign of vulnerability, from a window left ajar to a door with only a single cylinder lock. They'll also be trying to see where you keep your keys. Don't give thieves the chance: keep your valuables out of sight and out of reach.

No matter what emergency they're claiming, check it out. You can confirm a real crisis by having a look from your windows, with the door shut. Offer to call the emergency services and assess their reaction. Just ensure the 999 services know that you are making this call on behalf of someone who has come to your door for help, otherwise, if it's a fake emergency, you'll be in the shit. If you do let someone in, never leave them on their own anywhere other than the doorstep, and always do a 360-degree search of your property afterwards to ensure nothing has been stolen.

How to protect yourself and your loved ones

If you're woken by a strange, unrecognizable noise at 2 a.m., it can only mean one of two things: your partner has chronic indigestion or you have an intruder in your house. The question is: what do you do? Do you investigate and potentially put yourself in harm's way? Or do you wait for the intruder to reach you and pretend you're asleep?

Confronting a burglar is not something to be taken lightly. Burglars are known to carry weapons and you don't want to end up the victim. The last thing a burglar wants is a confrontation with the owner, but force on him and the consequences could be dire. Your immediate aim should be to form a barrier between you and him, but try to get all your family into one room first. Shut your bedroom door and lock it, place a chair back underneath the handle or push some heavy furniture against the door. Call the police and then attract attention outside by making as much noise as possible. Open your window and, if necessary, throw something through it so that you can attempt to alert a passer-by.

If you awaken to find an intruder inside your bedroom, feign sleep. Remember: at night, you'll be the sleepy one and not them. Most professional burglars just want to grab what they can and get out, but the less experienced can be nervous and trigger-happy.

If you find an intruder standing over you, act immediately. You need to raise the alarm as soon as possible. Throw any objects handy – alarm clocks, a drinking glass, books, even your laptop – and aim them at the intruder's face and head.

TO ATTRACT HELP: Make more noise than a cat with its tail stuck in a crocodile's mouth.

GET OUT OF TROUBLE – BIG PHIL'S TIPS

IN BRITAIN, the law currently states that it is acceptable to use reasonable force to protect yourself or others in order to prevent a crime. However, you must only do what you believe is necessary in the heat of the moment and not use force which a reasonable person would consider excessive. My personal feelings on this are that I would sooner be judged by twelve than carried by six. If an intruder should attack me and I feel my life is threatened, I will use whatever I can lay my hands on to defend myself, and with luck remain alive to explain my case. One of the most effective methods I use is to sleep with a powerful torch near my bed. One blast of light from this will temporarily blind an intruder, giving me time to strike out at them and also move away more easily.

Temporarily blind the intruder with a powerful torch . . .

. . .this will buy you time to make your next move.

FORENSIC-STYLE TACTICS: WHAT TO DO IF YOU SUSPECT THAT YOU'VE BEEN BURGLED

Nothing equips you better for the unexpected than to be prepared. An intruder in your home can be a frightening experience that can turn nasty at any point, so it's down to you to do all you can to defend your own safety and that of your loved ones. Here's how to use precaution as your armour and give yourself a hassle-free time dealing with the insurance company.

How to effect the 'drive-past'

If you're coming home one night and see movement in your house or a light that you know you never switched on, it's possible that you may have an intruder. As a safeguard, consider a drive-by recce.

The rules: If you SUSPECT that there is someone in your house, do not enter. CONFIRM the situation from a safe distance and RETREAT to your car, or, if you're on foot, to a place of safety such as a neighbour's house or a nearby shop. Raise the ALARM and call the POLICE. Your first thought should be for your safety and that of your family. A burglar that is surprised may lash out and the consequences could be fatal.

REMEMBER: SCRAP Suspect, Confirm, Retreat, Alarm, Police

How to know if you've had an invader in your home

Sometimes it pays to act like a crime scene investigator, especially when you return home and you know something just isn't right. Knowing the exact position of all your valuables around the home is vital: it will tip you off if you've been burgled and it's also important for your insurer in the event of a claim.

Always take photos of your rooms and your possessions as a useful record of what you own. The average break-in will be revealed by an open window, a broken pane or a smashed lock, but not all burglars are so obvious. On closer examination, a lock may reveal tiny scratch marks indicating that it has been picked. You may even find lock-picking tools discarded nearby.

Treat your house as a crime scene if you suspect you've been burgled. If the Old Bill stands any chance of catching someone for the crime, you must preserve as much evidence as possible. Even a cigarette butt may contain enough DNA to identify someone. Once you are safe, try not to move or touch anything.

Have furniture and other items in your home been rearranged? Some burglars will take smaller items that are less noticeable. Footprints or signs of soil, gravel or grit near entrances could indicate that someone has been in your home.

The most popular items stolen in a burglary include:
- ▶ **Smartphones**
- ▶ **Cash**
- ▶ **Laptops**
- ▶ **Bicycles**
- ▶ **Home entertainment equipment**

When my house was burgled, I realised that something was wrong when I couldn't get my key in the lock – the burglars had broken in at the rear and deadlocked my front door so they wouldn't be caught in the act. Once I knew that I'd been burgled, I started to preserve any evidence, but not before securing my family in case the burglars were still around. The last thing you want is to go bowling in and end up getting a beating from a burglar or junkie.

SECURITY: LOCKS, ALARMS, LIGHTS AND CAMERAS

Before you start to install security devices, take a walk through and around your house and do a 360-degree assessment of your weaknesses. Imagine you're a burglar; what would you look for?

What can you see from outside, through the windows? Are there tempting goodies on display? Around thirty-eight per cent of us are guilty of this – showing off what we have – and then we wonder why we get burgled.

Don't hide keys under doormats or inside flower pots, leave a spare set with a trusted neighbour or relative or buy a push-button operated key safe. Those that are police approved built like a tanks, so a big deterrent.

Is there anything left lying around that a burglar could climb on to, so giving them access to an open upstairs window? Always keep all windows closed and doors locked when you're out. About twenty-nine per cent of us regularly leave our homes unsecured.

Remember also to cancel newspaper or milk deliveries if you go away: seventy-five per cent of us fail to do so.

DON'T THINK A SMALL WINDOW WILL PUT A BURGLAR OFF

ANY GAP larger than a human head is accessible. Some burglars are so thin they have to run around in the shower to get wet, while some gangs will use kids to go through the smallest of spaces. Keep all windows locked, no matter what the size.

Locks

If you have only a single cylinder lock on your door, a burglar will be in your house quicker than one flap of a hummingbird's wing. Most insurance companies regard anything less than a five-lever mortice lock or an anti-snap cylinder lock as a security risk.

Ensure that you also have a dead lock on your doors, to be opened from the inside only. Consider internal locks on doors – time-consuming to use but massively effective – and ensure all of your windows have locks, and that you use them.

Alarms

Despite the nuisance of being woken up by the neighbour's cat tripping the motion-sensor burglar alarm, these are a deterrent. Modern systems allow you to choose from a vast array of services from a simple alarm to sophisticated maintenance and monitoring contracts, all at a cost of course, but they can bring peace of mind.

Don't be fooled into pretending you have an alarm, though – burglars aren't stupid and know the telltale signs. The same goes for the sign 'Beware of the dog'. Unless you actually have a dog, don't even bother – burglars will simply call your bluff.

Sensor lights

Motion-sensor lights around the outside perimeter of the house are useful. A burglar isn't going to want to announce his arrival under the equivalent lighting of a football stadium, but they can be a nuisance if the local wildlife and pets trigger them on and off all night. The alternative is daylight-sensitive low-energy lighting. It provides a continuous subdued illumination, is cheap to run and ensures your house is always illuminated after dark.

When you're out, use timer switches on lights and even radios or TVs. This is an easy way to give the illusion of your presence and, let's face it, there's nothing like the nightly soap to scare off the burglars.

LIGHT UP ANY DARK CORNERS
WITH MOTION-SENSOR LIGHTING

Ensure that you position the sensors so that all areas where a
burglar could hide are covered - back and front.

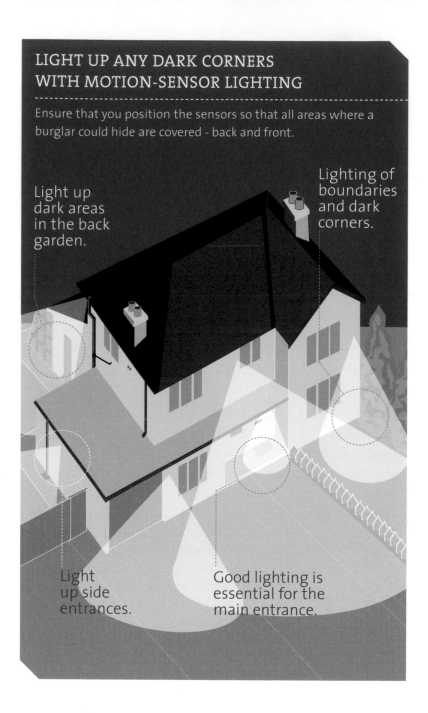

Light up
dark areas
in the back
garden.

Lighting of
boundaries
and dark
corners.

Light
up side
entrances.

Good lighting is
essential for the
main entrance.

Cameras

CCTV that is kept operational is a worthwhile investment, and while it doesn't always deter burglars (some seem to forget that the little red light means they're being filmed!), the footage could help the police identify the thief.

THE GARDEN AND YARD: HOW TO KEEP THIEVES OUT

Most of us want to enjoy some peace and privacy in our garden or yard, but all too often our open spaces become an invitation for unwanted visitors. Don't get caught out – with a little thought, you can make your garden and yard a deterrent to all those with bad intentions.

Bins, collections and deliveries

Bins should be placed outside only on collection day – and not days before – preventing anyone from having a good snoop through your stuff. If you don't want them to be used as a ladder by a burglar, chain them up (away from the house). If you are leaving items for charity or scrap collectors, take them to the gate. As with the bins, you don't want anyone unknown having access to your garden. Try to ensure that any delivery people only have access to where you want them to have access and prevent them from seeing more than they should.

One man's waste is another man's gold. Don't put sensitive information like bank and credit card statements in any bin unless they've been shredded. Burglars are usually well networked and you could find your information being used by identity thieves to commit fraud and worse. The golden rule is to shred any personal documents.

Sixty-five per cent of all UK fraud cases in 2012 involved the use of identity details such as those found on bank statements. Be careful what you throw away in the rubbish.

Garden valuables

Theft from gardens is a growing problem. Expensive garden furniture, children's toys and even plants and garden ornaments are all potential rich pickings for a passing burglar. Insurance companies will confirm that the minute the clocks go forward and the days get longer, claims on garden theft soar. Most crooks would have the fillings out of their dead relatives if they got the chance, so don't ever think anything is safe.

Some of the most popular items on burglars' lists include power tools such as drills, saws and planers, followed by forks, rakes and spades, and finally ladders and electric lawnmowers. That's not to say that they won't remove your barbecue and your patio furniture if you let them – some might even take your garden gnomes! Always identify your property with your name or postcode, either with a UV marker pen or labels, and take photographs – it helps when the

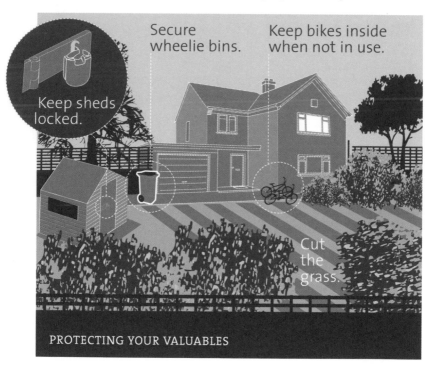

PROTECTING YOUR VALUABLES

insurance company wants proof of what was stolen. Remember: putting your name on items doesn't mean they won't get stolen, it just means that the thief knows who he is stealing from.

An untidy, overgrown garden says you're away. Long grass is useful to a burglar who wants to hide out of sight. If you can't maintain it yourself, it pays to hire someone who can, or do as I do and cut everything back to the bare minimum. Keep all furniture and tools covered, stored away, locked or bolted down, and keep the children's toys and bikes inside when not in use.

Don't promote things like your next holiday abroad. It's all well and good showing off down the local, but you don't know who is listening: loose lips sink ships. You could well be giving someone a heads-up of your impending absence, so do your gobbing off when you get back.

FIRE IN THE HOME: HOW TO SURVIVE A DISASTER

Most of us never give enough thought to what we'd do in an emergency, but I'd strongly advocate that everyone considers the most likely escape routes, should the worst happen. Again, a little forethought can prevent a tragedy.

ADVANCE PREPARATION IN CASE OF FIRE

EXAMINE EACH ROOM in your house and look for two ways out. If the door is one, the second is most likely a window. Look for a route which may allow you to escape on to a neighbour's roof, or keep a collapsible ladder inside for use from an upstairs window. Ensure that all windows are operational and that any security screens can be opened. Practise so that you can do this quickly and make sure all members of your family know how.

Surviving a fire

Time is of the essence in a fire. In thirty seconds a small flame can grow into a major fire. In two minutes the fire can become life threatening. In five minutes, an entire home can be engulfed in flames. Remember: the heat and smoke from a fire can be more dangerous than the flames. Temperatures can rise to 100 degrees at floor level and to 600 degrees at eye level. Poisonous gases can make you disorientated and sleepy, and eventually kill you. If you wake to a fire, your only thought should be of escape: there is NO TIME to grab valuables.

Get out fast, as soon as you hear your smoke alarm – seconds count. Aim for your first exit, testing any door handles to see if they're hot. If they are, use your second exit. If smoke is blocking the door, or coming around the door, use your second way out. Open any door slowly. If heavy smoke or fire is present, shut it quickly. Your first thought should be to avoid the thick smoke and poisonous gases which accompany all fires. Get as low to the ground as possible and crawl under the smoke. It will collect along the ceiling first.

If you can't escape, close all doors and cover gaps and cracks with tape or cloth. Stay at the window to attract attention using light coloured clothing or a torch.

IF SOMEONE HAS LOST CONSCIOUSNESS

Tie their wrists ...

...and pull them out.

If you catch fire, drop to the ground and roll back and forth until the fire is out – never run: the air will simply fuel the fire. Cover your face and hands. If others are on fire, but unable to get to the floor, smother the flames with a blanket or towel.

If someone has lost consciousness and they're too heavy to lift, tie their wrists together with a sheet or a cord, loop your head through their arms and use your body weight to pull them out of there.

When and how to tackle a fire in the home

Successful firefighting relies on the speed of the response and the appropriate action. If you cannot put out a fire within seconds, chances are that it will burn out of control, leaving you with no means of escape.

Two of the best items you can keep in the home are a fire extinguisher and a fire blanket. Choose a fire extinguisher that is appropriate: electrical fires require a very different extinguishing agent to those involving cooking oil. Only use pressurized water for putting out flames on carpets and furniture. Always ensure that any firefighting equipment is easy to access in the area it's most likely to be needed, and that it's kept in good working order.

REMEMBER: Do not put yourself at risk: if in any doubt, always call the fire service first.

The fire blanket: These come contained in a wall-mounted box. Keep in the kitchen and use to extinguish chip-pan fires or to wrap around someone whose clothing has caught fire.

The dry powder fire extinguisher: This is a multi-purpose extinguisher that is effective for most items, including textiles, electrical fires, flammable gas and liquids BUT NOT COOKING OIL.

The wet chemical fire extinguisher: Used for tackling fires involving oil, such as deep-fat fryers. Equipped with a long nozzle, it allows you to coat a layer of foam on top of the burning oil from a distance.

2 CUTTING ABOUT

'LEAD, FOLLOW OR
GET OUT OF THE WAY.'
22 SAS

HOW TO SAFELY NAVIGATE MODERN-DAY STREETS

On foot: how to handle gangs, muggings and aggressive dogs
By car: how to avoid theft, car-jacking and road rage
By motorbike or bicycle: how to gear up and stay safe
Public transport: how to stay safe on buses, tubes and trains
Hitchhiking: travelling safely for free
Urban chaos: what to do if you're caught up in a robbery, shooting or riot

IT'S YOUR GIRLFRIEND'S BIRTHDAY and you've decided to treat her to a romantic evening at the new exclusive French restaurant in town. Following a fine meal and lots of wine, you're both ready for bed. As you head for the local taxi rank 400 yards down the road, you notice a gang of youths on the opposite side of the street smashing bottles and vandalizing a bus stop shelter. In the dim street light you hope they won't see you, but then you hear one of them shout, 'What you lookin' at?' If you're quick, you can sprint to the busy main road and the taxi rank, but if you delay, you'll have no choice but to face the youths and defend your girlfriend. Should you head back to the restaurant and take cover? Make as much noise as possible to attract help? Or should you use whatever you can find as a weapon and take them on?

BIG PHIL'S ADVICE: The number-one rule in any potentially violent encounter is to avoid it at all costs. If you can find a safe escape route, take it. Cross the street or look for a nearby shop – anything to avoid a confrontation. If you are cornered with no way out then you have two choices: defend yourself the best you can, or use whatever items are near at hand as weapons.

In a world that rests for no one, rule number one in the survival game is to keep your wits about you. Turn your attention off for one second and that's the time you'll get mugged, fall off your motorbike or become the target of a street scam.

Everywhere you go there are opportunities for crime: queuing up to use the cash machine, waiting for the bus with your expensive camera slung over your shoulder, or parking your car in the usual quiet side street. You can go about your daily routine without so much as a sniff of trouble, and then one day your attention drops and so does your wallet – straight into the hands of a thief. Always be on your guard and never take anything for granted. Stay alert and stay safe.

ON FOOT: HOW TO HANDLE GANGS, MUGGINGS AND AGGRESSIVE DOGS

Violent gangs

You never know when you might find yourself confronted by a gang – violent or otherwise; it's a situation any one of us could face. Our best defence is to learn to understand violence and interpret the early warning signs.

If you encounter a gang, you need to assess the situation quickly. In the Special Forces we were taught to carry out a reconnaissance: to survey the land and weigh up the risks. I remember a Sergeant Major of mine, Chad Cain RIP. He'd been at an incident involving a minor incendiary device and suddenly decided to calmly walk away. Two minutes later the whole street blew up where he'd just stood.

'F*** me; I didn't see that coming,' I said. With complete composure, he turned around and answered: 'I did.' He had suspected that something was up and didn't hang about to find out what.

AVOID KNOWN HANG OUTS

SELECT ROUTES where you know there are going to be friendly people around and avoid times of day when streets are deserted. If you spot trouble and see an easy exit, take it. Do not hang about to see what happens next. If you can detect intent, you stand a good chance of preventing any threat to your own safety.

First ask yourself: can you safely avoid the gang by turning around and making a swift exit? If you can, do.

Watch out for behaviour from the gang to see if they're checking you out. They may not be interested in you at all, in which case keep your gaze ahead of you. If you do catch their eye, try not to look in a way that signifies contempt; just acknowledge and move on. Your number-one aim is to avoid confrontation at any cost. Gang members desire respect: take that away and you pose a threat.

Walk confidently and avoid looking like a victim. Would-be attackers can judge your vulnerability from the way you move. Your body language must convey strength, not weakness. Keep your head high and your shoulders back and take measured, purposeful strides. Don't nervously look away from someone – direct eye contact demonstrates that you're not easily intimidated.

If it's only verbal name calling, ignore it. Keep walking, and start to look for any potential escape routes.

Not all groups of youths are out to cause trouble, but good intentions don't matter if they don't lead to good actions. When lads and girls are in a group together, the lads will be more likely to show off, so stay aware. If it does appear that they've spotted you as a potential target, the game changes and it's time for you to take some action.

If things turn noisy, the rules change and you need to alert people to your predicament. Use whatever self-defence skills you have; kick

The first sign of trouble is when someone shows intent to harm. This is the point where it's got to be all about self-defence rather than avoidance. Recognize that point and you have time to prepare, including looking around you for any potential weapons that you can use.

cars to set off alarms and look around you to see what you could use as a weapon. The more fierce and aggressive you are, the better: your aim is to defend yourself and get the hell out of there. Wait until you're safe before raising the alarm and making a report to the police. See *Chapter 9: Self-defence, SAS style* (p214).

If you carry a personal alarm, make sure that it delivers a deafening sound. Some people might choose to set off car alarms or break windows to attract attention, but I can deliver more noise than the lot of them. In essence, I don't give a f*** about how much carnage I cause, as long as I live to tell the tale. Standing in front of the judge is better than lying in front of the priest.

Mugging

This is a common crime but it's deeply unpleasant for the victim. The main rules are: keep your valuables hidden from beady eyes and never carry more cash or gadgets on you than you actually need. My uncle Steve has always got a wad of money on him. It means that, rather than losing a few quid to a mugger, he'd end up losing the lot.

Dress down and avoid looking like a tourist. If you dress flash, you're a target. Muggers love tourists who are often naive, loaded with cash and cameras, and distracted. But I often see people who are completely unaware of what's going on around them because they're buried in their £300 smartphone: they're just begging to be robbed.

Stick to well-populated areas and those with street lighting.
Leave the dark back alleys to the cats and rats, and steer clear
of parts of town that are known to be dangerous. Don't wander
around with a map, looking lost: muggers are skilful at sizing up
a person's body language, and anyone who looks vulnerable will
make a nice and easy target.

Stay alert to your surroundings and avoid distractions. A
favourite trick of muggers and street thieves is to ask for the time.
While you look at your watch, they'll have their hand in your pocket
quicker than you can blink. Another trick involves bumping into
you and then, while you're apologizing for being clumsy, your
wallet's doing a runner. Some pickpockets even carry razor blades
and will cut through your pocket or bag without you even realizing.
If you often use your mobile in public areas, beware of the exits at
underground stations in London. Most people desperate for a signal
reach for their phones the minute they surface and – bingo – it gets
snatched. It doesn't need the brains of an archbishop to work out
this is easy money for a thief.

**Always separate your valuables, such as money, credit cards
and ID,** so that you're never carrying them together. That way,
if something does get snatched, you haven't lost everything.

If you can, always carry a 'mugger's wallet' with limited cash
inside that you can hand over instead of your real one.

AVOID ADVERTISING WHAT YOU'RE CARRYING, SUCH AS A LAPTOP OR CAMERA

WHEN I WAS LUGGING A BAG of diamonds all around the
Middle East, I certainly wasn't going to be shouting it from the
rooftops, so I stuffed them inside an old sports bag and no one
was any the wiser.

If the shit hits the fan, you can try attracting attention by screaming 'fire' – out of curiosity, people will always turn to look.

If all else fails, consider your safety the main priority and remember your possessions are replaceable. Rather than face an injury or fatality, it's always better to give up your valuables and protect yourself. But don't just hand them right over – you need to make an escape and this is your opportunity. Throw your wallet or handbag as far away as possible and then do a runner in the opposite direction.

THOSE MOST AT RISK of mugging are men between the ages of 16 and 25 after an evening out at a club or pub.

Walking safely at night

If you can afford it, take a registered taxi home, or else get a lift from someone you know. Travelling on foot is not the safest at night, but, if you have no choice, follow these rules to get home in one piece:

Stay in well-lit areas where there are people and traffic. Keep your wits about you and stay aware of those around you. Avoid making eye contact with anyone who looks suspicious.

If you can, stay near the kerb, facing oncoming traffic to avoid individuals in cars coming up behind you and grabbing your bag.

Walk with purpose. Know where you're going and don't hesitate.

Avoid wearing any clothing or accessories that might draw attention to you. If you've been out for the night, make sure that you've got a coat to cover up any evening dress. For ladies in heels: they might look nice, but they also make you a more accessible target. I'd suggest swapping into flats for an easy escape and keeping the heels handy for an attacker's face.

Keep your mobile phone switched on and in your pocket. Ensure the emergency services are on speed dial. Always let someone, either family or friends, know when you leave somewhere and when you reach your destination (whether that's home or the venue). This is something I do religiously. It saves others worrying and gives you peace of mind that someone is watching your back.

Stray or aggressive dogs

If you're a dog lover it's hard to acknowledge that some dogs can be a danger. National statistics show that out-of-control dogs, and the injuries they cause, have become a serious concern. In a single year, 6,450 dog bites resulted in hospital admissions. Around ten per cent of those required plastic surgery. A confrontation with a snarling dog is not to be taken lightly, especially when children are around. Understanding dog behaviour and knowing what to do in the heat of the moment could help prevent any injury to you or your loved ones.

If a dog displays aggressive behaviour, such as growling, snarling or snapping, stay calm. Try using verbal commands that most domestic dogs are trained to obey, like 'no', 'down', 'sit', 'stay' or 'go home'. Avoid any kind of arm-raising, which could make the dog more aggressive. Keep your hands in your pockets or by your side and protect your fingers by making a fist. Larger dogs may aim for your throat, so protect this area of your body with your arm.

Don't smile – showing your teeth to a dog can make it think you're going to attack.

> ## JUST BECAUSE A DOG BARKS, DOESN'T MEAN IT WILL ATTACK
>
> THIS 'DOMINANT' BEHAVIOUR is normal. However, a dog that has stiffened with its tail held high, and is staring and snarling at you with bared teeth is on the aggressive.

Don't run – you're likely to awaken the 'prey instinct' in the dog
and they will simply hunt you down. If you're jogging and a dog
goes for you, stop and stand still.

Find a solid stick, newspaper, coat or shoe, to use as a barrier
between you and the dog's teeth. Poke it firmly down its throat
until it gags. An umbrella is a great item to keep handy. Open it to
confuse the dog and it will attempt to attack the middle – the most
difficult part to grasp. If there is nothing to hand, use the street
furniture as a barrier: parked cars, bicycles, dustbins, fences or gates,
as long as you get something between you and the hound.

Keep your fists clenched.

Use an object as a barrier between you and the dog.

DEALING WITH AN AGGRESSIVE DOG

If the dog does manage to get hold of you, do not pull away as the dog will only tighten its grip and you'll end up with serious injuries. Your best option is to push in and down to try to get the dog to gag or lose its balance. After any dog bite, you should stop any immediate bleeding and attend your GP or local A&E for a rabies and tetanus jab.

BY CAR: HOW TO AVOID THEFT, CARJACKING AND ROAD RAGE

A car is more than just a convenience: it can offer protection from the elements, minimize the potential risks of journeys on foot or by public transport and also even, in some extreme cases, act as your shield. However, without the right precautions, your car can invite crime and danger into your life in an instant. Here are my tips for a trouble-free life behind the wheel. Also check out *Car crash* in *Chapter 6: Man-made disasters* (p132) for how to avoid being one of the thousands who die every year on our roads.

Protecting your car from theft

The main rule is never to leave anything of value on display. Even a coat or a plastic bag can look inviting to a thief. If you can't remove your valuables, at least hide them from view, preferably in the locked boot of your car.

Be aware of who is about when you park up; a thief will often be lying in wait for a suitable target. If you feel uneasy about someone, move on. Always close all the windows and lock the doors when you leave your car, even if it's only for a brief moment. Thieves need just seconds to make a steal.

Mark any equipment, such as your stereo, with your car registration number, either using an ultraviolet marker pen or a tamper-resistant label. Registering items on an electronic register provides additional security. Secure your wheels with locking wheel nuts.

Vehicle thefts account for sixteen per cent of all crime in England and Wales.

Deterrents: Older cars are at risk of being broken into and hotwired by joy riders looking for an easy spin. If you haven't got an immobilizer, get a wheel lock. Newer cars are computerized and won't operate without a programmed key – one of the reasons car thieves will try and break into your house first and take your car keys. Deter thieves from stealing your vehicle or the valuables inside by having an alarm installed. The attention generated by the noise will often mean that it's just not worth it to a car thief.

How to prevent a carjacking

Carjacking means hijacking your car, often with the threat of violence. A prevalent and growing problem across the world, it is now so rife in South Africa that road signs alert drivers to the dangers. Carjacking is believed to have grown at such a rate as a result of car manufacturers devising new security measures to elude thieves. What's happened is that predatory thieves have simply changed tack and try to secure their desired goods by a more direct method. Follow these basic tips to stay safe.

Keep all of your car doors locked and the windows closed, especially in built-up areas and at traffic lights. Be aware of who is around you and your surroundings at all times and look out for pedestrians who seem to be near to your car.

Always keep some space between you and the vehicle in front. We were always taught in the Special Forces to look for 'TYRES and TARMAC' in front of us, to allow us enough space to manoeuvre if things turned noisy.

Use the middle lane in traffic when waiting at a junction or the traffic lights – it makes it that much harder for a potential carjacker to reach your car.

Be wary of anyone trying to make you pull over, unless it's the police. Carjackers are well known for persuading potential victims that there is something wrong with their car. Drive on and check

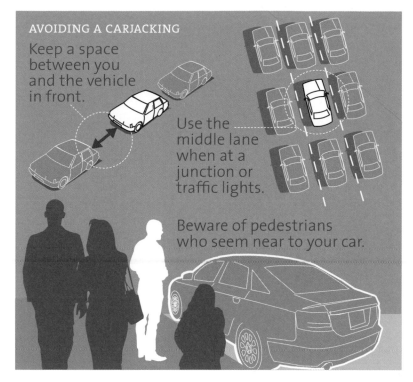

Keep a space between you and the vehicle in front.

Use the middle lane when at a junction or traffic lights.

Beware of pedestrians who seem near to your car.

your car in an area where there are plenty of people around – never get out on a deserted road where you're vulnerable. If you are bumped from the rear, stay in your car to get a visual of the driver. If there is more than one person in the car, lock your doors and wind the window down only a fraction so that you can talk to them but they can't grab you.

Key areas to beware of carjackings

- ▶ **Areas with high crime** rates.
- ▶ **Car parks** that are isolated.
- ▶ **Congested areas** and traffic jams.
- ▶ **Remote rural roads.**
- ▶ **Junctions** where you have to stop and give way.
- ▶ **Residential drives** and gated communities.
- ▶ **Petrol stations.**

YOUR CAR IS A TEMPORARY SAFE HAVEN AND YOUR BEST WEAPON

I HAVE NO QUALMS about jumping a red light or taking an illegal U-turn if it means I get home alive. Equally, I will go for you sooner than surrender if you are attacking me. If you have a phone with a camera installed, film the carjacking incident, or, to be safe, ask someone travelling with you to do it. Always report any violent behaviour to the police.

Staying safe during a carjacking

If someone is trying to take your car, you need to assess the situation quickly. If you're in a public area, you may be able to shout for help, but if you feel that your life is at risk, it's best to comply and let the carjacker have your car. Avoid a hijacking situation at all costs. If necessary, throw the keys far away from you and then run. Better to let them have the car than end up getting injured.

Road rage

According to a national survey, half of all car accidents are caused by aggressive driving. In a list of the top ten most irritating problems drivers face, cutting up or failing to use indicators came top. Road rage can, and does, cause accidents and sometimes fatalities. If a driver turns violent, or you feel your safety is threatened, you need to act and get away from the situation fast. Follow these guidelines and you could save yourself a trip to A&E or worse.

Learn to recognize the signs of road rage and the early warning signs of imminent danger. If you spot an erratic driver – one that's weaving through traffic or driving too fast – they could easily be your typical road-rager. Your best course of action is to stay clear and never engage in confrontation. If someone cuts you up on the road, let it go – anger easily results in accidents. If you mess up on the road, apologize and avoid any provocative responses.

If you meet the driver from hell and it looks like it's about to get personal, remember: your car is your shield. Keep your windows up and your doors locked and keep moving until you know that you are safe. If you think that you are being followed, come off route. If they remain in your rear-view mirror for three sides of a box (for example, left, left and left) then it's likely that they're on your tail. Film the incident on your phone if you can (or ask your passenger) and let the other driver see that they've been captured. Avoid dead ends, junctions and traffic lights, and aim for free moving roads or busy areas where they're less likely to attack, or head for the nearest police station. Whatever happens, do not lead them to your front door.

Top tips to lose a road-rager

- In daylight, fake your brake lights with your headlights.
- Use sudden turns or quick U-turns without indicating to lose a tail.
- If you have to drive through a red light or down a one-way street, be careful.

BIG PHIL'S **REAL LIFE TALES**

I HAD AN INCIDENT LAST YEAR on a busy road on my way to Dorset. I accidentally cut a van up while turning off at a roundabout. I knew straight away that there was going to be trouble: the driver was flashing his lights and he and his mate were working themselves up into a right old lather.

It was heavy traffic and eventually they overtook me, gobbing off and pointing as they travelled past. When they stopped at some traffic lights, I left the gap between me and the car in front as large as possible. As soon as I stopped, they were both out of their van. I knew their intent was to get me, so as soon as they approached the car I drove at the gap I had just made. The lights changed to green, and while they were jumping for their lives – their eyes out on stalks – I made my getaway with a smile on my face.

GET OUT OF TROUBLE – BIG PHIL'S TIPS

If you feel that your life is at risk, you may need to resort to extreme tactics. For emergencies only:

If another driver attempts to get into your car, use every means to escape. Make noise to attract attention and if necessary mount the pavement to get away. If the attacker comes to your door, and you have room, reverse into them aggressively on full lock – use the handbrake to lock the back wheels while accelerating backwards (see illustration). This will block their attempt to get at you, giving you time to get your car out of there driving forwards or in reverse. Familiarize yourself with these manoeuvres before attempting them for real.

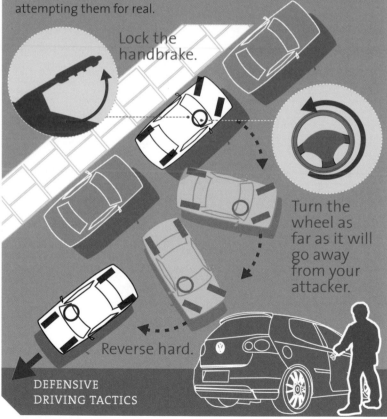

Lock the handbrake.

Turn the wheel as far as it will go away from your attacker.

Reverse hard.

DEFENSIVE
DRIVING TACTICS

BY MOTORBIKE OR BICYCLE: HOW TO GEAR UP AND STAY SAFE

Two wheels may be more nimble than four, but they're also more vulnerable. The old adage 'cyclists should be seen and not hurt' stands true. Whether you're a cyclist or a biker, wearing the proper protective clothing, helmets and high-viz gear may not make a fashion statement, but could save your life.

Bikers: wear the right gear. Choose long, thick trousers that will protect you from the hottest parts of the bike. Keep your top half covered in a long-sleeved jacket which is fitted around the wrists. Thick, full-fingered gloves are a must to give you a good hold and protect against injury, and strong footwear with a good non-slip grip on the sole – but no laces – will ensure that you have full control of the pedals. Finally, always wear a helmet with either a visor or some goggles to ensure good visibility and to protect your eyes against the wind, rain, snow and dust.

Cyclists: wear the right gear. Always wear a helmet. And something high-viz too.

Bikers: know your bike. Learn your bike's power and braking performance. Handled incorrectly, you can easily skid or go over the

BIG PHIL'S **REAL LIFE TALES**

I WAS TRAVELLING to my local petrol station on my bike once and I thought, 'F*** it, I won't bother with the proper gear, I'll just stick my helmet on.' As I parked up, I flicked the centre stand out but it went down a pothole. I jumped back on the bike to save it from falling over and burnt my leg on the pipe. I never dropped the bike, but my leg proper hurt. If only I'd worn my leathers, it would never have happened.

handlebars, so practise in a safe environment until you know how much brake power to use between your front and rear brakes.

Cyclists: know your bike. If you are not in full control of the gears or brakes, or not able to stop suddenly or to ride confidently with one hand, you shouldn't be on a bike, far less a road.

Bikers and cyclists: beware of wet or icy weather. Even the most skilled of you needs to take care in these conditions.

Bikers and cyclists: know how to position yourself in moving traffic. Be aware of the traffic around you and other driver's blind

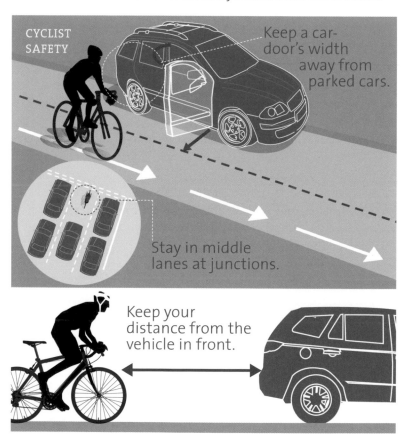

spots. Stay away from the kerb and at least a car-door's width from parked cars to avoid a mashing. When you approach a junction, keep clear of other vehicles and always try and stay in the middle lanes. Keep your distance behind a vehicle; if you cannot see their mirrors, they cannot see you. For cyclists without indicators, use clear hand signals and look behind you frequently, especially when changing lanes and before any manoeuvre.

Bikers: never overtake if you cannot see the road ahead, especially on bends.

Cyclists: never undertake – it's a death trap.

PUBLIC TRANSPORT: HOW TO STAY SAFE ON BUSES, TUBES AND TRAINS

Travelling by bus, tube or train is less risky than walking home, but they can still be potential hot spots for thieves. When waiting for a bus, try and stay in the most brightly lit spot you can, in full view of passers-by. The same goes for tubes and trains – move where there are more people.

A second-class ride is better than a first-class walk.

Don't sit next to someone who you feel might be a potential threat. Stay close to the driver on a bus if you feel safer, or try to sit in a carriage on a train that has plenty of other people around. I like to avoid having people sit behind me, if possible. If I'm with a mate, we'll always try and sit with our backs to one another – it's called all-round defence and you can achieve it without any real effort. Failing that, sit where any cameras can cover you.

Keep valuables out of sight. Hide your mobile phone and avoid revealing anything that can identify who you are or where you live. Thieves are opportunistic and are more likely to attack if you're alone. If someone does harass or assault you, shout to other passengers, the guard or driver, and make as much noise as possible.

If the situation is getting out of hand, I have no qualms in pulling the emergency cord – that's what it's there for – just make sure that you're not going to make the situation worse before you give it a tug. If you're on a tube, try to follow the recommended advice and wait until you're in a station before raising the alarm.

When you get off a bus or train, avoid walking home in the dark. Either have someone collect you from the station or try and walk home with a passenger who travels the same way. Always try to vary your route. If someone is lining you up for an attack, they'll probably know your routine, so alter it regularly. My kids always ask me why I take a different route each time – it's simple: ROUTINE KILLS. It's a habit that I shall take to my grave.

HITCHHIKING: TRAVELLING SAFELY FOR FREE

Hitchhiking is a great way of getting about if you're strapped for cash; however, if you want to do it safely, it's wise to know the lay of the land. Here are some ground rules to keep you safe and help you arrive at your destination in one piece.

Position yourself in a place where drivers can pull in safely. Make sure you're visible to drivers from about one hundred metres, giving them a chance to assess whether they think you're worth the risk. Wear visible clothing, especially at night. When you get in, make sure the door opens from the inside.

Think about what you're wearing. When I've been hitchhiking around Europe I've made it obvious to any driver that I'm English by wearing a Union Jack T-shirt or something similar. As a general rule, drivers tend to pick up hitchhikers that remind them of themselves, so dress according to where you are in the world.

Always choose your driver if you can. Good places to secure a lift include petrol stations, truck stops or motorway services. Truck drivers are usually monitored by their company and are less likely to risk any funny business. Ask them which direction they're headed in and assess their reaction to gauge their personality. Watch out for signs of drunkenness or a lack of eye contact. Trust your instincts and, if in doubt, don't be afraid of refusing the ride.

> Don't be walking around with a face like a beaten favourite if you're dressed like a tramp and nobody stops.

Film your journey. Pretend you're documenting your journey on Facebook or as a home movie for your friends. In reality, you'll be getting shots of the vehicle, the make, colour and registration number and a mug shot of the driver to send to a trusted friend. Tweet or post it on Facebook ASAP, to let people know your current whereabouts should something go wrong. Always think outside the box.

Place your emergency contacts on speed dial. Ensure that your mobile phone has all your important numbers on speed dial, including the emergency services. Before any trip, make your family or friends aware of where you are and have a code word to use in case of emergency. If you find yourself in trouble, use this in a conversation or in a text and make sure that it stands out to your friend or relative.

GET OUT OF TROUBLE – BIG PHIL'S TIPS

IF PUSH COMES TO SHOVE and you feel that your life is at risk, it's time to resort to drastic action. If the car stops at the lights, make a quick escape. If the driver won't stop, try pulling the parking- or handbrake to cause the car to slow down, but REMEMBER: avoid any dangerous manoeuvres if the car is travelling at high speed or on a bend, as the car is likely to go out of control. Always keep your seat belt on until the driver has stopped. They might brake hard in an attempt to knock you out.

In many countries, it is now legal to buy self-defence weapons like tasers or pepper spray. If you have one in your possession, now is the time to use it. As as last resort, carry some toilet paper and a lighter in your rucksack, light the paper and throw it on to the back seat, forcing the driver to pull over.

Hitchhiking for women

Many people think that it's more dangerous for women to hitchhike than men, but the truth is it doesn't have to be.

Use your body language appropriately. Dressing flirtatiously may win you a ride, but it could also attract a whole heap of trouble. Carry a sign making it clear that you're hitchhiking and carefully observe people's behaviour towards you before you get in their vehicle.

Don't be afraid to defend yourself. Always carry a can of hairspray or deodorant and spray it into the eyes of the driver if you find yourself in danger – just make sure that it doesn't blind the driver to the extent that he can't see where he's going and you end up in a road crash.

URBAN CHAOS: WHAT TO DO IF YOU'RE CAUGHT UP IN A ROBBERY, SHOOTING OR RIOT

Getting caught up in the midst of any major criminal act can be scary and potentially life-threatening. If you have the chance to walk away before getting involved, do so, and contact the police, providing as many details as possible. If you're unlucky enough to find yourself trapped, the main thing to remember is to stay calm and try not to panic. Most incidents are over quickly and there's no point in being a dead hero. Staying focused can protect your safety and help you remember important details and observations that could later prove helpful to the police. Remember: these are not the occasions for any Superman heroics.

Robberies

Robbery is defined by the use of force or the threat of force prior to or during a theft. Around 67,000 robberies took place in the UK last year involving banks, businesses and private homes. If you get caught up in one of these incidents, it's important to remember that the robbers are only intent on obtaining their loot and getting out, rather than hurting you. If you follow their instructions, the ordeal isn't likely to last very long.

Don't try to defeat the robber.
The most heroic thing you can do is be observant, pragmatic and remember anything useful. In the heat of a robbery, adrenaline is running high and robbers are likely to be nervous

> ### HOW TO IDENTIFY ROBBERS WITH THE A–H
>
> Observe the following, but do so without being obvious so as to avoid provocation.
> - **Age**
> - **Build**
> - **Colour and clothes**
> - **Distinguishing marks**
> - **Elevation** (that's height)
> - **Face**
> - **Gait**
> - **Hair**

and trigger-happy. If they tell you to lie on the floor, do it. Any sudden movement is likely to provoke a violent response, so stay calm and quiet. As we were taught in the army, if you get captured, act the 'GREY MAN', the one who goes unnoticed and who has nothing to offer.

In 2012, around twenty-one per cent of robberies recorded by UK police involved a knife or sharp instrument.

Remember: do not touch anything after an incident. Evidence is everything. If you can, observe the direction in which the robbers headed and whether there were any accomplices in a waiting car.

Shootings

It depends on where you live, of course, but getting caught up in a shooting is thankfully rare in most places around the world. Mass shootings in public areas do happen, however, and especially where gun laws permit the ownership of a gun. If you should find yourself in one of these situations, it's worth keeping in mind what the military and police are taught. Here are my own tips from personal experience.

Remain aware of your surroundings when in any public place. The first thing I do when I enter somewhere is look for the exits; making a quick getaway can save your life. Check people out and be alert to anything that is even remotely suspicious.

In the event that a gun goes off, get down quickly to the floor and stay down. Anyone standing up is an easy target.

Try to put distance between a gunman and you. Keep out of the line of fire: if you can't be seen, you can't be shot. Stay low and move quickly in a zigzag pattern. Get away from the area and find good cover. If you're inside, find a room to hide in, create a barricade with furniture against the door, close any blinds, turn off the lights and take cover away from doors and windows, staying quiet. Make sure that your mobile is set to vibrate.

GET OUT OF TROUBLE – BIG PHIL'S TIPS

IF SOMEONE IS KILLING PEOPLE all around you and you feel that your life is at risk, something has to be done. If you can get out of the way and escape to safety, then do so. But if you find yourself trapped and there's no way out, then you have to make a decision. Either you try to keep a low profile, even to the extent that you play dead – or you fight. As a group, you stand a better chance in bringing the shooter down than you would as an individual. Use improvised weapons such as chairs, computers and fire extinguishers – anything you can to strike the gunman and disarm them.

Consider setting off fire alarms and use a lighter for smoke alarms and sprinklers to cause confusion while you get out.

Phone or text the police as soon as you can do so safely and without attracting attention and, when they arrive, follow their instructions quickly but calmly. Any sudden shouting or running may make the police think that you're a threat.

Riots

Civil unrest is becoming increasingly common across the world and so are the chances of it turning into a riot. The causes can be anything from a shooting by police, economic collapse, political rebellion, even a football game. An angry mob is an unpredictable one and potentially the cause of fatalities. Even normally rational and calm people can become rampaging lunatics when part of a mob. Wherever you are in the world, there are some simple precautions you can take to avoid the worst.

Stay alert to police crowd control tactics. Always think about your exits and escape routes. Don't get hemmed in; move down the flanks of any riot crowds to avoid getting crushed. If you can't get out, try and distance yourself from the rioters. Make sure that your hands can be seen and do not make any sudden movements. Many of the police will be as scared as you and might be lashing out. As soon as you can, move to a place of safety, away from the riot. International hotels can be a safe intermediate haven – if nothing else, you can have a cup of tea. Alternatively, use your smartphone to locate a nearby safe spot.

Kettling: British police forces use this method to contain riots or troublesome demonstrations. Kettling can often mean being forced to remain in one place for up to eight to ten hours. If you can spot a kettle forming, move away quickly. Watch out for extra police arriving in vans and, if they begin to move across exit points and roads, get out.

Water cannon: Previously used for fighting fires, this high-pressure hose is used around the world to break up riots. Those hit by the powerful stream of water are at high risk of eye and head injuries. Avoid approaching the front line, where deployment of water or the use of batons and horse charge is most likely. Good places to aim for are doorways which can provide some protection.

Tear gas: Tear gas canisters are normally shot from a gas gun, so if you hear a shot, look up and try to avoid being in the path of the canister. If you know you are going to be in an exposed area, use glasses or even swimming goggles to protect your eyes, but don't wear contact lenses – the gas will adhere to these and your eyes will burn. A cloth soaked in vinegar or lemon juice can help you breathe, and you can use saline solution or liquid antacid and water (half, half) in a spray to rinse your eyes.

Dress appropriately. Cover up to avoid being hurt by sharp or flying objects, but avoid anything that might label you as a rioter – so no hoodies. A motorcycle helmet comes in useful if bricks or large items are being thrown, but once again beware because it might look like a threat to the police.

Cash and ID. Just in case you need to pay off rioters or looters or arrange quick transportation, always have a small amount of cash with you. If you're abroad, keep your passport and visa with you and make sure that you have *in case of emergency* contact details, should you get injured. One mobile is essential, two is better, so keep a spare in your bag.

Move down the side of crowds to avoid being crushed.

Watch out for police moving across exit points.

Hotel

SURVIVING A RIOT

3 THE SOCIAL SCENE

'LIFE IS A SERIES OF DRILLS
CULMINATING IN DEATH.'
BIG PHIL CAMPION

HOW TO PROTECT YOURSELF WHEN YOU'RE HAVING FUN

Drink and drugs: drunks, overdoses and how to
stay out of trouble

Drink spiking: avoidance tactics

Date rape: precautions and escaping from dodgy
situations

Spotting trouble: reading nightspots like an SAS
trooper and how to stay safe

Kebab shop trouble: avoiding flashpoints and getting
home in one piece

Eating is cheating: how to drink right through the
night and survive

Keeping a lookout: the buddy system and shark
watch for nights out

IT'S FRIDAY NIGHT and you're at one of London's top clubs with your mates from work. The drink is flowing and it's that time of the week when you can forget about your job and the boss. Most of your pals are on the dance floor, attempting to make some moves, when you spot one of the girls, Sarah-Jane, talking to a group of blokes who strike you as looking decidedly dodgy.

Sarah-Jane is a sweet girl, but a bit naive, and these guys are not exactly the sort that you'd take home to meet your mother. Worse still, you're sure that you've just seen one of them drop something into her drink. You sense Sarah-Jane could be in real danger if you don't step in, but how do you break up the party without a punch-up? Do you call a taxi and get one of her girlfriends to accompany her home? Do you tell the club management and hope that they call the police? Or do you pretend that you're her boyfriend and tell the blokes that she's coming home with you?

BIG PHIL'S ADVICE: If you suspect that someone's drink has been spiked, the first thing to do is warn that person and discard the drink. If you believe that they're at risk of a sexual attack, try to remove them from the situation calmly, and find someone that can be trusted to accompany them home. Avoid making a big scene, though, as you could end up on the receiving end of a beating or worse.

When you're out on the town with your mates, a few drinks and some laughs can be the perfect antidote to a hectic week. Until, that is, someone has one too many drinks and the punches start flying. It can go off quicker than a prawn in a heat wave, so keep your eyes open.

Whenever we went on the piss, we would always follow that principle. With drink spiking often a potential risk, it was all too easy to become prey to thieves and those with bad intent, and the so-called 'shark watch' was our way of ensuring everyone in our group got home safely.

I learnt this lesson the hard way when, early on in my career, at the age of nineteen, I was sent to Kenya. The furthest I'd ever been was France and suddenly here I was at a beach bar in Watamu. Naively, I took a cigarette from a local who was proper friendly towards me and my mates. Within a few minutes, it was goodnight – I was completely stoned. Luckily, my mates spotted I was in trouble and I was escorted back off to my bed.

In the Regiment, watching one another's backs was second nature: loyalty to your brothers in arms at all costs.

Don't let others ruin your fun. If you're out and about with your mates, keep in mind some simple rules and you'll have a night to remember instead of one you'd rather forget.

DRINK AND DRUGS: DRUNKS, OVERDOSES AND HOW TO STAY OUT OF TROUBLE

Alcohol is one of the leading causes of accidents, with more men dying from drink-driving than any other group. In the UK, one in thirteen adults are dependent on drink and 33,000 people die each year due to associated health issues and related incidents. While it can be fun, alcohol is a lethal substance if mishandled.

Illegal drugs on the social scene are prevalent and it's often impossible to know their strength or purity. Drug dealers have only one object – profit – in mind, meaning some drugs are far more harmful than at first realized. The lethal cocktail of drugs and alcohol can cause fatalities and also make the user extremely vulnerable.

In recent years, incidents of drink spiking and date rape have been on the increase, with females the most common victims.

Know the signs of drink spiking and the precautions to take, and you can protect yourself from this vile crime.

Drunks: how to recognize the early warning signs and how to avoid trouble

For many of us, alcohol is a pleasant way to relax. Some can down pints and still stay standing; others fall over after one or two drinks. Knowing your limit is vital if you don't want to end up in a dodgy situation.

Spotting a drunk: Drunks are far more likely to put themselves and others in dangerous situations and, if you're on the receiving end, it pays to know what to do. Typical signs that someone has had one too many drinks include slurred speech, stumbling, embarrassing and noisy behaviour, and even violent reactions. The number-one rule is to avoid saying anything that might provoke aggression. Stay calm and reassure them.

A friend in need: If the drunk is your friend, you need to stay with them until they're out of danger. Get them away from the alcohol and then get them home, where they can sleep off the drink. Drunks are particularly vulnerable to unsavoury individuals who could well attack them. Try to prevent them from having any more alcohol by buying them soft drinks – if they're truly drunk, they probably won't even notice.

Do your best to help your mate avoid physical injury by guiding them to a seat. If they need the toilet, either to relieve themselves or to vomit, help them and stick around in case they collapse or slip and knock themselves unconscious. Never let someone who is drunk lie on his or her back or stomach: the risk of choking on their own vomit is high. Use the recovery position – on their side, with one leg bent – and ensure nothing is restricting their mouth (see illustration on p60 and *Essential emergency treatments* in *Chapter 10*, p244).

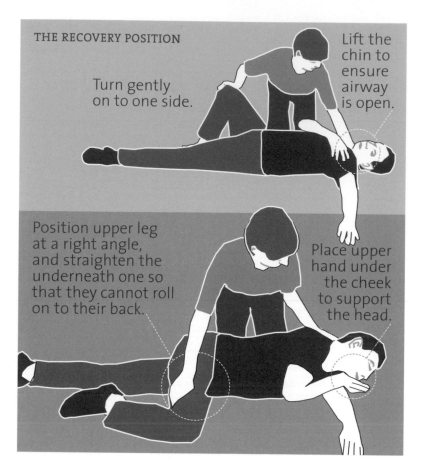

THE RECOVERY POSITION

Turn gently on to one side.

Lift the chin to ensure airway is open.

Position upper leg at a right angle, and straighten the underneath one so that they cannot roll on to their back.

Place upper hand under the cheek to support the head.

If you can't watch over them, try and find someone who can.
Check that they're breathing and responding to being woken occasionally. If their breathing slows to less than eight breaths per minute – and they don't awaken – they're at risk of alcohol poisoning. Look for other signs, like blue lips and fingertips, cold and clammy hands and a rapid pulse. Call an ambulance immediately.

One too many: If I'm hanging out with my mates, I'll get a couple of sly waters down my neck to dilute the effects of drink a little. But if this doesn't work and you think you've had one too many, you need to consider cutting loose.

Drink-drivers

Drink-drivers kill, so it pays to be sensible about your own habits and recognize the signs of drunkenness in other drivers.

Common signs are driving too fast or too slow, drifting in and out of lanes, rapid braking, driving too closely to other vehicles and responding slowly to traffic signals. Try to keep your distance from any vehicle like this. If the road isn't wide enough to allow you to pass safely, stay behind. If you can make a note of the vehicle, model type and registration number and the exact location that you've seen the car, call the police and report the incident. A driver who can't handle their car is an accident waiting to happen.

If you're partying and are likely to drink, do not take your car. The legal limit in the UK is thirty-five microgrammes of alcohol per hundred millilitres of breath: no more than two cans of beer. Don't be fooled into thinking you can sober up – you may feel fine but your reaction times will be dimmed by the alcohol. You can buy a breathalyser, but I always think it's best to just leave your car behind if you are going to drink at all. Leave your breathalyser at home and use it to see if you are clear-headed enough the next morning to drive.

Drug addicts

Drugs, like alcohol, alter behaviour. If someone has an addiction, whether it's to drink or drugs, the threat of violence is greater. Many common drugs in use today, like cocaine, are psychoactive

THOSE THAT CHOOSE to take recreational drugs can usually be spotted by their behaviour: frequent trips to the loo (often in pairs), highly talkative and manic, overly loving and laughing at things that just aren't funny. Some of the symptoms are similar to being drunk but they are usually more pronounced. I make no judgement on what people want to do with their lives, but for my own peace of mind I like to identify who may be a potential threat. It's the same as walking into a strange environment and identifying the emergency exits – awareness keeps you one step ahead of the game.

substances that impair the judgement and can cause the person to lose their grip on reality, posing a very real violent threat. It can make people madder than a meat axe and just as vicious, so watch out for them.

Drug overdose

A drug overdose, either accidental or intentional, is not to be taken lightly. It can result in permanent brain damage and even death. If you find someone who you suspect has overdosed, call an

When I took part in Channel 4 Television's *Drugs Live* I underwent a blind trial to determine the effects of ecstasy. I knew within minutes that I had been given the drug – it was like I was being taken over. Most people on the trial enjoyed it, but if it had been raining women in bikinis, I'd rather have been washed down the drain with a binman, it was such a hideous experience. Just because your mate says it's good, doesn't mean it will be. The choice is yours.

ambulance immediately. Look for any drugs lying around and give them to the paramedics when they arrive so that they know what they're dealing with.

If an overdose hasn't caused unconsciousness, it can make people behave in bizarre ways, promoting aggression and violence, a tolerance for pain and in some cases a type of 'super strength'. Stay away and do not place yourself in physical danger.

DRINK SPIKING: AVOIDANCE TACTICS

Drink spiking is an increasing issue for anyone who enjoys pub and club culture. No matter whether you're male or female, heterosexual or gay, you can still become a victim. Rendered unconscious and unable to defend themselves, victims are vulnerable to all sorts: rape, theft, GBH or simply someone's idea of fun. The most common types of drugs in use are sedative drugs like Rohypnol, ketamine, GBL and GHB (liquid ecstasy), but recent research has also discovered the use of MDMA (ecstasy) in cases of date rape. The effects of this particular drug, which can make you develop feelings of affection for strangers, can impair personal judgement, leaving the victim open to assault. So much for the so-called 'love drug'.

It's crucial that you are able to recognize the altered state of mind that drugs can produce; that way, you can flag it up and get

SIGNS OF DRINK SPIKING

THE MAJORITY OF PEOPLE who have been victims of drink spiking wake the next morning with absolutely no recollection of the night before. Within five to thirty minutes of consuming the drug, many victims experience paranoia, disorientation, nausea, hallucinations and confusion, often with blurred vision. Many still feel the effects of these drugs the next morning. Typical date-rape drugs make a dangerous cocktail when mixed with alcohol, creating a very powerful anaesthesia effect.

help straight away. I am convinced that, with the ecstasy trial, I would have become very violent had this experiment happened outside a controlled environment. I looked to Wendy, my partner, who was present throughout, to reassure me that things were okay. If you think that you've been drugged unwittingly, you must stop what you're doing and seek help immediately.

How to protect yourself from drink spiking

Never leave your drink unattended. If you need to use the toilet and don't feel that you can carry your glass in there, ask a friend to watch it for you. If possible, buy drinks with a screw top and carry the bottle with you at all times. Always buy your own drinks and watch as they're being prepared. Drinking from bottles in busy clubs means that you can keep your thumb over the opening between sips – this will stop anyone dropping anything into your drink.

Beware of a stranger offering to buy you a drink. You might be flattered, but it's an easy way for you to fall victim. If for any reason you feel that your drink may have been messed with, ditch it. If you see someone spike a drink, make sure that no one drinks it and inform the manager or house security. It's best not to confront the perpetrator unless you are confident that you can deal with the situation.

What to do if you think your drink was spiked

If you're feeling the effects, such as hallucinations, drowsiness and nausea, get someone that you trust to take you to the nearest

TRY AND KEEP SOME OF THE SPIKED DRINK

ANY REMAINING DRINK can be used as evidence. Ask the bar manager to keep it for you. If you don't have any major symptoms but still believe that your drink was spiked, call the police and give the remains of any drink to them. Drink spiking is illegal and can result in a sentence of up to ten years in prison.

A&E and tell them you think that your drink was spiked. Most drugs usually leave the body within twelve to seventy-two hours after they've been taken, some even sooner. GHB is undetectable in your blood within six to eight hours and within twelve to eighteen hours it will be untraceable in your urine. Get a blood and urine test carried out as soon as possible.

DATE RAPE: PRECAUTIONS AND ESCAPING FROM DODGY SITUATIONS

An increasing number of cases reported in the media have made date rape a well-known phenomenon. Unfortunately, when drugs are used most are virtually untraceable in the blood or urine in as little as twelve hours, and some even less. Go straight to A&E or the police if you think you have been a victim. The quicker you do, the more chance you have of gaining proof against a suspect.

Date rape

Once thought of as an issue solely affecting women, research has shown that men are also targeted: mostly men on men, but also women on men. Date rape can affect anyone, but there's no denying that women are still more likely to be a victim. However, prosecutions are few and far between because victims can rarely remember the event or are too embarrassed to come forward. It's worth remembering that date rape drugs are not only used to facilitate rape. There have been several recent cases in the media where a woman has used drugs to render a man unconscious, faked a sexual encounter and legged it with all his valuables.

Precautions to avoid a date-rape situation

Common sense and an awareness of your behaviour and that of others is a priority, whether you're a man or a woman, gay or heterosexual.

▸ **Avoid parties** where drugs and alcohol are used to excess. Date rapists and their victims are often intoxicated.

▸ **Never use alcohol** or drugs as a method to boost your confidence when trying to date someone: your judgement won't be clear.

▶ **Beware of anyone** who seems to be plying you with drinks. If you're drunk, you may be less aware of the reality of a situation.

▶ **Always take a friend** to a party so that you can watch out for each other. (See *Keeping a lookout*, p73)

▶ **Be aware of your appearance** and body language, particularly if you're a woman. Dressing provocatively could lead others to think that you want to have sex. It never justifies rape, but you should be aware that some individuals are led by these kinds of visual things.

▶ **Trust your instincts.** If someone is coming on too strong and getting possessive or pushing you to have sex when you don't want to, make your exit – fast.

▶ **Be confident** and assertive. Know your own sexual limits and how far you are prepared to go. If you are uncomfortable, make it clear by saying NO and move away.

SIGNS TO RECOGNIZE

IF YOU THINK that you've been the victim of a date-rape drug, you'll likely feel many of the symptoms noted in *Signs of drink spiking* on p63. The two most common drugs used are GBH and Rohypnol due to their muscle relaxant properties. They can both have extremely dangerous side effects.

GHB: Otherwise known as liquid ecstasy, this drug can induce seizure-like activity, including a coma, which can last about one to two hours. Because it leaves no odour and the effects wear off quickly, schoolchildren have begun to use it as an alternative to alcohol.

Rohypnol: This was originally produced as an anaesthesia. Odourless and colourless, Rohypnol tablets, better known as 'roofies', are easy to slip into someone's drink. In high doses, the drug causes loss of muscle control, amnesia and loss of consciousness, and the effects can last eight to twelve hours.

GET OUT OF TROUBLE – BIG PHIL'S TIPS

IF YOU END UP in a situation where you are about to be raped, the only form of defence is attack. Remember: whoever is doing the raping has to expose their sensitive parts, so this is your opportunity for escape. It may even be possible to wait for the perfect moment and then strike. Your attack needs to be done violently, utilizing anything you can lay your hands on: bedside lamps, handbags, high-heeled shoes, knees and elbows are all devastating if plunged into the right areas. See *Chapter 9: Self-defence, SAS style* (p214).

Target the sensitive areas in your attack.

Responsible dating

▶ **Don't assume** that just because someone is flirting with you that they want to have sex with you.

▶ **If you're turned down** by someone, accept their decision and realize that it's not a personal rejection; they just may not be into you in that way or in the mood for sex.

▶ **Always accept** someone's decision: NO means NO. Respect them and don't pressure them sexually.

What to do if you think you've been date-raped

Your first priority should be your well-being: go to hospital for a check-up. Any medical tests carried out in hospital can be used as forensic evidence by the police, later. If you can, try not to shower, change your clothes, brush your teeth or even wash your hands, as this can remove essential evidence of a rape. You should also report the incident to the police and try to give a description of your attacker and any details that you can remember of the incident. Later, a medical check for STIs and pregnancy is advised.

Getting home safe and sound

Think ahead and either pre-book a licensed taxi to take you home or look up the times of the last train or bus. Never walk home alone – get a friend to accompany you. Try and stay in areas with lots of street lighting and away from dark and lonely alleys. Ensure that your mobile and other valuables like cash are out of sight. Always keep a spare set of keys and some money on your person – either in a coat pocket or in a shoe.

USE SOCIAL MEDIA

A SMALL MESSAGE on your Twitter account saying that you're on your way out or on your way home will at least alert people to your whereabouts should something go wrong. You might even be able to cadge a lift off a mate heading in the same direction.

SPOTTING TROUBLE: READING NIGHTSPOTS LIKE AN SAS TROOPER AND HOW TO STAY SAFE

Every club attracts a certain clientele and, if the management is up to scratch, they should know how to handle any trouble that kicks off. Do your homework, know the signs to look out for and save yourself a whole heap of aggravation. Don't let others ruin your night out.

Reading clubs and pubs like an SAS trooper

Just by looking at the clientele of an establishment, and its security operations, you can tell a hell of a lot about the way a pub or club is run. Unfortunately, some clubs already have a well-known reputation for attracting fights.

How to give a club a quick 'once over'

▶ **See what is going on** outside.

▶ **Walk through** to see what the action is like inside. If the bouncers stop you, say you're looking for a friend. If they let you in, this will afford you the time to have a quick look around and pie it off if you don't like the place.

▶ **Try not to bundle in** mob-handed. When arriving at a venue, the last thing you want to do is telegraph it to those who may take a dislike to you.

Beware of clubs that either have no security or too much. Most clubs have security on the doors and even metal detectors to check for knives and guns on entry. This is one way of ensuring that those who are already drunk, or are intent on conflict, stay outside. However, if a club has an unusually high level of security, it may well be because it needs it – and again, you may wish to give it a miss.

Two-for-one offers don't always spell trouble. Special offers are not always a sign that the place will be crammed to the doors with bingers. Check out the tone, the music and lighting to gauge what sort of place it is – you might find yourself surrounded by a busload of old-age pensioners out for an evening on the cheap.

Club and pub checklist

Once you're in a venue, you can assess the risks by doing a quick scan.

▶ **Is the place** overcrowded?

▶ **Are the exits** to stairs, doors, bar and dance floor congested?

▶ **Is there** no monitoring of those entering the venue?

▶ **Are meals,** snacks and a range of soft drinks not available?

▶ **Is the music** offensive?

▶ **Are the toilets** and the general appearance of the place dirty? (If these essentials are not maintained then the rest of the venue is unlikely to be.)

▶ **Is unacceptable stuff** like drug use/dealing, vomiting and behaviour of a sexual nature tolerated?

If you answer yes to most of these, find another venue.

GET OUT OF TROUBLE – BIG PHIL'S TIPS

SAFETY IS PROBABLY the last thing on the average person's mind when they're out on the town, but it pays to take precautions and to know what to do when the proverbial shit hits the fan.

Two is better than one: Always travel in twos if you can – on your own you're vulnerable to anything and everything.

Cash in a dash: Don't be left struggling to find a cashpoint, or, worse, finding yourself robbed. Always keep enough for a taxi fare somewhere safe on your body: in a shoe, tucked in your underwear or, for women, down your cleavage.

Keep family and friends informed: Always tell someone where you are, either by text or social networking. If you can't get home and your mobile goes dead, hopefully someone will come and collect you.

Taxis: Always get the taxi to drop you at your door; trying to save money by walking part of the way is asking for trouble.

A fist full of keys: If the shit has hit the fan, and you find yourself confronted by a mugger in a back alley, keys can be a useful weapon but should be employed only with the force appropriate for the situation. Place each key in between each finger, the sharp edge pointing out, and form a fist. This is very useful for jabbing anyone threatening your safety. (See *Chapter 9: Self-defence, SAS style* (p214))

Stiletto stab: Usually I'd advise women to wear a sensible pair of shoes so that they can make a quick getaway, but there is an advantage to the stiletto – it makes a very useful improvised weapon. Perhaps keep them handy in a bag.

KEBAB SHOP TROUBLE: AVOIDING FLASHPOINTS AND GETTING HOME IN ONE PIECE

You've had a great evening, everywhere is closing and it's time to head home. The only place still open for a quick meal is the nearby kebab shop next door to the taxi rank: ideal because you can grab a lift home. Unfortunately, everyone else seems to have had the same idea and most are staggering around drunk out of their skulls.

Closing time can mean flashpoint hell as too many tired, drunk and irritable individuals converge on scarce resources such as food and a ride home. Follow these guidelines to avoid the trouble hot spots.

Most of the gobbing-off will be all shine and no shoes, but steer away from the loudest ones.

Flashpoint hell

It's a time police and ambulance crews dread as trouble spills out on to the streets and one incident soon becomes twenty. Contrary to popular belief, fresh air does not sober you up but can accentuate the effects of a night out by enhancing the drop in body temperature caused by alcohol, leading some to feel confused and dizzy, or, at the very least, more drunk. These individuals – who would probably rather continue partying – are now in a queue for a taxi or a meal: the perfect combination for a flashpoint. Taxi ranks and fast-food places situated next to busy nightspots are among the worst for trouble. Here's how to avoid any hassle.

Do your homework. If you're in an area which is full of fast-food joints and bars and pubs, think twice – they're likely to be ideal haunts for those on the night-time circuit. Look for locations that also include licensed restaurants which are food-led rather

Look for places with adequate street lighting. Well-lit environments reduce crime by twenty-one per cent according to studies.

than alcohol-led. Areas with a high number of restaurants appear to reduce the number of alcohol-related incidents and hospitalizations. Residential properties nearby can also improve the safety of an area, as no one wants trouble on their own doorstep.

Don't trust CCTV to protect you in a busy city. Statistics show that it's great for protecting car parks but, where alcohol is involved, most culprits are so drunk that they don't even realize they're on camera. One thing CCTV does ensure is a rapid response from the emergency services.

EATING IS CHEATING: HOW TO DRINK RIGHT THROUGH THE NIGHT AND SURVIVE

If you don't want to be falling over before you reach the dance floor, make sure that you eat before knocking back the drinks. Food lines the stomach and protects your liver and brain from the effects of alcohol, meaning that you're less likely to get drunk quickly. Choose anything that contains fat and protein, even fruit will slow down the absorption of alcohol into your bloodstream. If you want to stay healthy, go for meat, poultry or fish, nuts, cheese, bread or pasta. If you don't care, fish and chips, pizza or even a hamburger will do. One of the best hangover preventions is to drink lots of water in between your boozing: one glass of water for every alcoholic drink and another few before heading to bed.

The dreaded hangover: cures that work

If you didn't follow the eat-before-you-drink advice and you've got a head that feels as though it's gone ten rounds in a boxing contest, try the following. Proper renegades will recommend 'hair of the dog', but this will only lead to drunkenness and definitely won't sober you up, that's for sure. My favourite is a full English breakfast – it may not be the healthiest option, but it will make you feel better straight away.

BIG PHIL'S ESSENTIALS FOR THE MORNING AFTER

Eggs: Apart from being a great protein source, eggs contain the amino acid, cysteine. In brief, this will help your body break down the by-product of alcohol that makes you feel so lousy. An eggnog is definitely a potential hangover cure.

Dried apricots: Everyone always thinks bananas, but a cupful of dried apricots has double the amount of potassium you'll find in one banana. After a night's drinking, the body is usually low in this mineral due to alcohol's diuretic effect. Other foods with high levels of potassium include raisins, dried prunes and yogurt.

Orange juice: Fruit sugar can help get rid of toxins in the body after a night of drinking. It will also rehydrate you.

KEEPING A LOOKOUT: THE BUDDY SYSTEM AND SHARK WATCH FOR NIGHTS OUT

A night out can quickly turn from fun to disaster, so make some ground rules in advance. If you're going to meet a friend for a night on the town, always operate the buddy system: you watch out for them and they watch out for you. Going solo is an open invite to the criminals lurking in the darkness. If you're going out with a group of mates, assign one of them to keep shark watch on the group as a whole. If you are moving between venues, this system also helps to prevent people getting left behind.

The buddy system

When I was in a war zone, watching out for one another was second nature, and it's no different when you're down the local pub or club having a few beers with your mates. In many ways, when you're relaxed – with the help of a pint or two – you can be at your most vulnerable to those with bad intent.

You might be in an unfamiliar town, surrounded by people you don't know, or on a large-scale 'piss-up', either way, always agree with your mate that you'll keep a lookout for each other. Having someone cover your back and smooth the way is priceless. If they're a good mate, they'll always recognize when things have gone too far and when someone's in real trouble. Be on the lookout for your wingman at all times.

I like to sit where I have a vantage point. When I go into a pub or restaurant, I want to see what's going on. I especially want to see the main entrance as this is more than likely going to be where you'll spot trouble.

I was out with my partner, Wendy, an old regiment mate and his missus, and Wendy said to me, 'This is the first time we've sat down with your back to the door.' And I said, 'That's because Rob's got it.' You know which mates you can trust and those you can't. With mine, I'm lucky enough never to have to tell them to watch my back, because they already have it.

GET OUT OF TROUBLE – BIG PHIL'S TIPS

ALWAYS KEEP A CHECK on each other's movements. If one is buying beer, the other covers his back. Always have someone watch your unguarded drink if you head off for a pee. Be aware of the signs of drugging and watch out for any unusual behaviour. If any of you suspect something isn't right, alert one another. Always keep everyone on the same page.

Shark watch

Every time you go out in a group and you know that you're going to be drinking until you're legless, you should assign one of your mates to be on shark watch. That means one member of your group – either the driver or someone who won't be drinking that night – should be assigned the role of remaining super-vigilant, like a shark. They'll spot any potential dramas, sort out trouble and help anyone who has had too much to drink, and they'll also look after the group's money.

We've all been there when someone is so drunk that they're out for the count, so much so that they'll probably wake up with a missing eyebrow or two. What you don't want to find is people who aren't part of your group taking liberties. The mate on shark watch is there to ensure anyone in a vulnerable position is removed safely and that everyone gets back home in one piece.

4. THE CYBER SCENE

CYBERSPACE IS FULL OF FREE LOVE, SERIOUS HATE, BIG PROMISES, EASY MONEY, BULLSHIT AND LIES. DECEIVING PEOPLE ONLINE IS NOW ALMOST COMMONPLACE. HERE'S HOW TO AVOID BECOMING A VICTIM.

HOW TO STEER A COURSE THROUGH THE DIGITAL MINEFIELD

Social networks: the promises, pitfalls and dangers
Hooking up: online friends and relationships – how to do it safely
Internet security: safeguarding your identity online
Shopping, selling and banking online: how to avoid the fraudsters
Internet nasties: cyberbullies and trolls – what to do
Internet scams: what to look for and how to deal with them

YOU MET LISA on a dating website. She's 6'1", a natural brunette with brown eyes and a GSOH. It's been several weeks of lengthy emails at all hours of the day and night and now she's finally asked to meet you. You can't believe your luck. Lisa is super smart, fearlessly brave and judging from the photo she sent you, beautiful too. She's told you all about her work as a doctor – risking life and limb to save lives in dangerous locations. She's been caught up in enemy fun fire, kidnapped and once even battled a crocodile that had sneaked into camp. Now she's declared her undying love for you and wonders if you could be the one to help her fun a new school for orphans. Are you dreaming or is this for real? In the back of your mind you're wondering whether your mates are setting you up, or worse, that Lisa is one of those fantasists manipulating her way into your life and about to take you for all you've got. Do you risk getting caught up in a situation that you'll regret? Try to find out whether she's telling the truth or turn your back on a potential once in a lifetime opportunity?

BIG PHIL'S ADVICE: Do your homework on your prospective date. Check out their profile on Facebook, Google and Linkedin. If things don't add up suggest a pre-meeting chat on a service such as Skype – that way at least you can find out more about them in the safety of your own home. If all else fails, make sure that you meet them at a public location where you're not endangering your safety. If in any doubt, don't hesitate to walk away.

In the UK, eighty per cent of households have internet access and ninety-one per cent of us own a mobile phone. From dating to banking, booking holidays to finding a job, nearly every part of our existence is now organized online, with even our social lives managed by the likes of Facebook and Twitter. But with ease and convenience comes danger, especially for the unsuspecting. Internet theft, cyberbullying, false personas and online dating disasters: our twenty-first-century interconnected world is now the playground of conmen, conwomen, cheats and criminals alike. Where children are concerned, the internet is full of dangers. Keeping your child safe can be as simple as making them aware of the risks and using parental controls. Sitting behind a computer screen or smartphone might seem a safe place to be but don't be lulled into a false sense of security – take precautions and protect yourself and your loved ones.

SOCIAL NETWORKS: THE PROMISES, PITFALLS AND DANGERS

Across the world, seventy-two per cent of adults now use social media, with 699 million international Facebook users. While most of us can probably list our friends in the real world on two hands, online the number could easily run into thousands. Tracking friends from our past suddenly becomes easy, meeting new people even easier as traditional handshakes get replaced by 'poking'.

Social networking is unrivalled in allowing us to promote and share our personal and professional worlds, but there are drawbacks to this vast community. In revealing intimate details, we attract those

TAKE CARE WHEN ACCEPTING FRIEND REQUESTS FROM STRANGERS

IT MIGHT LOOK GOOD having 5,000 friends but can you trust all of them? Some could be identity thieves looking to access your private information.

who are only too willing to exploit our personal information for their own good. It also offers potential employers or partners, as well as law enforcers, a ready-made character profile of you – and one that you may prefer remains private. The first thing anybody does when they want to check you out is Google your name to see what comes up. Follow some essential rules and you can have all the benefits of social networking with none of the drawbacks.

How to protect yourself when social networking

You've partied your way through the weekend. As a bit of fun, you decide to upload the photos to Facebook for all your friends to see. Now it's Monday morning, you're back at work and just about to sit down when your boss summons you to his office . . .

Keep an eye on your privacy. If you're going to post personal photos of your social life, or any personal details, make sure that only your friends have access via the privacy settings, or don't post. Also, remember that any information you type on your friends' pages can be viewed by everyone else as well.

Be careful what you write on Facebook pages. An innocent note about your holiday trip to Spain could be viewed as an open invite to burglars who'll clean you out of house and home.

Try Googling your name to check how your identity is being used. You can even try search sites like White Pages. If you're unhappy at being on these, look for the link to remove a listing.

Current and prospective employers may find your social profile page and that could include some embarrassing photos, so think carefully about the information you put up online.

Be alert to Facebook ad malware. Some event invitations are scams so watch out when emails arrive, and don't enter your passwords if anything seems suspicious.

HOOKING UP: ONLINE FRIENDS AND RELATIONSHIPS – HOW TO DO IT SAFELY

More than nine million of us have accessed dating websites. Whether you're in a relationship or not, the ease and potential choice of partners makes online dating one of the fastest growing trends. One survey estimates that a third of all relationships are now found online, but, just because you find a profile and photo that looks like your ideal mate, the reality may be quite the opposite.

The temptation to lie about our age, weight, profession and hobbies is all too strong for some and we've all heard the horror stories. The other risk is that most of us offer too much personal information in the hope of finding a mate. This ultimately makes us vulnerable, not only to scammers and sexual predators, but also to the marketers that dating agencies often sell your details on to, sometimes without your consent. Also, any information you provide to online dating agencies remains as a permanent record and could be used against you in the event of a court case.

Regardless of all the downsides, people do find successful relationships online, so how do you separate the oddballs from the real deal and protect your safety and your dignity? Follow these guidelines and you'll most likely find your perfect match.

Dating online

So you've plucked up the courage to give online dating a go, but where do you start?

Dating sites: free or fee? A free online dating service is an open door to all, including the weirdos and the outright dangerous. With no payment, there's no record of credit card or location – in other words, they're unaccountable. If you want to begin safely, it's best to pay. Look for reputable sites that are recommended by people you trust. Check out their credibility by reading case histories and reviews. Most offer a trial period for free, but make sure you cancel your membership before the trial is up.

BE HONEST

IF YOU'RE HOPING to eventually hook up with your online date, don't lie or submit a photograph of yourself that was taken twenty years ago. You might get away with a few years off your age, but if you're serious about a relationship, stay away from the big fibs.

Know what you want before you begin. Are you looking for a long-term relationship or just a casual encounter? Friendship that could lead to romance or an adult no-strings-attached fling? Just as with any conventional dating agency, it's all about profiles and identifying your ideal match. So know your type and be specific. If you want someone with similar interests or who speaks a certain language, target the agencies that offer that service.

Keep your personal details secret. Sign up for a free email account and keep it for online dating only: do not reveal your personal email address, your full name or any other details, such as your telephone number or address. Until you know who you're dealing with, trust no one. Ask for their telephone number first and, if they refuse, be wary. There are plenty of married people and individuals with less than honourable intentions using online dating services.

Get personal. You can tell a lot about a person from the way they answer questions and how willing they are to share personal details. If they seem reluctant to reveal much or appear controlling, ask yourself why. After you get to know them better, find out what relationships they've had in the past and how long they lasted. Is the photo on their profile recently taken? If not, ask for one. If you suspect any lies this early on, trust your instincts and move on.

Meeting up

If you're serious about someone then there'll come a time when
you want to meet them. Always agree a daytime rendezvous in
a public location, preferably one that you know well, such as a
cafe or restaurant where there are
plenty of people around or one
that's covered by CCTV cameras.
If you're unfamiliar with the
location then do a recce. I do
this everywhere I go if I'm
meeting someone for the first
time. Arrive early so that you can
assess the environment again at
the meeting.

FIRST DATE RULES: Never agree to
meet at your home or
someone else's and don't
accept a lift to a venue.
If your date asks this
– be suspicious.

**Tell family or friends that you are meeting someone for the
first time.** Have a plan so that you know exactly where you're
going rather than making ad-hoc arrangements. Give as much
information as you can to your friends and family: the name of the
person you're meeting, their phone number, where you're meeting
and when you expect to be home. If necessary, get a friend to call
you at a certain time in case you want an excuse to leave.

Make sure that you know what they look like before you meet.
Either ask them for a recent photo or a clear description. If you've
arrived at your rendezvous and no one matches the profile,
use your mobile to call them and see who answers. If you have
reservations about anything, now is the time to make a run for
it before direct contact is made.

**If your date doesn't turn up at the agreed time, they may be
running late or they could have gone to a different rendezvous.**
If they suddenly change the meeting place at the last minute,
be suspicious and don't be afraid to cancel, especially if you're
a woman. Keep everything on your terms and stay safe.

Do not share any personal details with your online date.
A small white lie here and there is better than presenting an
open book and making yourself vulnerable. Everything remains
classified until you know them better: safety is your priority. Do
have several questions to ask them, though – this is your chance
to assess whether they could have relationship potential.

When you're back home safely, don't forget to let your friends
and family know.

Romance scams

Unfortunately, where emotions are involved, we are all
vulnerable, and there are plenty of unsavoury characters out
there only too willing to take advantage. In one year, a study
revealed that, out of 2,028 British adults interviewed, over half
had been conned out of money by an online romance scammer.
Sadly, they thought they'd found love, only to pay the price with
a broken heart and a broken bank account.

Scammers are highly clever and know the tell tale
personality traits that make an individual more likely to fall for
a scam. Education is the best prevention. Save yourself a whole
lot of heartache by looking for the following warning signs:

SCAMMER'S TRICKS

▶ **Financial information:** Beware of people asking about your financial status early on in a relationship, or showing keen interest in your personal details.

▶ **Sob stories:** Don't fall for the sick mother routine or the grandad who desperately needs money for an operation to save his sight.

▶ **Individuals posing as members of the military:** Research these Walter Mitty types online and check out supposed military documents. Commonly used false documents can be found on the web.

▶ **Love in an instant:** If your date declares their undying love for you in only a matter of weeks, alarm bells should ring – especially if they suddenly ask you to mail a package to Africa.

▶ **Check them out:** If you're in any doubt, check out your date online at romancescam.com. Here you can confirm whether they're a scammer or not, the types of photos they use and the most likely scams.

INTERNET SECURITY: SAFEGUARDING YOUR IDENTITY ONLINE

ID theft is one of the fastest-growing crimes and accounts for two-thirds of all cases of fraud. Personal information such as your full name, date of birth, address, national insurance number and internet logins are like gold dust to criminals.

The average person has around twenty-six online accounts – everything from banking to shopping – and yet we fail to safeguard our personal information with the most basic of precautions. The online world can feel relatively safe compared with the high street, but don't be fooled. Anything that is connected to the internet, like your computer or your phone, is a potential security risk. You wouldn't walk around the streets flashing all your cash around, so why leave your most valuable information readily accessible online? Here's how to create an online fortress that can keep the criminals at bay.

Online security basics

It pays to ensure that you have all the essentials.

Protect your computer by adding a firewall and anti-virus software. This is the first step to avoiding theft. Some products may be free but only use reputable companies and always install any updates. Ensure operating systems are set to 'auto update'. Use a site checker to test out the safety of a URL: if there is no certificate, beware. Most anti-virus software should alert you before installing software as well. Check that you have an anti-spam product for emails – fraudsters often gain access through email first.

If you've been sent an email with an attachment, think before you open it. Unless it's from someone that you know and trust, leave it. Be certain that your virus software checks all downloads and attachments before opening them, to be extra sure.

Before entering any payment details online, look for the golden padlock either in the lower right-hand side of your screen or on the address bar. Also make sure that the URL begins with 'https'. This ensures that any purchase you make is protected by a special security protocol.

Watch out for redirects and pop up boxes. Always look at the address box to see if the URL changes to something else that bears no relation to the company's URL. If it does, think twice before entering sensitive information such as passwords.

Keep your eye on the end of the URL. This determines in which country the website is hosted. If you're expecting to be linked to a UK or US company and the web address ends in '.ro' or '.ru' you should question whether it's legitimate.

Delete cookies and browser history regularly. Browsers and cookies keep records of the web pages that you visit as well as login details and passwords, making them readily available to fraudsters. If you use a public computer, be sure to clear your browser and cookie history afterwards.

SECURE BANKING – WHAT TO LOOK FOR:

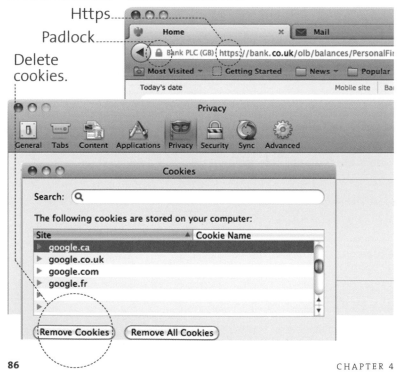

Https

Padlock

Delete cookies.

CHAPTER 4

Protecting your identity online

Every time you enter personal details online you're opening yourself up to the risk of ID theft. Without adequate protection, everything stored on your computer suddenly becomes an open book to the wolves out there – and, trust me, they know every single way of accessing anything worthwhile. Scams, malware and phishing: if you want to survive the wild west of the internet, take the time to read the following and protect yourself by every means.

LIMIT YOUR PERSONAL INFORMATION

EVER SINCE SOCIAL NETWORKING SITES took hold of our lives, we've all become more relaxed about sharing information with strangers. Statistics show that those who spend more time social networking are twice as likely to become victims of ID theft as the rest of the population. Never reveal your exact date of birth or any information that could be used to answer security questions on bank logins.

Phishing: Thieves have become highly skilled at copying the layout and style of a bank's emails claiming that your account has been hacked and that you need to contact them with all your account details immediately. No bank would ever require you to hand over confidential information online. If in any doubt, contact your bank directly and check. Look out for spelling mistakes in the email or errors in the layout and if the address is not one that normally comes from your bank, be wary.

I don't like logging into any of my email accounts on shared computers. Public computers are fine for things like Google and YouTube but risky for anything private. If you have to log into an email account, make sure that you don't tick the box that remembers your details and always log out.

**IMPORTANT INTERNET
BANKING ACCOUNT UPDATE**

Dear SirsMadam,

We wear unable to verify your account information
during are regular database verification process. This
might be due to one or more of the folowing reasons:

1. A recent change in your personal information
(i.e. change of address).
2. Submitting invalid information during initial
enrollment process.
3. Inability to accurately verify your account
information due to an internal error within our
database management systems.

We would require the renewal of your records to
forestall a re-occrence of any future problems with
your online service. However, failure to update your
records might result in your account being supsended.
Please note that your updating of records will not
affect nor interupt your banking services. Please
CLICK HERE and renew your account information.

Spear phishing: Social networking sites leave us prey to thieves
who can access the names of our friends and family, even jobs.
Consequently, if we get an email from someone that we recognize,
we automatically trust it. Read every email carefully and don't click
links or attachments, especially if they ask for personal information.
Never log in or enter any of your details on a site accessed via an
email link, and if you see one signed by 'Customer Relations' with
no contact information, bin it – it's a scam.

How to spot if you've been a victim of ID fraud

Once a year, contact the major credit organizations for a credit
report. Some are free, others charge a small sum but it's worth it.
If you discover credit card accounts that have been opened in your
name but that you have no knowledge of, raise a fraud alert on
your credit report, which will stop further accounts from being
opened. Ask your bank if they have some form of credit-monitoring

service. Once a fraud has been identified, keep a record of all correspondence and conversations made. Contact your bank and ask them to stop any suspect transactions. They will report any criminal activity to the police. Follow up any calls with a letter in writing. Change passwords and banking logins.

SHOPPING, SELLING AND BANKING ONLINE: HOW TO AVOID THE FRAUDSTERS

UK consumers now spend on average £1,083 per year online. In a short space of time we've gone from frequenting shops in the high street and shopping centres to using our iPads and smartphones to buy and even sell online. Instead of queuing for hours at our local bank, we can now run our finances from the comfort of home, all thanks to the internet. But while the benefits are many, they're not without risk. Each time we go online, we're vulnerable to fraud, identity theft and more. Take the following precautions and you should be able to shop worry-free.

How to bank safely

Every bank has its own online system for customers, and some are better than others. Here are some pointers to keep you and your money safe when you're banking online.

Keep your computer's security up to date. This means ensuring that you have all of the latest updates and patches, from your virus software to your operating system. Do this and you'll be able to avoid ninety-nine per cent of fraud and theft online.

Familiarize yourself with your bank and credit card statements. Go through them every day, if you can. The first sign that someone may have stolen your ID is via your credit card and bank. Don't presume that fraudulent payments will always be for large sums of money: many thieves charge small amounts and hope to slip under

SCAM-PROOF PASSWORDS

▶ **Keep banking passwords separate from all others.** If scammers manage to steal one password, they'll clean you out elsewhere.

▶ **Do not share your password, even with family or friends.**

▶ **Never choose a word that could be found in a dictionary,** try to make up a phrase that means something to you, such as 'I love New York'. Use the first letter from each word: ILNY. Add a number or two, perhaps someone's birthday (not your own), such as 12. Add one more layer by using your initials and perhaps keep them lower case, so the final password would read: ILNY12pc.

the bank's automatic radar, so keep an eye out for all payments that you don't recognize.

Beware of calls and emails asking for your online details. If you weren't expecting a call from your bank and are suspicious of the caller, or have received an email you don't trust, telephone your bank for confirmation.

Beware of using free WiFi. Avoid using free or public-access WiFi to purchase goods. An internet cafe could well have someone logging your keystrokes and, in turn, your credit card details and password. Always make sure that you have anti-theft protection as part of the security software installed on your tablet or smartphone. If you're banking online from home via a wireless network, check the security settings on the wireless router are activated. Never do any confidential work such as online banking on a WiFi network that is not secure. Anyone else on that same network can access all of your information.

How to shop safely

Online shopping carries a high risk: sixty-five per cent of card fraud is committed without the card being present. For the fraudsters, it's a business that is highly profitable, with around £3.5 billion lost to card fraud across the world in 2012. But it's not just a case of a trader taking your money and failing to deliver the goods; the bigger crime is where a large number of stolen card details are used to buy goods which are then sold to launder the money.

Check the privacy and security policy. Every online shop has one of these, telling you what information they collect, how they protect the information and with whom they share the data collected. If a shopping site fails to have sufficient security or retains your card details longer than normally allowed, then they're leaving their customers open to theft.

Use a credit card, not a debit card, for online shopping as you will be covered by the bank's automatic payment protection insurance should you fall victim to fraud. As credit cards are usually monitored more closely for patterns of fraud, there's a better chance of any crime being spotted earlier. It also ensures that it's only your credit card that's hit and not your bank account being emptied.

Never give your online password or PIN to anyone. No legitimate shopping site will ever ask for your online bank password or your PIN, only the CV2 number on the back of your credit card will be requested. This number should never be stored after the transaction has been completed, so if you are able to make new purchases without entering this detail, request that they delete your card details.

USE A VIRTUAL CREDIT CARD

THESE CAN BE USED for all online and telephone shopping across the world and can be one way of preventing theft as the card details are useless to a thief. You don't even need a bank account.

THE GOLDEN RULES OF BUYING AND SELLING ON EBAY

For happy shopping and safe selling online, follow this advice:

The buyer's golden rules

▶ **The seller's feedback:** Always read and check that a seller's feedback is for items sold and not for buying items from other sellers. Some sellers buy feedback to make potential buyers believe that they are a legitimate seller.

▶ **New or established seller:** If a seller is new it might not be the wisest of decisions to buy an expensive item from them. With no track record, it could be that they're a scammer hoping to ensnare vulnerable prey.

▶ **What do they sell?** Check which products the trader normally buys and sells. If their main line of business is computers, it might be strange that they also retail clothes. Their account may have been hacked so it's worth double-checking.

▶ **Protection:** eBay provides buyer protection, so check that the product you are purchasing is covered. If you pay for your item via PayPal, you will receive additional protection.

The seller's golden rules

▶ **Know what you can sell and what's illegal.** Try selling a pair of prescription glasses and you'll swiftly discover that they're prohibited. But sex enhancement pills and the odd stuffed animal are freely bought and sold.

▶ **Watch out if a buyer offers to give you a banker's draft that far exceeds the asking price.** If they then ask you to forward the overpaid amount via an instant cash transfer service, such as Western Union, beware. If it sounds dodgy, it usually is.

▶ **Always verify the name on a credit card matches the contact address.** If you are in any doubt, ask the credit card company to confirm that payment has been made before you send the goods.

▶ **Be aware of fraudsters who ask for refunds under the guise of false buyers.** Check eBay messages to validate their claim first before refunding any money and, as a back-up, always use the original payment method.

INTERNET NASTIES: CYBERBULLIES AND TROLLS – WHAT TO DO

Bullying can happen in all walks of life, from the day we toddle into primary school to the rat race of work. In most cases, a change of school or job can solve the problem, but online there's no escape. Protected by the safety of a computer screen or smartphone, an online bully is likely to be more threatening and tormenting than they'd ever dare to be face to face.

Recognizing cyberbullies

You can be innocently voicing your opinion online and, before you know it, you've become the new target of senseless bullies whose only aim is to cause distress. You may well be told nonsense like: 'you deserve this' or 'you're sick', all to provoke a response.

Cyberbullying is usually carried out directly via text messaging, blogs and social media or by using others to help bully the targeted victim.

The harasser might pose as the victim and get hold of their account, or create one in their name and start posting hate-filled messages. The victim's friends soon retaliate and an online war of messages begins. If the cyberbully wants a speedy result, they'll pose as their victim in online hate groups, or even sex offender chat rooms. It turns particularly ugly if a victim's mobile phone details are posted online.

CYBERBULLY FACTS

A mobile phone is the most common means for cyberbullying among teenagers.	**Girls are twice as likely** as boys to be both the victim and the perpetrator of cyberbullying.	**Forty-three per cent of teenagers** say they have been the victim of bullying online.	**Victims of bullying** are at greater risk of committing suicide.

How to prevent a cyberbully attack

Social networking sites have promoted a free and easy exchange between users online. Just as some of us open our mouths without thinking, so our online communications can be reckless. But the internet highway is not a law-free zone. Those posting offensive and abusive messages can often find themselves arrested and behind bars.

HOW TO PROTECT YOUR CHILD FROM CYBERBULLIES

▶ Teach your child how to stay safe online. Show them how to set up privacy settings, especially on social networking sites, and how to report content that they find upsetting to a service such as Childline. Advise them not to share any personal information online, such as their name, address or telephone number.

▶ Talk to your child, little and often, about what they do online and watch out for any unusual behaviour, such as excessive secrecy. Encourage them to tell you if anything makes them feel frightened.

▶ Avoid buying your child a smartphone until they're old enough to understand what they should and shouldn't share online. Consider limiting the use of smartphones in your child's bedroom and the hours in the day that it can be used, but don't overreact – no internet can also mean no friends.

▶ Look out for signs that your child is being bullied online, such as becoming withdrawn, not wanting to go to school and becoming tearful, especially after using the internet. If you discover your child is a cyberbully, explain to them that the written word can be just as harmful as the spoken.

▶ Cyberbullying is not a criminal offence in the UK, but threatening behaviour and harassment are, so contact the police if you think your child is being cyberbullied. Collect all the evidence you can, such as emails, postings on social networks and texts. Mobile phone companies have specialist departments who can help with abusive texts.

ONLINE SEXUAL PREDATORS – WHAT YOU SHOULD KNOW

▸ Be aware of any online friendships your child develops. Paedophiles often strike up relationships using a false online identity – often that of someone similar in age to the victim. Help your child to recognize the danger signs when the online chat becomes sexual.

▸ If your computer has a webcam, take care that your child is not being manipulated to expose themselves.

▸ Stay alert to any face-to-face meetings instigated by a so-called online friend. Make your child aware of the risks and teach them what is considered unacceptable behaviour.

▸ Get to grips with netspeak, the shortened text that your child will use online. Knowing that YOLO means 'you only live once' or LMIRL 'let's meet in real life' can help you defeat the online predators.

▸ Sexting: Tell your child not to take or send any photos that they would not feel comfortable sharing with everyone. Anyone caught sending indecent pictures of a person under eighteen could face prosecution.

Think first; write later. Always consider what you're going to write and treat people in the same way as you would like to be treated. If someone says something online that annoys you, don't be provoked. Ignore them or use your social networking settings to block them.

Facebook friend or foe? Always consider whether you really want to add someone as a friend. If in doubt, block them out.

How to deal with cyberbullies. Do not respond to the bully. These people love to see pain in others and will do anything to achieve a reaction.

Don't participate. Don't watch someone else being bullied; stand up for them and report the situation.

INTERNET SCAMS: WHAT TO LOOK FOR AND HOW TO DEAL WITH THEM

The world is full of scams and scammers, and on the internet it's a free-for-all. With no regulation, these con merchants can run riot stealing and deceiving the vulnerable. Just as we become wise to one scam, another springs up in its place. Many scams are for small gain, but run on a massive scale to maximize profits. From the famous Nigerian '419' scam to email lottery scams, fraudulent competitions to money laundering and begging letters – it's easy to fall prey to the internet wolves. Follow these simple rules and safeguards and you can keep them at bay.

Are you being scammed?

Check online at www.scamomatic.com. Just copy the email text and paste it into the search box and their software will check to see if it's a known scam.

To find out if a website is genuine, try www.scamadviser.com and they'll give you a rating that will tell you whether it's safe to use.

For a useful forum go to www.scamwarners.com.

Your computer is infected: This pop-up alert claims that your computer has been infected with a virus, and is very convincing, but don't be fooled by their offer of a solution. The screen grab that looks like your computer's scan is just a con to get you to click on the link and buy the 'Antivirus software'. DON'T. Thieves will install malware, rendering your computer useless, and they'll also have grabbed your credit card details. Click on the 'X' to close the window and if it doesn't let you, try Ctrl-Alt-Delete to shut it down. If you're in any doubt, run a real anti-malware program to establish that your system is safe, before doing anything else.

Mobile apps: Beware of downloading apps from 'open' app stores. iPhone apps have their own security protection, thanks to

FACEBOOK FAKE EMAILS

ALWAYS STOP TO CHECK any link that asks you to click on it, even if it's from a friend or someone you know. Most good anti-virus software will scan links before opening documents. By holding your mouse over the link, you can establish whether it's genuine or not by checking the address or use a browser plug-in that will allow you to preview shortened URLs.

Apple, but those that operate from an open system for Android are sometimes capable of stealing passwords or banking details. Always ensure that the app developer is a reputable company and, if in doubt, find out what other people think of them via reviews.

Money for a friend in need: If you receive an email from a mate stuck for cash in some foreign land, double-check to see if it really is from someone you know. Scammers may have taken hold of your friend's email account hoping to ensnare you as an unwitting victim. If in doubt, check out their story through other friends, their Facebook page or via an alternative email.

5 NATURAL DISASTERS

HERE'S HOW TO DEAL WITH
MOTHER NATURE'S SHOCKS
AND SURPRISES, AND BE
PREPARED FOR THE WORST.

'NO CITY ON EARTH HAS THE
RIGHT TO BE THERE.'
BIG PHIL CAMPION

SURVIVING NATURAL DISASTERS

Avalanches: surviving a snow slide and essential equipment
Hurricanes and tornadoes: recognizing and surviving storms
and twisters
Landslides: what to do when the earth moves like water
Earthquakes: how to stay alive when the earth starts to shake
Tsunamis: beating the killer waves
Volcanoes: what to do when one erupts
Floods: staying afloat in your home and on the roads
The big freeze and the scorching heat: surviving temperature
extremes
Wild animal attack: what to do when face to face with tooth
and claw

YOU'VE SIGNED UP for a backcountry snowboarding holiday in the US – seven glorious days of freeriding on pristine, powder snow. It's your second morning and a fresh fall of snow overnight has created an unblemished blanket of white. As you set off down the slope, you relish the serene solitude, but just as you're settling into your stride the peace and quiet is broken by voices up on high. As you look behind, six snowboarders are making their way down from the starting zone towards you, but that's not the only thing that's heading your way. With a whoomphing noise a huge layer of snow is sliding towards all of you at increasing speed. Do you shout to the other snowboarders to alert them? Try and move to the side to get out of its way? Or do you call the emergency services while you still can?

BIG PHIL'S ADVICE: Avalanches come in all kinds of shapes and sizes, but the most deadly is the slab: a large block of hard snow – often as big as a car – that fractures away from the less stable snow beneath. If the slab is already heading your way, the only thing you can do is keep going. Within seconds it will reach speeds of sixty to eighty miles per hour as it travels down the slope, so it's futile to try and out-ski this moving mass of snow. Your best bet is to pick up speed ahead of it and then immediately steer to the side, left or right, so that you're out of its destructive path.

On a planet increasingly menaced by torrential rain, earthquakes, tornadoes and tsunamis, a natural disaster is often only one step away. The more we travel to inhospitable places thinking it will never happen to us, the more we fool ourselves. Natural disasters claimed the lives of 9,655 people in 2012 and displaced or affected 124.5 million.

Compared to some years, it's a remarkably low figure. In 2010, the Haiti earthquake alone caused 222,570 fatalities. In natural disasters, you're often at the mercy of powerful freak occurrences that can wreak havoc and take lives within seconds. In all my time travelling, I have witnessed most natural phenomena and can confirm that nowhere on earth is excluded from Mother Nature's wild ways. My rule is never put anything down to chance. It's impossible to predict every natural phenomenon but, with an understanding of the laws of the planet, a good knowledge of basic survival techniques and sufficient preparation, we should all be able to increase the odds of staying alive.

AVALANCHES: SURVIVING A SNOW SLIDE AND ESSENTIAL EQUIPMENT

Avalanches are dependent on several factors: the weather, location and terrain, including the condition of surrounding slopes and sun exposures, the depth and layers of snow, and human behaviour. Most avalanches occur within twenty-four hours of a heavy snowfall: the more snow that falls, the greater the pressure on the weak points. Around ninety per cent of avalanche fatalities, however, are triggered by human activities. As skiers, snowboarders and those on snowmobiles move down a slope, the extra pressure exerted on the snowpack creates fractures resulting in a dry snow slab avalanche.

While predicting an avalanche is difficult, surviving one is possible. Here's what you need to know.

Basic preparation

The safest approach to any avalanche is to avoid it at all costs. Before you even think about venturing out on a slope, do your homework: consult the local avalanche advice centre for a current weather forecast, find out what the avalanche danger rating is and check the snowpack conditions.

Despite the common misconception, noise does not trigger an avalanche. However, too many people on the slope at once can do. If you're travelling with a group, try to spread out; it also means that, if an avalanche does occur, the survivors can help the victims, or at least advise rescuers of their location.

Be aware of everything happening around you. Look for recent avalanche activity: any fracturing, sloughing or wet slides on the slopes or ridges. Listen for hollow noises and whoomphing sounds when moving across the surface: the snowpack may be fracturing. If the snow doesn't appear to support you, it's not safe.

THE SLAB AVALANCHE

Dry: The dry slab avalanche accounts for more deaths than any other type of avalanche. Often triggered by skiers or those on snowmobiles, these occur when a large top layer of hard snow forms over weak, soft snow beneath. As a skier travels over the layer, a fracture occurs within the weak layer, releasing the upper slab. Within five seconds it can reach speeds of sixty to eighty miles per hour, and as it builds up pace it will break up into ice-hard chunks that can injure or entomb victims.

Wet: The wet slab avalanche is triggered by thawing snow and can cause a whole slope to slide. It travels much more slowly, at around ten or twenty miles per hour, and has an appearance a bit like concrete pouring down a slope. Although less likely to cause a fatality, if you're caught in its path it can still give you a serious injury.

The dry powder avalanche: Usually occurring after a fresh snowfall, it starts to move as a soft slab but gathers speed and width as it travels down a slope. As the snow is lifted on the air, a powder cloud forms, but beneath it is a speeding mass of snow: a mix of air and ice particles. Travelling at speeds in excess of one hundred miles per hour, this powder avalanche can create a risk of suffocation if inhaled. Although less dangerous than the dry slab avalanche, if caught in one you can easily be pushed over cliffs or end up buried in concrete-like snow.

Choose gentler slopes for skiing: the steeper the slope, the greater the likelihood of an avalanche. Slopes that have an angle of between thirty and forty degrees provide perfect conditions for the snow to slide. If you have to travel down a section that you're unsure of, seek an alternative route, or travel one at a time to keep tabs on each other.

Try to avoid the side of a mountain that faces the prevailing wind as this can cause large amounts of snow to gather in one place, increasing the likelihood of a slab avalanche.

Surviving an avalanche

In a rapid snow slide, you're likely to get swept up in its path and will most likely crash into anything that lies along the way, including rocks and trees. At impact, snow will fill every available orifice, including your mouth, ears, nose and eyes. You'll lose your bearings quickly and may not know which way is up, becoming entombed in an impacted mass of snow that will make it impossible to move or, worse still, breathe. Chances are that your clothes will be ripped from you, too. If you want to survive this experience, try and remember some basic rules.

THE BEGINNING OF AN AVALANCHE

AT THIS STAGE you still have the chance to escape. If a slab of snow begins moving underneath where you're standing, you need to act immediately. Try moving to one side or running uphill so that you are above the fracture and on stable ground. If you're already skiing and you trigger a slab, the only thing you can do is keep moving. Use your skis or snowmobile to build up speed and distance from the avalanche and then attempt to steer sideways to get out of the pathway of the fast-moving snow. The snow moves fastest at the centre of the flow, which is where most of the snow will accumulate, so the further away from this you can be, the better.

If the snow knocks you down, get rid of as much equipment as you can or it will pull you down into its depths. If you're skiing off-piste, never use the wrist straps on your ski poles, so that they can be discarded quickly in an emergency. Your best chance of survival is to remain on the surface of the moving snow.

If you're on your back, attempt to backstroke your way up the hill with your feet pointing downward and your heels digging into the slab of snow to try to slow your descent (see illustration).

If you can, grab on to a tree, but remember avalanches can travel at between sixty and eighty miles per hour, so this sounds easier than it is.

If you find yourself being rolled by the snow, try and hold your breath and curl up into the foetal position. Use your hands to protect your face.

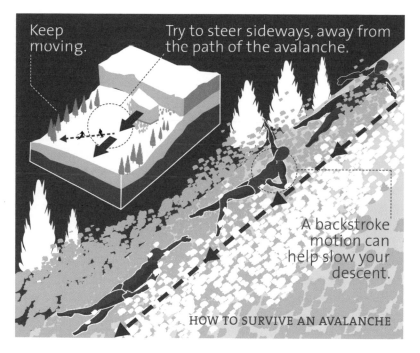

Keep moving.

Try to steer sideways, away from the path of the avalanche.

A backstroke motion can help slow your descent.

HOW TO SURVIVE AN AVALANCHE

As the slide stops, the snow will begin to harden around you like cement. You have only an instant to try to make some air space around your nose and mouth. Fold your arms in front of your face to give yourself as much room as possible and use your body to move from side to side to make more space. If you're near the surface, push one arm or leg up to try and break through the surface of snow so that rescuers can spot you. Take a big breath to expand your chest and give you extra breathing room. One of the key causes of death in an avalanche is suffocation, claiming around ninety per cent of victims.

REMEMBER: If you're buried alive in snow, your chances of survival depend on how far from the surface you are and how much room you have to breathe.

Essential equipment

To avert an avalanche disaster is to go prepared and that means taking the right equipment for the job and knowing how it works.

Transceiver or beacon: If you get buried by an avalanche, this piece of technology will help rescuers find you. Combining a radio that transmits and receives electromagnetic signals, it is highly effective at locating you. Always ensure that you set it to 'transmit' when you start out and not 'receive', as the latter will mean you'll be out in the cold a lot longer than you expected.

Shovel: It sounds basic, but it can move snow five times as fast as your hands, and in an emergency that's vital. If you're backcountry skiing, always carry an aluminium shovel in your backpack for a light but effective lifesaver. Metal is far more effective than plastic for removing avalanche debris.

Ski pole / probes: Once the beacon has located a trapped skier, they could be buried so deep that they're not visible from the surface. A probe can lessen the time it takes to pinpoint their body before expending energy digging, and it's the only way to penetrate the dense debris from the avalanche. Most collapsible probes are light and compact and far longer than ski-pole probes. Otherwise, you could use a long tree branch as an alternative.

HURRICANES AND TORNADOES: RECOGNIZING AND SURVIVING STORMS AND TWISTERS

Hurricanes

Hurricanes are common if you live in a coastal area off the Atlantic or Gulf. When this tropical storm kicks up, you could find yourself facing the full force of winds travelling at seventy-four miles per hour and above. The destructive power of a hurricane is immense: trees are uprooted and ripped right out of the ground, any remaining are left twisted and bent – a permanent reminder of the force of nature. Vehicles and buildings can be torn apart and debris sent swirling into the air until finally the storm moves on, leaving only wreckage and chaos in its place. Never be fooled into thinking a hurricane will lose its power over land: trees and buildings can weaken the power of a storm through resistance, but some storms retain their strength. Unlike a tornado, a hurricane can linger for days, wreaking havoc in the process, but fortunately this slow progress allows for several days' preparation.

THE SIGNS A HURRICANE IS ON ITS WAY

IF YOU CAN READ the signs of nature, you can help yourself prepare well ahead of time.

▸ **Changes to the sky:** A greenish-black spooky colour means a storm is on its way.
▸ **Cloud formation:** Look for quick-moving or rolling clouds.
▸ **The smell of the air:** A fresh, clean edge to the air means a hurricane is looming.
▸ **The sounds:** Listen for the sound of rushing water that gets louder as it moves towards you. An eerie silence after a thunderstorm usually means the eye of the hurricane is passing over you.
▸ **Debris:** If bits are falling from the sky or rotating, it means the storm is moving nearer and it's time to get out.

Surviving this deadly phenomenon relies on recognizing the signs and either battening down the hatches or getting as far away as possible.

How to survive a hurricane

Preparation is your greatest armour. Know your home's vulnerability and, if you live in an evacuation area, devise an action and protection plan to be used in the event of a disaster. Prepare a disaster kit with all the essentials: water, non-perishable food, lighting and heating. Use local news and weather reports to understand the type of hurricane and any associated risks.

The safest place during any powerful storm is the basement. Failing that, keep away from windows and aim for the middle of the house, taking shelter under a weighty table. If you're out driving and see the storm approaching, abandon your car and find shelter in the nearest building.

Make your home windproof. Use strong storm shutters on any windows or glass and lock them to keep your windows protected –

or attach plywood to the window frame. Windows can be covered with a protective film so that the glass doesn't shatter if they break. Make sure doors have three or more hinges and use security locks that can be dead-bolted. Roofs and garage doors should be strengthened with bracing on each of the panels.

Home basics: Buy a small generator that will keep the essentials, like a fridge, running for a short time. Ensure that you have batteries for torches and camping equipment that would allow you to cook in the event of the electrics or gas going out.

Tornadoes

Unlike a hurricane, where you may have days to prepare and evacuate, a tornado can develop within minutes. A tornado is a column of air that rotates violently across the land, creating wind speeds of up to 110 mph, and in some extreme cases 300–500 mph. These terrifying twisters are formed when the sun increases the temperature of the ground, promoting warm, moist air to travel upwards and collide with the cold, dry air above. Usually accompanied by powerful thunderstorms, a tornado is a powerful hazard that can sweep buildings away within seconds.

THE 'SUPER SPEED TORNADO' FACTS

THE OLD SAYING GOES, 'It was so windy, it could knock a dog off its lead.' Here's what the experts say:

▶ **113–157 mph – Considerable damage:** Trees are uprooted, cars are lifted and mobile homes severely damaged.
▶ **158–206 mph – Severe damage:** Roofs are torn off buildings and trains overturned.
▶ **207–260 mph – Catastrophic damage:** Houses with weak foundations are completely blown away.
▶ **261–318 mph – Decimation:** Cars are lifted and thrown one hundred metres. Few buildings remain standing.

DIFFERENT TYPES OF TORNADO

THERE ARE THREE MAIN TYPES of tornado. Most occur over land, but occasionally one can travel over water. Know the difference and you can take precautions accordingly.

Wedge tornado: The most dangerous of tornadoes but fortunately also the rarest. Shaped like a wedge, the base of these tornadoes can be as wide as one mile. Spreading across land, and usually at the heart of a thunderstorm, they can produce extraordinary amounts of debris.

Rope tornado: Better known as the 'twister', these are common. Shaped like a funnel or an 'S' shape, it's easy to think of these tornadoes as weak, but the truth is they can still do serious damage.

Water spouts: These tornadoes form over water and are the least harmful. Small in width, they often measure only about fifty metres. Once they hit land, they normally lose their power and dissipate.

Staying safe when a twister arrives

Listen out for a tornado warning on the local weather forecast and take shelter immediately. As with hurricanes, the safest place is away from windows and doors and at the lowest possible level. That could be the basement, a low spot towards the centre of a building, or in an office stairwell.

If you're outside, stay away from parked vehicles and move to a building quickly. If you're stuck in a vehicle, don't try and act the superhero and out-drive the tornado. The rotation of air can reach speeds of over 300 mph and your vehicle is likely to be tossed around like a toy if you're in its path. Do the sensible thing: find a building to shelter in or lie down in a low area and protect your head with your arms.

LANDSLIDES: WHAT TO DO WHEN THE EARTH MOVES LIKE WATER

Landslides occur when water accumulates in the ground, changing the earth into a fast-flowing river of debris and mud. With the ability to travel several miles, landslides can grow in size and power within a very short space of time, killing thousands.

Various causes can predispose an area to this huge earth shift: everything from erosion and human activities like excavation and mining to the main triggers of heavy rainfall and earthquakes. With a growing population, more road construction and increased rainfall, landslide incidents are on the increase worldwide. If you know the signs to look out for, you can make an escape, but time is of the essence and every second counts.

How to survive when a landslide hits

If you get caught in the path of a landslide, move away from the debris flow as quickly as you can. If you can't escape, protect your head with your hands and curl up into a ball. Even in its aftermath,

THE SIGNS OF A LANDSLIDE

▶ **Sounds:** Cracking of trees or rocks knocking could be the first signs of a landslide, or a faint rumbling sound that gets louder. Look for a small trickle of mud. A landslide can escalate quickly and a little falling mud can suddenly turn into a torrent.

▶ **Rivers that turn muddy:** If you see this, or a dramatic increase or decrease in the water flow of rivers or streams, it could mean a landslide, is on its way.

▶ **Earthquakes and torrential rain:** Both of these can trigger a landslide so stay alert and move to safer ground.

▶ **When driving, look out for debris:** Fallen rocks, collapsed pavements and mud on the road all can indicate a landslide is on its way.

you may not be safe. Further slides may occur now that land has been disturbed. Debris, like trees, could be strewn across roads and bridges, walls may be weakened and electric and gas supplies damaged with the risk of explosion or fire.

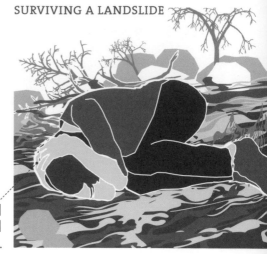

SURVIVING A LANDSLIDE

Curl into a ball and protect your head with your hands.

EARTHQUAKES: HOW TO STAY ALIVE WHEN THE EARTH STARTS TO SHAKE

When layers of the rocky outermost crust of the earth begin to grind against one another and eventually break apart, the force results in an earthquake. The length of time it takes for those layers to break apart determines whether it's just a minor shaking of the earth, or a major seismic event destroying buildings and everything in its path. Surviving an earthquake depends largely on where you're located and the immediate action you take. Follow these guidelines and you heighten your chances of coming out the other side alive.

Signs that the earth's about to move

Scientists often attempt to predict earthquakes but ,with the exception of major quakes, they often arrive without warning. Despite constant monitoring of changes in seismic waves and the earth's electrical and magnetic properties, earthquake forecast is far from perfect.

MOTHER NATURE'S EARTHQUAKE PREDICTORS

REMEMBER THAT AN EARTHQUAKE is more common when several of these precursors occur together:

▶ **Temperature rises:** Months before an earthquake, the average temperature of an area increases. On the day of the earthquake it will usually be five to nine degrees higher than normal.

▶ **River flow increases or decreases:** One or two days prior to an earthquake, water levels will suddenly appear to rapidly increase or decrease. Fountains may appear in the ground and wells will rise.

▶ **Electrical interference:** As the temperature rises, electromagnetic waves used by radios, telephones and televisions are adversely affected. One to three hours before an earthquake, mobile telephones may start to malfunction, with interference most common.

▶ **Animals:** About ten to twenty hours before the earth starts to shake, animals become disturbed. Birds give out panic calls and won't sit in trees; pets and domestic animals, like horses and cows, resist being tied up and may act aggressively.

▶ **Human behaviour:** Physiological symptoms may occur, like headaches, migraines, breathing problems, heart disorders and a sudden rise in blood pressure. In high-risk areas, hospitals see a seven-fold increase in individuals attending as outpatients, while the number of childbirths occurring is eight times greater than normal on the day of an earthquake.

When an earthquake strikes

If you've never experienced a major earthquake, it's easy to think it's all a lot of fuss about nothing, but when the earth shakes violently and the ground moves back and forth several feet per second, events occur so quickly and with such violence that you have to act fast.

'Drop, cover and hold on.' The instant you feel the first jolt of an earthquake, get down on your hands and knees to stop yourself from falling. Get under a table, hold on to it and move with it, if necessary. If you have nothing to take shelter under, position yourself next to low-lying furniture that will not topple over on to you. If you're in bed, research shows that you should stay there and cover your head with a pillow.

TO STAY SAFE: The corner of a room offers the greatest chance of survival. In a collapse, a natural triangle will form there.

Keep away from anything that might break. Stay away from the most dangerous parts of a building – the windows and the façades – as these will be the first to collapse in an earthquake. Do not stand in the doorway of a modern house. Older houses used timber frames with their inherent strength, but modern doorways are no stronger than any other part of the house, and they will fail to protect you against the most dangerous aspect of an earthquake: falling objects.

Take cover underneath a table.

SURVIVING AN EARTHQUAKE

ESSENTIAL EQUIPMENT AND ACTIONS BEFORE AN EARTHQUAKE

IF YOU LIVE in an earthquake-prone zone, it's worth creating an earthquake kit that includes the following:

- Fire extinguisher
- First-aid kit
- Mobile/smartphone, with batteries
- Battery-powered radio, charged up
- Torch and batteries

Remember:

- Turn off gas, water and electricity.
- Don't use any form of flame – like matches or candles. Gas leaks are common in an earthquake and you don't want to blow yourself up.
- Secure furniture, such as TVs, bookcases and lamps so, when the room does do the mamba, everything stays put, and fix down ornaments with Blutack or Velcro tape so that they don't fly around like lethal weapons.
- Plan where to meet family and friends after an earthquake.

After the shaking has stopped

Stay tuned into the radio for the latest updates. Use your mobile to monitor social networking sites and alert people to your situation. Stay out of damaged buildings in case they collapse (see *Buildings and bridges: how to stay alive if they collapse* in *Chapter 6: Man-made disasters*, p152). Be aware of debris: windows are likely to be broken in buildings and cars. Most of all, stay away from the beach: the ground may have stopped shaking, but this is the time when a tsunami can hit, so listen out for government warnings.

TO STAY SAFE: If you're near the sea and you fear that there may be a tsunami, even without official confirmation, move to higher ground immediately.

TSUNAMIS: BEATING THE KILLER WAVES

Whenever an earthquake occurs near or under water, always beware what may follow. Any kind of earth movement beneath the ocean can displace a huge volume of water, creating a series of monstrous waves, better known as a tsunami.

Unlike ordinary waves, a tsunami's wavelength is far longer: up to sixty miles in length with a height reaching tens of metres, and some can even travel across 300 miles without losing power. The result is a hugely destructive force, capable of extinguishing land and life. Listen out for national warnings, but also stay alert for the natural signs that precede a tsunami – identifying them may be your only chance of survival.

KEY EVENTS THAT CAN PRECEDE A TSUNAMI

IF YOU NOTICE any one of these events, get out quickly and move to higher ground.

▶ **Earth shaking:** An earthquake is the first warning of a tsunami, but it's not always the biggest quakes that trigger this destructive phenomena. If the ground shakes forcefully, pack your bags and move to higher ground, away from the water's edge.

▶ **Tide withdrawal:** If the ocean suddenly pulls back from the shore, revealing fish and reef – RUN. When the ocean returns, it's likely to be as a fast-moving wall of water.

▶ **Ocean roar:** If you hear an eerie roaring sound from the direction of the ocean, get out quick – a tsunami is most likely on its way.

▶ **Animals:** Pets and wildlife have an innate sixth sense when it comes to natural phenomena. If you see animals crowding together or attempting to find shelter, take it as a sign that something's not right. Get out while you can.

SURVIVING A TSUNAMI

▶ **Find something that floats:** Doors, fishing equipment, rafts, even tree trunks – any of these items may already be in the water with you.

▶ **Leave your possessions behind:** The only thing you should grab is your emergency kit and your family and then get the hell out. As a last ditch, all you can do is save yourself; you will be no good to anyone dead.

▶ **Wait for the all clear:** A tsunami can last for hours, so don't return until you've received the all-clear signal. Check in advance to see what this is. Don't be fooled into thinking the waves start big and then diminish. The waves often grow bigger as the tsunami unfolds.

▶ **Aftermath:** Debris will be strewn everywhere, including dead bodies, so the risk of disease is high. It is important to find fresh water and food provisions, as well as to maintain high levels of sanitation.

Prepare for the worst

If you live in an earthquake and tsunami-prone area, take the time to figure out an evacuation plan with several safety routes and options for shelter. As with other natural emergencies, put together an emergency survival kit that can be grabbed quickly the minute you know a tsunami is on its way. (See *The emergency survival kit* in *Chapter 11: Big Phil's locker*, p258.)

At the first warning sign, head for higher ground inland, preferably among hills and mountains. Move away from all sources of water: sea, coast, lagoons. If you cannot travel far, get up as high as you can. Climb on to solid building rooftops as far away as possible from the incoming waves. If there are no buildings, look for a tall tree and head upwards. Trees are at risk of being swept away by a tsunami, so choose one that is strong and sturdy and preferably has branches to rest on – you may be there for some time.

VOLCANOES: WHAT TO DO WHEN ONE ERUPTS

When one of these bursts forth, there's a sky-high explosion of boiling lava, rocks, ash and gas. Whereas an earthquake originates from the outer layers of the earth grinding together, a volcano is found inside the thinning areas of the earth's crust. Luckily, so far, we've not had a super-volcano strike; its sheer devastation would cause a level of destruction equal to a world nuclear war.

Signs of eruption: what to look for

Once a volcano becomes active, experts are able to detect the warning signs from its seismic activity, providing a fairly accurate indication of when an eruption is on its way. For the layman, there are more obvious clues, but remember: when the smoke is so thick the dogs have stopped barking, it's too late to learn the clues.

Always be aware how near you are to a volcano. Many holidaymakers may not even know that they're staying in a volcano hot spot until ash is spewed everywhere. Keep tabs on the local media and social networks: they'll be pumping out the news if there's even the slightest chance of an eruption.

VOLCANO CLUES

▶ Look for swelling or bulging of the ground, cracking of the surface and noticeable activity around hot springs near the volcano.
▶ A smell of rotten eggs will be apparent as carbon dioxide and hydrogen sulphide escape into the air. Steam alone is not a sign of an immediate eruption, as this can often be found in a dormant volcano.

Preparations to avert the danger of a volcano

Whether you live near to a volcano or you're on holiday in a high-risk area, you should always be prepared for an eruption. Ensure that you are familiar with the escape routes. A local hazard-zone map will indicate the risk factor for your location, including the likely path of lava and debris flow and the depths of ash fall. Keep an ear on the radio the moment a volcano erupts. This will keep you updated on events around you and help you assess the situation and your route to safety. Always keep an emergency survival kit near to hand with all the necessities. (See *The emergency survival kit* in *Chapter 11: Big Phil's locker*, p258.)

When the lava flows

Local emergency crews may order an evacuation – don't ignore this, even if at first it's only a recommendation. People have died because they have failed to take immediate action.

Move to higher ground, especially if you are in a valley. Lava, mud and debris can be deadly if you're on lower ground – try and stay on a hill on the opposite side of a volcano. Be aware of flying hot rocks as you travel.

Avoid deadly gases. When a volcano gets going, poisonous gases are pushed into the air, killing anything in their path. Use a mask or respirator, or at worst a damp piece of cloth to protect your lungs from the ash. Do not drop to the ground, as the most dangerous gases are to be found low down. Stay indoors if you can and close windows and doors until given the all clear by authorities. Seek medical attention for immediate emergencies like gas inhalation, burns or injuries.

FLOODS: STAYING AFLOAT IN YOUR HOME AND ON THE ROADS

At least 3,527 people died in floods across the world in 2012. It only takes a few torrential storms and, within hours, fast-rising water levels can cause rivers, streams and lakes to overflow. Just fifteen centimetres of fast-flowing water can knock you off your feet; sixty centimetres will float a large car. Stay clear of streams, ditches, swamps and any low-lying areas. A flash flood can happen in any one of these places, far away from the storm clouds that bring the rain.

Nature's tip-offs

Look out for flood indicators and act accordingly. If clear water, for example in a stream, becomes muddy or is suddenly full of debris, then a flood is more than likely on its way. The clap of thunder upstream is another confirmation that trouble is afoot. Move to higher ground or aim for the upper storeys in a house, or the roof. Stay there until you can be rescued by the emergency services.

HOW TO PREPARE BEFORE A FLOOD

▶ **Make up an emergency flood kit and keep it handy.** Include a torch with spare batteries, blankets, warm waterproof clothing, bottled water and non-perishable foods. Don't forget to include baby food and care items if you have little ones. A first-aid kit with prescription medicine and household insurance documents are all must-haves.

▶ **Move anything valuable upstairs.** Don't leave any expensive items of furniture, anything of personal value or any electrical equipment downstairs.

▶ **Put any flood protection items you have in place,** such as airbrick covers or sandbags (a pillow case or plastic bag packed with earth will suffice). Put the plugs in sinks and baths and weigh them down with a heavy object to stop the water rising up into your house.

What to do in the event of a flood

If water is entering your house, and if it is safe to do so yourself, turn off the gas, electricity and water supply as soon as possible. Do not touch any electrical items that are standing in water. Collect essential items, including pans and bottles of fresh water and food, and move these along with everyone else – pets included – to higher ground that has a means of escape. You should include enough non-perishable food and bottled water for three days. Most active people require at least a gallon (4.5 litres) of water per day for drinking.

WARNING: Don't walk or drive through flood water. All kinds of debris will be in your path, including open manholes. Flood water can become contaminated with sewage, so be careful to avoid contact or wash hands well.

Driving in floods

Avoid driving in flooded areas as there's a good chance that your vehicle will quickly be swept away. If the flood water begins to rise around your car, get out immediately and, if you can, move to higher ground. If you are crossing a ford or an area which has been flooded, don't stop the car – keep going. The car will force a wave behind but, if you stop, the wave will go into the exhaust and you will come to a halt. Check your car's brakes as soon as it is safe to do so.

DANGEROUS WATERS

15 **centimetres** of water can reach the under-neath of a car and cause it to malfunction. The car is likely to stall and you can easily lose control.

30 **centimetres** of water and the car will begin to float.

60 **centimetres** of water is enough to sweep away a pick-up truck.

IT'S THE MOMENT that everyone has been waiting for, when the rain stops, but you're not out of danger yet. A flood can leave behind some nasty surprises.

▸ **When the water recedes,** the ground and roads may have weakened and be close to collapse, so take great care when driving.

▸ **Electrical and gas supplies may be out and power lines down,** which can electrically charge flood waters, so stay clear.

▸ **Ensure drinking water is safe to drink,** as sewage and debris may have contaminated supplies.

▸ **Beware of bridges and any building** that is surrounded by flood water, as a flood can seriously weaken the structure.

THE BIG FREEZE AND THE SCORCHING HEAT: SURVIVING TEMPERATURE EXTREMES

As our weather system becomes more unpredictable, the chances of extreme conditions increase. From freezing cold to sweltering heat, you don't need to be in the desert or Antarctica to encounter a survival challenge. Should the body's core temperature shift just a couple of degrees either way, the consequences can prove deadly. Here's how to beat the challenges of our ever-changing climate.

The bitter cold

Keep it loose and keep it layered. Choose several layers of clothing that are loose-fitting rather than one or two thick items. The aim is to trap the warm air next to your body rather than keep the cold air out. When you get too warm, you can simply remove one of those layers. Choose at least three layers: the inner *wicking* layer; the middle *warm* layer, and the outer *wind and waterproof* layer. Wool is good for the inner layer of clothing as its fibres will naturally trap warm air and draw perspiration away from the body, but don't overspend on thermals – any layered clothing will have the same effect.

Don't lose heat through your head. Always wear a hat or cover your head with a hood. Statistics vary as to just how much heat is lost from the head, but it's true to say that, if you want to stay warm, a hat is essential.

Warm feet and hands; warm body. Use a thin inner layer underneath a thick outer layer for both socks and gloves. Choose

RECOGNIZE THE SIGNS OF FROST-NIP AND FROSTBITE

WHEN THE AIR temperature drops below freezing, the body starts to divert heat away from the extremities to the body's core. While the essential organs remain protected, blood flow is reduced to the fingers, toes, nose and earlobes. If left long enough, the tissue will eventually freeze and die.

▸ **Frost-nip** affects the outer layers of skin, which begin to feel itchy and painful but are as yet undamaged. The skin may start off red and then turn an unnatural pale white colour, especially around the nose and ears. As the blood flow reduces, fingers and toes may feel numb.
▸ **Frostbite** is when the skin actually begins to freeze and ice crystals start to form within the living cells of the skin, killing them. Look for swelling of the skin and blisters that are coloured purple or black.

See *Extreme Cold* in *Chapter 10: The bare essentials,* p 250.

a wicking fabric that will pull the perspiration away from the body. Be careful not to make your shoe or glove too tight as you need some room to trap the warm air.

Keep active. The more you move, the better your circulation and body warmth.

Getting snowed in

Snow can be fun if you're on holiday, but when you're stuck in your house with no safe means of transport, it's a pain. Ensure that you have enough essential supplies to last you a week, including clean water, non-perishable food, such as canned fish, meat, vegetables and soups, dried fruit and nuts, and a means to keep warm if power lines come down. A small generator is worth investing in to provide heating and the ability to warm food. Failing that, ensure you have plenty of blankets and sleeping bags, and stock up on torches and batteries for lighting. Always keep emergency numbers near to hand in case you need medical assistance.

Snow gear

Snow goggles: Whether you're on the piste or mountaineering, you need to protect your eyes from the wind and glare. Remember that the sun's UV radiation levels will be stronger at high altitude due to the thin atmospheric levels, so always use goggles that block one hundred per cent of UVA and UVB rays. If you're in an area with variable levels of sunshine, choose photochromatic lenses that will self-adjust. If the snow is blowing in all directions, go for wraparound, but ensure that you can still see 180 degrees, from one side to the other.

Sunscreen: Spending time in the snow in alpine regions can be equally as damaging as the sun in Acapulco, with UV levels increased by the reflection from the snow. Always wear a sun cream with a minimum SPF of thirty to keep out ninety-three per cent of UVB rays. For fair skin, an SPF of fifty is recommended to protect you against ninety-eight per cent of the rays responsible for sunburn. If you want to block the sun's rays out altogether the best product to buy is zinc oxide.

What to do if you have to drive in the snow

If you have to travel, go prepared and allow plenty of time for the journey. Take blankets and warm clothing, including hats, gloves and scarves, and ensure that you have enough food and water for you and your passengers. Always carry a shovel in case you get stuck on the road and remember the following basic principles of driving in snow and ice.

Take the time to clear the snow from your car. Time and again I see drivers who've only wiped away a small square of snow from their windscreen and then drive off like an igloo on wheels. If you can't see out of your windscreen, you're risking your life and that of others. It only takes five minutes with a snow/ice scraper to give your vehicle a good clean, including your lights and indicators.

Don't forget the roof – a huge wedge of snow there can quickly slide across the windscreen when you brake, temporarily blinding you to any hazards.

Manual or automatic? If you're driving a manual car, you already have an advantage over an automatic. With full control over the gears, any wheel spinning can be kept to a minimum. Always begin in the highest gear possible, usually second gear. Let your foot off the clutch slowly, without pressing the accelerator, and the car should move forward. Keep the revs up with gentle acceleration. For automatic cars in the snow, select '2' instead of 'drive'; this will limit the gears and make you less reliant on your brakes. Use brakes in good time and gently to avoid skidding. Hold the steering wheel with both hands and keep your thumbs away from the inside. Any sudden move in the wheel and they'll break.

If you do slide, make a gentle movement with the steering wheel in the direction you want to go and then a fraction the other way to unlock the wheels. Don't attempt to brake sharply or use the accelerator until the wheels have come back under control. Use your clutch and come down in gears, then gently brake if needed once the car is moving in the right direction again. Allow for extra stopping distances in snow and ice and stay well back from other cars.

Keep your thumbs on top of the steering wheel rim to avoid injury in a skid.

Keep a good distance from other cars.

In a skid, gently turn the steering wheel in the direction you want to go, and then a fraction the other way until the wheels grip.

DRIVING IN ICE AND SNOW

Heatwaves

Excess heat will push the body to extremes, causing it to work extra hard to maintain its normal temperature, so stay cool by taking it easy and wear light, breathable clothes. If you're fit and healthy, a heatwave shouldn't cause you any problems, but for children, the elderly and those who are sick, prolonged heat can cause numerous health risks. In high temperatures, avoid smog-filled environments, as the air quality is stagnant and can affect breathing.

Symptoms of over-exposure to heat

Heat exhaustion: As the body tries to cool down, perspiration increases and vast quantities of body fluids are lost in the process. Without these fluids, blood flow to the essential organs decreases, putting the body at risk of heat stroke. Signs to look out for include fatigue, sweating, cool, clammy skin, dizziness, fainting, vomiting, headaches, muscle cramps and thirst.

Heat stroke: As the body's temperature control system malfunctions, it's unable to cool itself. Your brain is in danger of being cooked alive and your kidneys and liver are at risk of failure. Signs to look out for are a body temperature of forty-one degrees Celsius, nausea, rapid breathing, confusion, seizures and unconsciousness.

See *Extreme heat* in *Chapter 10: The bare essentials*, p251.

Protection against the heat

If you can't stand the heat, do something about it.

Indoors:

▶ **Make sure that air conditioners and air vents are insulated well.** Alternatively, install window reflectors to reflect the heat outside, or create your own with cardboard covered with aluminium foil. Place between the window and curtains for immediate coolness.

- **Use curtains or blinds** to keep morning or afternoon sun out.
- **Wear loose, thin clothing made of natural fibres,** like cotton or linen, around the house to stay cool.

Outdoors:

- **Limit your time outdoors to before 10 a.m. and after 4 p.m.** to avoid the hottest time of the day.
- **Wear long, loose clothes to cover up and stay cool.** T-shirts and shorts might feel like the right choice, but in very hot sun you need to keep your arms and legs covered to avoid damage from the UV rays.
- **Wear a hat to protect your head and face,** and to avoid cooking your brain. I always choose a wide-brim hat to keep my neck cool in the heat.
- **Find shady spots to cool off** and always wear a high-factor sun cream or a sunblock like zinc oxide.
- **Choose light colours to reflect the heat** and stick with cool fabrics or special sports clothes that are designed to absorb sweat.
- **A vest works wonders when it comes to keeping you cool.** Worn under clothes, it will take the sweat away from the body – the reason why so many locals in hot countries wear one.
- **Keep hydrated by drinking lots of fluids** but stay away from alcohol as this exacerbates dehydration.
- **Don't overeat and avoid rich, high-protein and hot meals,** which require more digestion and will raise your body temperature. Instead, choose salads, fresh fruits and vegetables.

WILD ANIMAL ATTACK: WHAT TO DO WHEN FACE-TO-FACE WITH TOOTH AND CLAW

It's rare to be attacked by a wild animal, but not impossible. Essentially, you have three choices: you avoid an encounter, you attack the animal or you play dead. If you decide to attack, then you'd better make sure that you have the means to win. Here's the A–Z of the animal kingdom and how to escape an attack from each one.

A–Z of surviving an encounter with the animal kingdom

▶ **Alligators:** Fighting back is your best chance to survive, as an alligator prefers an easy life. If you're grabbed by one, try to force its mouth open so that you can escape.

▶ **Alaskan moose:** Those with offspring may see you as a threat. If they try to kick you, curl up on the ground and wait until they've moved away.

▶ **Bees:** Most bees are very unlikely to harm you, but if you disturb a nest of killer bees, move off quickly. Head for cover in a car or building and protect your face with your clothing.

▶ **Dogs:** See *Stray or aggressive dogs* in *Chapter 2: Cutting about*, p37.

▶ **Elephants:** An aggressive elephant can be a fast mover, travelling at twenty-five miles per hour, so don't try to outrun one. Climb up a tree to safety or lie down with your hands on your face.

▶ **Grizzly bears:** Don't run. If you can, lie face down with your hands protecting the back of your head until the bear loses interest. If a bear is approaching you, try and make as much noise as you can: bang cans and scream to scare the bear away. I have done this with a honey bear in Brunei and it worked.

▶ **Hippos:** Avoid at all costs – they're horrible. Remember you will never outrun a hippo.

▶ **Jellyfish:** If you want to swim in deep water that is likely to contain jellyfish, wear a wetsuit to protect exposed skin. Some say that a pair of tights can be just as effective, as most jellyfish do not possess stingers long enough to penetrate the nylon mesh. If you are stung, pour vinegar immediately on to the wound and do not rub or cover for thirty seconds. Jellyfish stings can cause anaphylaxis that may lead to breathing difficulties or a heart attack, so call for emergency help immediately if you suffer any unusual symptoms.

▶ **Lions:** If things look like they're about to turn nasty, make as much loud and persistent noise as possible to scare them off. Throw anything within easy reach without turning your back or crouching down. Some people have had success using a flashlight or lights that flicker intermittently. If you are attacked, place your hands at the back of your neck and cradle your head between your elbows, tuck your chin into your chest and lift your shoulders to your ears to protect your throat.

▶ **Monkeys:** Avoid smiling at primates or using eye contact – it's seen as a sign of aggression. Give them some room and keep your distance, stay calm and only fend off the animal if it becomes violent.

▶ **Poisonous spiders:** If you're in a high-risk area for spiders, take some sensible precautions. Don't leave any clothing on the floor and shake all items well before dressing. Bang shoes on a hard surface before putting them on. Pull the bed away from the wall, avoid letting your bedding touch the floor and avoid any unnecessary frilly edges. If bitten, call for emergency help immediately, and in the meantime, rinse the bite with water and use ice to cool the area until help arrives.

▶ **Rhinos:** If one charges at you, aim for thick or thorny bushes, as they're less likely to enter these areas. Whatever you do, don't try and outrun one. Most rhinos can run at thirty-five miles per hour.

▶ **Sharks:** It sounds obvious, but stay out of shark-infested waters if you want to avoid an attack. If you must swim in these areas, don't wear brightly coloured clothing. Dark colours are less likely to attract a shark. Avoid sudden movement if you spot one nearby and try to stay as still as possible. If you do get attacked, strike the shark's gills and other sensitive areas. Aim for the nose and not its mouth, unless you want to lose an arm or leg.

▶ **Snakes:** Avoid tall grass, logs or any rocks where a snake could be hiding. Cover up and wear boots and long trousers. Be aware of water snakes, if you're swimming in rivers or lakes.

Not all snakes are venomous. Beware of those with a triangular head that indicates a venom gland. Non-venomous snakes normally have a round head. If bitten, don't attempt to suck or squeeze the venom out, as you can seriously risk infection and damage to the tissue. Try and identify the snake that bit you, as each snake's venom requires a different antidote. Keep the wound below heart level to ensure that blood circulation to the snakebite is slowed, thus preventing the poison spreading too far within your body, and seek urgent medical help.

▶ **Wolves:** A wolf is more likely to be scared of you, but if you do encounter one that's getting curious, attempt to make yourself look bigger than you are. Throw anything you can to discourage the wolf from coming closer – rocks or tree branches – and always make sure that there's no food around to attract wolves or any wild animal.

6 MAN-MADE DISASTERS

'IF A PLANE COMES DOWN, IT DON'T MATTER IF YOU'RE IN FIRST CLASS OR ECONOMY: YOU'RE ALL IN THE SHIT.'
BIG PHIL CAMPION

SURVIVING MAN-MADE DISASTERS

Car crash: drivers, passengers and pedestrians – how to stay alive

Sinking ship: when something's wrong – preparation and escape

Air disaster: enhancing your chances of survival

Train crash: preparation and survival

Buildings and bridges: how to stay alive if they collapse

Nuclear power station leak: what to do if you're hit by radiation

SCENARIO

YOUR GRANDPA ALWAYS DID SAY, 'Never travel on anything with wings or a rudder.' He may have only ever travelled as far as Blackpool but, as you lie in your cabin bed, his words come disturbingly back to you. It's your third night at sea on the 141,000-ton mega-cruise ship, *The Royal,* and you've just been awakened by an almighty bang and a groaning noise as the ship shudders to a halt. Whatever's happened, it sounds terminal. You can hear no alarms or people running down corridors; perhaps you were just having a bad dream? But as the ship suddenly tilts to the right – along with most of the cabin's furniture – you realize that you're in trouble. Should you try and find out what's going on? Wait for the ship's crew to tell you what to do? Or do you race for the muster station, grab a life jacket and head straight for the lifeboats, super-quick?

BIG PHIL'S ADVICE: In any impending disaster, being prepared can save your life. Always pay attention to the safety drill at the start of your journey. This will inform you of the location of three vital things: the muster station (or gathering place in an emergency), the lifeboats and your life jacket, as well as how to put it on. Make it your priority to learn the quickest and safest route to the muster station – you may need to find it in the dark – and take the time to practise putting on your life jacket.

A disaster can happen to anyone, usually when you least expect it. The much-publicized luxury cruise liner capsizes or your first-class train carriage with an impeccable safety record suddenly derails. Without warning, your life gets turned upside down by a freak occurrence. So what can you do to avert the crisis-from-hell?

Having a strategy can make all the difference to your survival when your back's against the wall. As your heart and adrenaline go into overtime, your survival depends on how quickly you can react to the situation, what action you decide to take and, interestingly, the choices you made before the accident even happened.

CAR CRASH: DRIVERS, PASSENGERS AND PEDESTRIANS – HOW TO STAY ALIVE

Each year 1.24 million people are killed in car crashes across the world. That's enough to fill around 1,965 large passenger planes. Despite modern technology and the latest advancements in vehicle safety, car crashes continue to harm more people than any other form of transport. Statistically, they are the leading cause of death among people aged between three and thirty-three. Smash-ups can happen for all sorts of reasons, but the outstanding cause is the driver behind the wheel. From texting friends to driving when drunk, accidents happen when the mind of the person driving is anywhere but the road. Modern vehicles are now created with safety in mind, so, even in the event of a crash, you're likely to be protected from serious injury. But here are some tips on how to maximize your chance of surviving with little more than a bruise.

Drivers: prevention is better than cure

One of the biggest differences we can all make to road safety is to improve our own 'driver behaviour'. I'm amazed to see drivers talking on their phones or sending texts while trying to negotiate a roundabout or even overtake traffic. Attention is everything on the road: without it, you're an accident just waiting to happen.

Observation: Don't just fix your eyes on the car in front; check out the car on your left, your right and even the one behind you, and ensure that you stay clear of the obviously distracted drivers. Know what's around you and you stand a good chance of avoiding a collision.

Hands and seat: Get your seat upright and close enough to the wheel that you can reach the pedals easily. If you can't see over the steering wheel, get a cushion. Your left hand should be at nine o'clock on the steering wheel and your right hand at three o'clock: this position gives you full control of the wheel – and the car – in all circumstances, including emergency stops. Beware of holding the wheel higher than this, as modern air bags may cause hand and wrist injuries.

Know your car's limits. If you've never attempted an emergency stop in your car, you won't know how your car's brakes respond. Practise this manoeuvre in a quiet, safe spot. If you have ABS, you should press the brake pedal as hard as you can until the car comes to a stop and then depress the clutch. Without ABS, press the brake pedal firmly, but not so hard that the wheels lock and you start to skid. Ease gently off the brakes and then press again.

Keep a safe distance from the car in front, even when you're in slow traffic. If you can't see their wheels, you're too close.

Look both ways more than once at junctions before you pull out. It's surprising how many times you'll miss a vehicle the first time because the frame of your car creates a blind spot.

Turn your head when changing lanes, joining a main road on a filter or overtaking a vehicle and check for cars in your way. Wing mirrors don't always give you a complete view of the vehicles around you.

Watch your speed and your attention. Department of Transport statistics for road accidents reveal that careless, reckless and speeding drivers caused the most accidents over the course of one year: a total of 19,328, of which 272 were fatalities. Compare this to the ninety-nine accidents caused by slow drivers, three of which were fatalities and it brings home the lesson that cutting down speed and taking care on the roads really does save lives.

Choose light and bright. Studies have revealed that the lighter the colour of your car, the safer you are. Light colours reflect more light and can be easier to see from further away, especially in bad weather conditions. White or silver cars were shown to have the fewest accidents – even in daylight – while black, brown, grey or red cars had the highest number of collisions. Red is surprising in that list, but apparently our peripheral detection of this colour is poor.

Keep your headlights switched on. As is law in many countries, I always drive with my headlights on in daytime, which very few other people do in the UK, unless the weather is bad. At the very least, always ensure that you use dipped headlights in the rain and at night.

Choose your time to travel wisely. Public holidays, evenings and weekends are the most dangerous times to be on the roads. Most car crashes occur between 5 p.m. and 7 p.m. on a weekday, or on a Saturday. Statistically speaking, the best day to travel is a Tuesday.

Make sure that your car is well-maintained with regular servicing and MOT: if it isn't roadworthy, it shouldn't be on the road. Get into the habit of checking all the essentials, such as tyres, brakes, oil, radiator and windscreen wipers and washers.

Give your eyes and ears a regular MOT. It sounds obvious, but people often forget to get their eyesight and hearing checked regularly. If you can't read a licence plate from a distance of 20.5 metres (67 feet) then it's time to book an appointment with an optician. Hearing is equally important, so that you can hear what's going on around you – another reason not to wear headphones while driving.

Passengers: essential safety tips

Your passengers will often include your loved ones, so protect what's most precious to you with some simple but effective precautions.

Use the car seat head restraints to prevent whiplash injuries and provide support in a collision. To be effective, most head restraints require some adjustment. Always make sure that the top of the restraint is as high as the top of the head, and that it is gently touching the back of the head. Any gap means that the neck will bend back on impact, causing injury.

Follow the law for child seats. Any child under twelve years of age or less than 135cm in height must use a car seat. For infants up to three years old, always remember that it's illegal to use a rear-facing baby seat in the front without deactivating the air bag on that side.

Passengers in the middle back seat: Research shows that sitting in the middle of the back seat in a vehicle is the safest place when travelling. Passengers are better protected from near-side impact crashes and, in the event of a rollover collision, suffer less rotational force than those positioned by a window. Fatalities are around sixteen per cent lower than anywhere else in the car.

Always wear a seat belt, no matter where you sit. It pays to belt up. In a study, it was found that those who wore seat belts were three times more likely to survive a crash than those who travelled unrestrained. Make sure that the lap belt lies across the pelvis and not the stomach, and the shoulder belt is across the chest.

How to increase the odds of surviving a car crash

Every choice that we make in life has its consequences, and nowhere is this more true than in a car. Whether you're the driver or passenger, wise choices can increase your chances of walking away from an accident – injury free.

Always carry a first-aid kit in your car.

Buy a seat-belt cutter and window-breaker emergency escape tool. For a small cost, these neat devices comprise a special window-breaking hammer and a protected razor blade for slicing through seat belts.

Do not leave any unsecured items in your car. The pile of CDs and loose change on the dashboard can turn into lethal projectiles in a crash. Store all items safely away.

Try to sit at least ten inches from the steering wheel to avoid having your chest crushed by the airbag on impact.

If a collision with another vehicle looks imminent, do your best to minimize the damage. An impact at speed will significantly increase the harm caused. Brake quickly but with as much control as possible. Watch out for cars travelling either side of you where your vehicle is structurally weaker, offering less protection for the driver or front passenger. A side impact can cause serious injury.

At the moment before impact, try to contract your muscles to offer some protection to your bones, nerves and tendons. Brace yourself and clench the steering wheel at nine o'clock and three o'clock. Sit firmly back against the seat and look straight ahead – don't turn your head. If a car rear-ends you, lean back against the head rest. If you're braking to avoid a front collision, push your back squarely into the seat. Don't stoop towards the steering wheel in a crash, and warn your front passenger not to bend forwards. On impact, the air bag will inflate and could cause serious facial damage.

After a collision, switch off your engine and, if you can, get out of the vehicle and move as far away as possible, to an area of safety. After any kind of car crash, the risk of an explosion is high and so are the chances of being hit by another vehicle from behind. Be aware of vehicles around you, as you don't want to get run over.

Pedestrians: how to survive a hit-and-run

Be aware that using phones, iPads or listening to music on headphones can substantially reduce your awareness of what's going on around you. Always wear clothes that can be seen and, at night, choose light-coloured clothing and use reflectors. Stay alert to the traffic on the road: a distracted driver may not see you. And always try to engage eye contact with a driver before venturing out in front of them.

In a collision, instinct takes over. Rehearse the following moves and, with luck, you can put them into action and walk away alive.

If a car comes straight at you:

▶ Immediately turn away from the car so that you're facing sideways to the windscreen.

▶ If you can react quickly enough, aim to jump on to the bonnet – a little like you did at school in the high jump.

▶ Use your hand to break your fall.

▶ As the car sweeps underneath you, the impact will likely roll you into the windscreen before throwing you off. Try and protect your head (see box, p138) and keep your knees and feet together. What you must try to avoid is being pushed under the car and driven over. Remaining on top gives you your best chance of survival. Most new cars have shatter-proof glass and should absorb some of the impact of the collision.

PROTECT YOUR HEAD

YOUR HEAD is the one area of your body you must protect at all costs in a crash. On the moment of impact, try and remember to cover your head with your arms. Your forehead should be cradled between your elbows and your palms at the back of the head with your chin to your chest.

Surviving a car submerged in water

As torrential rain and floods swept Britain in 2012 there was a sharp increase in the number of drivers who drowned in their cars. While incidents are rare, it's worth taking the time to prepare and rehearse

SURVIVING A
HIT AND RUN

If a car comes straight at you, aim to jump on the bonnet.

Roll into the windscreen and protect your head.

the steps you need to take should such an event occur. You'll have just a minute or so to escape and, in those precious sixty seconds, you need to do everything you can to ensure your survival.

Prepare for impact. Most air bags will activate on impact with the water, so be prepared. Brace yourself with hands at nine and three on the steering wheel.

S-OW-O: Seat belt, Open Window, Out. Memorize this and use it if you find yourself inside your car and about to be submerged in water. Unlock your seat belt to give yourself the best chance of

A SUBMERGED CAR

A SEALED CAR takes approximately thirty seconds to two minutes to sink, and then around one to two minutes to fill with water. An open door will sink you and the car within five to ten seconds.

getting out. The car will nose-dive, as the engine is the heaviest part of the vehicle, so if you can't get out immediately, head for the back seat. Make sure any passengers are unbuckled and quickly open a window either before or very soon after hitting the water – but not a door. Electric windows will normally open for a short period after a car is submerged – some cars' power switches are designed to operate even after full submersion.

Smash a window. Once a car sinks, you'll be unable to open any door until the car has filled with water and the air pressure inside equals that outside. If you can't hold your breath for the two minutes this takes and you can't open the electric windows, you need to do whatever you can to break it open. Keep an emergency window-breaker tool in the glove compartment for this purpose or use an umbrella, laptop or any car tool, like a wrench. Failing that, you need to kick out the side or rear windows (not the windscreen, which is reinforced safety glass). Use the seat and brace yourself backwards directing all your force from your feet into the centre of the window.

Aim outwards and upwards. As the water pushes in through the open window, you need to push out. Take a deep breath and get out and up. Wait until you're clear of the car before kicking with your feet.

IF YOU'VE NOT MANAGED to open the window and escape, you may have one last resort and that's to wait until the car has filled with water and the pressure inside and out has equalized. As the water climbs, prepare yourself: make sure that the doors are unlocked and you have your right hand on the door latch, ready to open. When the water is just above chest level, take a deep breath and hold. Close your nostrils with the fingers of your left hand and open the door with your right (or vice versa, if the car is left-hand drive). Push out from the car and swim to the surface. Look for light or any bubbles and aim in that direction, avoiding any debris around you.

SINKING SHIP: WHEN SOMETHING'S WRONG – PREPARATION AND ESCAPE

A 158,000-ton cruise liner sinking to the bottom of the sea is not an everyday event, but big ships do go down, not to mention ferries. Whether you're a strong swimmer or a non-swimmer, the ocean is merciless. As soon as you enter the cold water, the shock may make it impossible to control your breathing. A healthy person should be able to remain conscious for between one and two hours in water that is ten to fifteen degrees Celsius (average ocean temperature) before succumbing to hypothermia. Floating is vital to surviving the perils of the sea, so always ensure that you know where the life jackets/personal floating devices are stored.

As soon as you get on board

I always take a quick 360-degree scan so that I know where everything is, especially the lifesaving equipment, the emergency exits, muster station (emergency meeting point), and the evacuation routes.

If you are in a cabin, make sure you know how to get out of it in an emergency.

Be certain you know where the life jackets are stowed and, if there are immersion suits, find out where they are and how they go on.

If you have driven your car on to a ferry, get out and head for the main decks as soon as it's parked up.

Alcohol in moderation: I'll have a drink on a ship if I'm not on duty or driving at the other end, but I'd never get completely out of it. That's one way of guaranteeing that you go down with the ship if the worst happens.

What to do when you hear the evacuation signal

The standard signal is seven short horn blasts followed by one long horn blast. The minute you hear this, you must evacuate. On a large ship, it's vital to stay calm: panic causes people to behave like a herd of wildebeest.

At the first sign of anything wrong, don't hang around waiting for the alarm: get yourself up on to the deck, keeping to the stairs rather than taking lifts and escalators, as these can go out of action quickly. Put your life jacket on, head for the muster station and

THE FIRST SIGN OF A SINKING SHIP

ONE OF THE FIRST SIGNS that a ship is flooding with water is that it suddenly becomes unusually stable. A ship in working order will roll slightly as it encounters waves; one that's heavy with water won't. A ferry that is in trouble will be virtually motionless – a worrying sign, as a ferry stabilizes itself through its rocking.

lifeboats, and listen out for crew instructions. Try to stay as dry as you can to avoid the risk of hypothermia. If you ensure that you're in position, it can help you get off alive. The whole process of evacuating the ship should take no longer than thirty minutes.

Be aware that the ship might begin to tilt, depending on whether water has already been taken on board. Most ships are now designed so that, even when they're on their side, you can still climb or walk to safety. Try to prepare for this by imagining which route you would take and what you could climb on. Seek out fixed objects large enough to shelter behind, but be aware of displaced furniture and catapulting or floating items coming your way.

Crew should instruct you into lifeboats but, if there aren't enough, you may have to rely on your life jacket or another floatation device and jump before heading straight for a rescue boat. Try to move away from the ship so that you don't get caught in any moving parts.

GET OUT OF TROUBLE – BIG PHIL'S TIPS

IF THE WORST COMES to the worst and you land in the water with no life jacket or floatation device of any kind, use your trousers, shirt or any form of material to make a temporary floatation device. This should buy you an extra hour or two and keep you afloat long enough for the rescue teams to find you.

Remove trousers under the water and put a knot at the end of each of the legs (or the arms of a shirt).

Hold the item in the air by the waist band and bring down sharply to trap air and then gather the fabric ends together. If you need more air, blow into them.

AIR DISASTER: ENHANCING YOUR CHANCES OF SURVIVAL

Across the world, thirty million airline flights are made each year. It's one of the most popular forms of travel and it's also one of the safest. Only ninety-nine air accidents occurred worldwide in 2012, causing 372 fatalities. Compare this with the one million fatalities across the world from car accidents.

Unfortunately, air disasters do happen and, at 10,000 metres (35,000 feet) in the air or at speeds in excess of 240 kph (150 mph), there's little the rescue services can do until the plane is on the ground. While you can't even board some aircraft with so much as a bottle of water nowadays, let alone your trusty survival tin and pen knife, there are a few handy items that I always manage to carry in my hand luggage and, in the event of a crash, I know I could easily find a stack of useful items in the debris.

Around eighty per cent of crashes occur in the first three minutes after take-off and the last eight minutes before landing, so take the time to learn what you can do in those precious few minutes. If you want to enhance your chances of survival, develop a 'crash plan'. Preparation could make the difference between whether you live or die.

Two items I always take on board an aeroplane

A SureFire Defender torch: A beam of unbeatable bright light to dazzle any attacker, but it's also fantastic in a survival situation where light is needed. It can even be used as a signalling device to the rescue services in an emergency.

Carabiner snap hook: Its uses are numerous, from emergency glass breaker to tourniquet tightener. For more uses, see *Survival choices: essential kit and improvisations* in *Chapter 11: Big Phil's Locker*, p275.

Decisions that could save your life

You might think that there's little chance of survival when the plane you're sitting on takes a nose dive, but statistics suggest that the odds of you making it out alive are quite high. Between 1983 and 2000, according to the National Transportation Safety Board, 95.7% of people involved in all plane crashes survived. Even in the worst plane crashes, 76.6% lived to tell the tale.

Safety briefing: When the cabin crew ask for your attention before your flight – don't tune out. Your survival may well depend on knowing the exact location of the emergency exits, how to put your life jacket on, and what to do in the event an oxygen mask falls in your lap. Count the rows between you and the exit: in a crash, it might be dark and you'll need to find your way to the exit door.

Choose your seat. Both the weather and the crash location can affect your survival. Some also believe that your choice of seating can have a bearing. I once asked a pilot where the safest seat was and he said that there wasn't one, as the plane was designed to fly, not crash. That said, there's evidence that sitting near an exit can help in making a quick escape. An analysis of the seating charts from over a hundred plane crashes discovered that passengers seated within five rows of an exit had a higher chance of escape and survival, while those seated in an aisle seat fared better than those in a window by six per cent. Some statistics have also shown that those who sit nearer the tail end of a plane, behind the wings, have a forty per cent higher survival rate. In an experiment on a real aircraft, as the plane hit the ground, all of the momentum was pushed forward, ripping off the front of the craft and the first eleven rows of seats inside. The seats towards the rear were undamaged. Maybe there *are* some advantages to flying economy.

Forget the booze. Alcohol might make the flight go quicker, but in an emergency you need your reactions to be as sharp as a tack. Stay clear of heavy drinking and avoid sleeping tablets as well.

This is an emergency

If you hear this announcement, follow crew instructions to the word.

If they tell you to put your life jacket on – do it. But don't inflate it until you're off the plane, as you'll make yourself too large to escape through the gaps in the plane's seating and fuselage once it's crashed.

Put your oxygen mask on. The moment the air pressure fails, you have ten to fifteen seconds to get your mask on and start breathing before you lose consciousness.

Tighten your seat belt in an emergency and keep it tight and low down under your pelvis at all times. In a crash, if the belt is loose, the G-force is increased. Wearing it low down means your pelvis will most likely sustain the force of the crash, and not your more vulnerable stomach. I always wear it tight when taking off or near landing.

Get into the brace position with your chin on your chest and your arms and legs tucked in; place a pillow on your lap and lay your forehead on top.

THE BRACE POSITION

Prepare mentally for where you might crash. So, if you're about to hit the ocean, try to grab something warm like a blanket and prepare for the cold feeling of the water hitting you, although it's unlikely to be as bad as you're expecting.

Wait until the aeroplane stops before assessing where you are. You could find yourself upside down, so try to orientate yourself before moving away from the crash debris.

Get out. A crash on take-off or soon after landing means any remaining fuel will catch fire. The first ninety seconds after an air crash is known as the 'golden time' for survival. Get out of the aircraft in that time and your chances of staying alive are good.

Smoke and fumes: In a fire, you need to avoid the poisonous fumes and smoke. Once the plane is on the ground, remove your oxygen mask and get out as quickly as possible. Stay low and stoop to avoid the fumes, but do not crawl on the floor as you may be crushed by other passengers as they make their exit. If you can, wet a cloth and keep it over your nose and mouth.

Crash landing in the water

Properly controlled, a plane can ditch safely in water and float, although at high speed it's more likely to disintegrate. Your survival relies on staying afloat and warm long enough to be rescued. Hopefully, you'll already have your life jacket on. On bigger planes, the emergency slides can also be used as rafts and will detach from the plane. They should include some limited survival stuff. Get on one and huddle together with other passengers to stay warm. Attempt to move away from any fuel spillage, which could catch fire.

Swimming techniques: Doggy paddle works well if you're fully clothed and need to conserve energy. Breaststroke is good for any underwater and long-range swimming, as it allows you to travel at speed without sapping your energy. Backstroke can relieve the

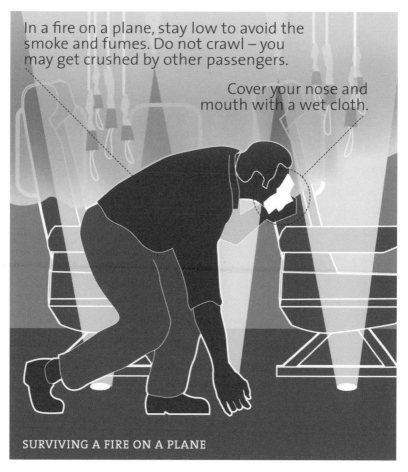

In a fire on a plane, stay low to avoid the smoke and fumes. Do not crawl – you may get crushed by other passengers.

Cover your nose and mouth with a wet cloth.

SURVIVING A FIRE ON A PLANE

body's muscles in between other strokes, and it is also useful if there is the likelihood of explosions underwater, as you reduce your risk of injury on your back.

Staying afloat: If you're in the water without a life jacket, you need to find something to help you stay afloat: a seat cushion or any debris that's floating nearby can help. If the sea is relatively calm, use your body's natural buoyancy: lie on your back with all your limbs extended. If it's cold and rough, you'll have to tread water to avoid hypothermia. If there are other crash survivors

SWIMMING STROKES

Doggy paddle

Breast stroke

Back stroke

Staying afloat

around you, group together; your shared body warmth can keep you alive and you'll be easier to spot by rescue teams. (See *Big Phil's tips* for making a temporary floatation device on p142, above.)

Bodily functions: If you end up in the sea in shark-infested regions and need to urinate or defecate, release it in small amounts – otherwise you might find yourself attracting unwelcome attention from sharks.

Crash landing in the middle of nowhere

Flight LANSA 508 is one of many flights that have crashed in the depths of the Peruvian jungle. The sole survivor, Juliane Koepcke, eventually made her way home because she understood the basics of outdoor survival. If your plane should come down miles from civilization, you need to know how to keep alive long enough to be rescued.

What resources are on board? If you're one of the few survivors and find yourself far away from any town or city, utilize what you can from the aircraft itself. Look for the obvious: food, blankets and medical gear, and then start thinking outside of the box. Even the remains of luggage may well have items that could help you survive. You could come away fuller than a fat girl's sock with food, water and even shelter, all in abundance. Be careful not to stay close to the crash scene if there is any fuel spillage and a risk of fire or explosion. See also *Shelter in extreme disaster situations* in *Chapter 12: Old skills revisited*, p279.

Finding help: If the plane has come down in a thick canopy of trees, there's a chance that it will have created a ready-made gap for signalling (see *The art of signalling* in *Chapter 12: Old skills revisited*, p293). If you have enough resources from the crash to survive for a few days or weeks, it may be better to remain at the crash site as the chances of being spotted by a rescue team are higher.

If resources are running out and there's no sign of a rescue, don't rely on the emergency services. Some jungles may be so deep that any signalling for help would be ineffective, so look for signs of life and, at the very least, a source of food and water. Start out moving downhill, if you can, where you're more likely to find a river or stream. Look for any signs that are man-made, such as fences, tracks and fires, and see where they lead.

TRAIN CRASH: PREPARATION AND SURVIVAL

Train disasters are thankfully rare. Improved design and safety measures have greatly enhanced the performance of our national train network in Britain, but human error and mechanical failure still account for accidents. If you travel regularly by train, make the effort to learn what happens in a crash and what you can do to enhance your safety.

What to do before a train crash: preparation

One of the most common types of rail accident is a derailment where one train leaves the track, jack-knifing or rolling on to its side. Misaligned rails, mechanical failure or excessive speed can all result in a head-on collision with another train. If you want to maximize your chances of avoiding injury, take note of the following tips:

Avoid clutter. Keep your bags and personal belongings stored securely in the luggage racks and avoid leaving bags in the aisles. In an emergency, anything not secured out of the way will either prevent a quick escape or be likely to fall on top of someone, a very good reason not to sit under luggage racks with lots of bags.

Identify your escape route. Know where the exits and emergency alarms are and familiarize yourself with the evacuation procedure.

What to do after a train crash: survival

When all you want to do is get the hell off the train, try and stay calm and listen to any information from the train crew. If none is forthcoming, it's time to find the quickest escape route, safely.

Move away from danger. Travel through the carriages using the connecting doors until you're well away from fire or other risks. Aim for the nearest exit or emergency door-release switch. Most train windows are reinforced, so don't attempt to break one, unless you have a pick axe handy.

Avoid train tracks. Once you're off the train, stay clear of train tracks: some are electrified and there's also the risk of being hit by approaching trains. Move up and out of the siding, if possible, and over any external fences.

If you are in a tunnel, you must get out. Just like any vehicle in a collision, a train could burst into flames. Within the close confines of a tunnel, the effects of any explosion are magnified, along with the potential for damage. There is also the risk of the train being hit by another train, injuring many more. There may be purpose-built exits but, if not, start walking towards the light.

If the train is on fire, cover your nose and mouth with a wet cloth, if you can, and keep low to avoid the smoke and poisonous fumes. Don't crawl on the floor, as other passengers heading for the exit may either trip over you or crush you.

If the train crash is in the middle of nowhere, in some far-flung place that only runs a train service once a week, then you might want to consider your options. If the weather is stormy and icy, the last thing you want is to be stuck out on some draughty hill, waiting for the emergency services. It is a risk, but if there doesn't appear to be any obvious sign of imminent fire or explosion, and the train carriage is still useable, it's worth considering taking shelter on board. Better this than dying of hypothermia in the name of safety.

BUILDINGS AND BRIDGES: HOW TO STAY ALIVE IF THEY COLLAPSE

Most modern buildings and bridges are extremely secure, but structural failure does happen, either through faulty construction or from the impact of natural phenomena like earthquakes and human action like wars or terrorism. A collapse of any building or bridge, tall or long, can crush a human body within seconds. No one can possibly forget the tragedy of 9/11, and the destruction of the Twin Towers that claimed so many lives. In this kind of mass-scale horrific incident, it's hard to know whether any action could have averted the loss of life, but a little basic knowledge and a keen awareness can always be of use.

What to do when a building starts to collapse

Find somewhere large and strong to shield you and take cover. Think 'Drop, cover and hold on' (see *When an earthquake strikes* in *Chapter 5: Natural disasters*, p112). Try to stay away from the inner parts of a building and aim to be as near to the outer walls as possible: your chances of finding an escape route are higher. Often the corner of a room along the outer walls of the house is the safest place to be. When I've travelled through bombed-out locations, it's often this natural triangle that still remains standing. Curl yourself into the foetus position for extra protection. Contrary to popular belief, getting under a doorway is the worst thing you can do, as you'll either be crushed by the ceiling, or cut in two with the doorway. Finally, never go near stairs as they are the part most likely to be damaged.

The building has collapsed but you're still alive

Surprisingly, if you've survived this far, your chances are pretty good. Before you rush to get up and out of there, stop and observe the situation. Is any part of your body trapped by debris? Has the collapse of the building left you upside down and disorientated? If in doubt, test yourself with the trusty saliva test.

Get help as soon as possible. If you have a mobile phone within reach, use it. Check to see if anyone is around you and then start yelling for help. Rest every now and then to conserve energy. Most rescue teams work to a system of stopping work on the hour, every hour, for five minutes to listen for calls for help. Specialist equipment is usually employed that can alert them to any sound or movement. If no one appears after a while, start to move any debris that's on top of you. Be very careful doing this, as you may end up dislodging other debris that could fall on you and trap you even more securely. Move slowly and carefully.

TO RAISE THE ALARM: Use your smartphone to call the emergency services but also to raise the alarm via social media sites like Facebook and Twitter.

Cover your nose and mouth with your clothing to filter your air. A cotton T-shirt or similar will help to reduce the dust from broken cement reaching your lungs.

If you're stressed and breathing fast, you could be hyperventilating, reducing the amount of carbon dioxide in the body. Restore your levels by cupping your hands over your nose and mouth and taking six to twelve normal breaths through them. Your breathing should return to normal. WARNING: If you have any symptoms of a heart attack (see *Chapter 10: The bare essentials*) or are a known diabetic, do not use this method, as you risk making your condition worse.

Getting others out in one piece

Even if you've escaped the falling debris, others around you might still be trapped. Rescuing someone who's pinned under pieces of cement and debris is a delicate process that should always, if possible, be carried out by expert rescue teams with suitable equipment. When a building collapses, it often creates voids – small spaces in which someone could be trapped but alive. The safest method to remove debris from someone buried is to carefully lift each piece from above vertically. However, it's crucial to avoid movement either side, as a support can easily be dislodged that could collapse on a survivor. That's why, in a major building collapse, it's always best to wait for the emergency services.

If someone is under minimal rubble, you may only need slight leverage. Table legs, fire extinguishers and cupboard doors can all be used to shore up debris to rescue someone. The surprising thing is that you often don't need to move an object in its entirety to be able to pull someone free. Even lifting it an inch can create enough space for them to be dragged to safety, or to enable them to wriggle clear. But again, it's essential that you make sure that your work won't have knock-on effects. Push or pull the wrong piece of rubble and, before you know it, you could cause a secondary collapse and an avalanche of bricks to come your way like a game of Jenga.

If someone is injured, especially with an obvious neck or back injury, do not move them unless they're at risk of immediate danger. Attempt to keep their neck and head still. Any movement can damage the spinal cord nerves and result in paralysis, so wait for the emergency services. For potentially broken limbs that have been crushed by debris, if you can remove any light debris without endangering them, do so.

Time is of the essence. Badly injured victims need emergency medical treatment within one hour. Shock and serious injury can create various complications, so your first priority is to call the emergency services out to them.

Surviving a bridge collapse

Whether it's human or natural causes, learn to recognize the signs of trouble and the action to take and you could save yourself facing a major disaster.

Always wear a seat belt when travelling in a car. In numerous collapsed-bridge incidents, those wearing seat belts were the ones who survived, even when the incident involved falling eighteen metres (sixty feet) off a bridge.

If a bridge starts to collapse, get your indicators on and get off the quickest and safest way possible, sounding your horn as you go. Passengers should yell warning to other drivers and people on the bridge to get out of there.

If you're heading for the water, prepare yourself to carry out an emergency escape underwater. See *Surviving a car submerged in water* on p137.

NUCLEAR POWER STATION LEAK: WHAT TO DO IF YOU'RE HIT BY RADIATION

We live in an age where the world's energy and electricity is increasingly provided by nuclear power plants. Naval vessels use nuclear propulsion to operate, and it sometimes seems as if every country that hasn't already got a nuclear bomb is attempting to build one. Is it any wonder that we're all terrified of a nuclear disaster?

In any such disaster where radioactive material is concerned, your best hope of survival is as much warning as possible.

Surviving a nuclear event

Whether the disaster is from a nuclear power plant or a dirty bomb (see *Chapter 8: Surviving GWOT*, p188), the key to survival is having enough time to prepare. A new scheme being operated by the UK's

National Security Council will aim to alert the public, via their mobile phones, to any major disaster, with information on where to receive help. However, in reality, the chances of receiving much notice of a nuclear disaster are likely to be slim. Radiation exposure usually comes from the particles that have been released after meltdown or explosion. Immediate exposure on the skin may be visible as burns, while any inhaled or ingested can cause short- and long-term damage.

Lessening your exposure to radiation

There's a limit to how much you can protect yourself from radiation. My advice is to create as many barriers as you can between you and the radiation. Here are a few ideas.

Distance: The further away you can be from a nuclear explosion, the better. Anyone within a sixteen-kilometre (ten-mile) radius of a power plant could be harmed directly, but radiation can only travel so far. Just eighty kilometres (fifty miles) further away and you may be safe, although anything in the open air, like water supplies, food and animals, could still be affected.

Get inside and close all windows and doors – remember, you can't see, taste or smell radiation.

Get upwind. If you can identify the wind direction, get upwind of the debris. If the debris is blowing away from you then you cannot be harmed.

Turn off air conditioning, heaters and ventilation. The last thing you want to be doing is sucking in any dust that's radioactive. Use a damp cloth to cover your nose and mouth.

Shielding: The more you can surround yourself with dense, heavy materials, the less likely the radiation is to reach you – even your home can provide some protection for a short while. Aim for any room without a window, like a basement or bathroom, to get as far away from the radiation as possible.

Keep up to date with activities outside by using a battery-operated radio.

Inform the emergency services, tap into government websites such as the Office for Nuclear Regulation in Britain, or the United States Nuclear Regulatory Commission, to keep a check on the situation, and use social networks to raise the alarm and monitor events.

If you're in a car, turn off your air conditioning and shut any air vents to prevent drawing in radioactive dust. Cover your nose and mouth with any clothing you have. Keep the radio on for advice from the authorities and keep travelling away and upwind of the power station.

If you've been exposed to radiation

If you think radiation particles have fallen on you, remove your clothes and shoes and place them both in a plastic bag. Seal the bag and place it away from any stores of food or water. Remove any food that you think has been contaminated and also store in a sealed bag. Keep these in a safe place until the authorities advise you of the correct disposal method. Shower thoroughly and change into fresh clothes. If you're feeling sick or have any burns, call for emergency medical treatment immediately, advising them that you may have been exposed to radioactive particles.

7 AWAY FROM HOME

TRAVELLING ABROAD ON BUSINESS OR HOLIDAY SHOULD BE AN ENJOYABLE BUT SAFE ADVENTURE, YET OFTEN IT CAN FEEL LIKE A TRIP TO THE LAWLESS WILD WEST. HERE'S HOW TO STAY OUT OF HARM'S WAY, AWAY FROM HOME.

THE DOS AND DON'TS FOR HOLIDAYING OR WORKING ABROAD

Prevention not cure: extra procedures to adhere to while abroad

Scams and street robberies: prevention tactics

Getting around abroad: avoiding road accidents and dodgy journeys

Drugs: how not to become an unwitting drug mule

Kidnap: how to avoid being snatched and what to do if you're abducted

Murder: how to holiday safely in dangerous destinations

Piracy: precautions and what to do if you're attacked

War zone: caught up in conflict and crossfire, the dos and don'ts

AFTER A FLIGHT OF TURBULENCE so severe that your stomach feels as though it's performed the dance of the seven veils, you arrive at Mumbai airport. Through the choking humidity, you're heading for the official taxi rank when a hand grabs you and ushers you in the opposite direction. Standing in front of you is the spitting image of Gandhi – all bald head and horn-rimmed glasses. 'This way, this way: luxury taxi.' He's as reliable as a cheap Chinese watch, has teeth like a nit nurse's comb and he's all over you like an ill-fitting suit. Before you know it, you're sitting in the back of his 'taxi' and being driven like a speeding bullet through the most crowded streets you've ever seen. As you try in vain to give him the address of your hotel, you're informed that it burnt down last week. Not to worry, he has the perfect alternative . . . Is this a scam? Is it a ploy to rob you of all your money? Are you likely to end up a kidnap victim or – worse – dead? What should you do and what should you have done?

BIG PHIL'S ADVICE: If you can, use a pre-paid or metered taxi to collect you from the airport. Always ensure that the driver provides proper identification to you before you set off. Never get into a taxi that is unlicensed and don't hail one off the street. Some unofficial taxi drivers will demand ridiculous sums of money once you're inside their cab, not to mention the numerous scams to divert you from your choice of hotel. If you get into trouble, call the police.

We all want a safe, relaxing and enjoyable holiday, but some of the more exotic destinations mean you're more likely to expose yourself to a range of dangers that you may not be prepared for. Between 2012 and 2013, the Foreign & Commonwealth Office helped

19,244 British tourists, from drug arrests to coach crashes, theft to death, you never can tell when you'll become the victim.

As more of us are working abroad, we must stay alert to the risks. We're no longer dealing with a few petty scams – abundant though they are; incidents now include full-scale criminal acts. In destitute countries, poverty-stricken residents will readily resort to kidnap if they think that there's the odd buck to be made from a Western tourist or businessperson, and we should all keep in mind the increased threat of hostility to many Westerners across parts of the globe. Finally, we shouldn't forget that even our best-loved tourist destinations – Egypt and Turkey included – are no longer guaranteed safe havens, as civil unrest transforms them into war zones.

PREVENTION NOT CURE: EXTRA PROCEDURES TO ADHERE TO WHILE ABROAD

Wherever you're headed, there's always the risk of some danger, but forewarned is forearmed, so here's my guide on how to be prepared for any eventuality.

Before you go

Ensure that close friends and family know where you are going and have a rough idea of how long you're likely to be away.

Do your homework. Check the Foreign & Commonwealth Office website for specific advice on travel to all countries across the world and tap into social media like Twitter and Facebook for the latest on dangerous hot spots and the dos and don'ts of local customs.

Plan to contact your country's embassy on arrival and advise them who you are and where you'll be staying, especially if you're visiting a particularly hostile country or one where there's political unrest. In the USA and Australia, you can register with your consulate ahead of your trip, in case of natural disasters or conflict outbreaks.

The essential documents

Passports and visas: Ensure that your passport is valid for your travel dates with at least six months to run before expiry. Obtain any required visas and check that they're in date. Some countries charge a fee to enter and leave, so ensure that you have the right currency or a credit card ready. If you have lots of previous stamps and visas, especially from high-risk countries, consider changing your passport before you travel. Certain embassies will refuse a visa if your passport reflects travel to a particular country (for example, Saudi Arabia if your passport indicates you've visited Israel); others won't issue an entry or exit stamp unless there is a blank page.

Keep your passport on you at all times. Also pack several photocopies or certified copies of your passport and visas. Leave a few in the hotel. Show these instead of the originals if asked to do so by anyone suspicious. A certified copy will provide official confirmation that the copy is an accurate version of the original. Any major British post office will be able to provide this service for a small fee.

Other travel documents. Check that you have your travel itinerary, tickets and reservations, travel insurance for your destination and planned activities, credit cards and driver's licence, if you're going to be driving.

Essential backup: Make two hard copies of all documents – leave one with a friend or family member back home and take the spare with you. Back up everything on a memory stick such as the UTAG ICE (In Case of Emergency) – and keep this with you at all times – and store a version on iCloud. You should also include important phone numbers, such as relevant embassies, consulates and any locally based organizations that can help if things go wrong, such as UN and aid agencies, as well as any vital medical details in case of an emergency.

Packing

See *The travel survival kit* in *Chapter 11: Big Phil's locker*, p264.

Medical essentials

Very few countries offer free medical care to foreigners, so always take out travel insurance and make sure that all potential accidents and medical emergencies are covered. Make a list of emergency numbers, including your embassy abroad and nearby hospitals. Just don't expect the same service as the NHS. If you're on prescribed medication, take enough to cover the duration of your trip plus an extra week, in case of any complications.

If you're travelling in a European Economic Area country, including Switzerland, apply online for the free European Health Insurance Card (EHIC) to allow you to receive state healthcare at a reduced cost or for free. **Remember,** though the EHIC is not a replacement for travel insurance, so it will not pay for private medical healthcare costs applicable in some ski resorts. It will also not cover the costs of flying you back to the UK in an emergency (or for any lost or stolen property).

Get the necessary vaccinations for your destination and take a basic first-aid kit, including, if necessary, anti-malarial drugs, a good mozzie net and the versatile shemagh scarf, which doubles as a good triangular bandage.

Money

You won't go far without it, so guard it carefully and make sure that you have enough money in the local currency or travellers cheques.

Don't carry huge sums of cash and, in case you are robbed, always split up any money that you do carry. Keep most of it in a money belt and a very small amount in your wallet. You could also, make yourself a dummy wallet to foil robbers, using a small amount of local currency padded out with paper.

Wear a covert money belt under clothes around the waist, and also position the pouch at your side or in front, where it's even harder for a thief to get at it. Alternatively, choose a leg wallet that fits around your thigh with enough room for your passport and some cash, or a neck pouch that sits underneath a shirt or blouse. Look for one that includes a scanner guard card or liner to prevent any unauthorized scanning of the radio frequency identification chips inside your passport or credit card.

Use alternatives to cash. I never travel with a lot of cash. Instead, I'll regularly transfer money online from my British bank account to a local bank in the country where I'm working. Mobile banking makes life easy no matter where you are in the world. I also always travel with two credit cards and a pay-as-you-go travellers' credit card, which you can put as much or as little money on as you feel comfortable with. I find this covers all financial needs.

Hotels and hostels: personal safety and guarding against theft

Ask for a hotel room that's not on the ground floor and is away from lifts and stairs, as they're the most at risk. When you're in your room, wedge a chair underneath the door knob so that anyone who picks the lock will still have trouble getting in. When you're out, keep the radio or TV on at a low level and hang the 'do not disturb' sign on the door.

Lockers or deposit boxes: In hostels or shared accommodation, use the individual lockers or deposit boxes, but make sure that you sleep with the key hidden on your body.

Safes: Some hotels and hostels may have safes, but be careful who you trust – often the staff can be just as light-fingered as the local thieves. Never hide something in your room – the staff will know every nook and cranny.

An alternative is to buy a padlock. Make sure that your luggage is locked and then lock your luggage to your bed.

Don't blab to anyone about what you own, such as expensive cameras or any of your other possessions. Networks of local thieves will be on the lookout for a new unsuspecting target. Keep your mouth shut and avoid becoming their next victim.

Not all hotels abroad have good fire standards. Some have no evacuation drill or fire-fighting equipment, others have interiors that are highly flammable. Make your own 'emergency plan' of how to escape safely, should things go wrong. For more advice on surviving fire, see *Fire in the home*, p27, in *Chapter 1: King of your castle.*

Out and about

▶ **Never share** your personal information with anyone.

▶ **Don't reveal** where you're staying, where you're going or anything to do with your schedule, to avoid becoming the victim of scams and other crime.

▶ **Vary your routes** and times every day so that you don't become an easy target for kidnappers and the like.

▶ **Find out what the appropriate dress code and local customs are** for the country you're visiting, as they can vary dramatically. What might be a perfectly innocent custom in one country can cause outrage in another.

▶ **Try and blend in.** One way is to buy and carry a local newspaper, even if you can't read the language.

Food and water safety

It's a fact of life that some countries don't have the same commitment to food hygiene that you'd expect in the Western world. My advice is, if in doubt, leave it out.

▶ **Just because the locals are eating something, doesn't mean that it's safe for you.** In some restaurants, keeping the meat under a carpet is the norm. I always insist on having a nosey in the kitchen to see what the chef is up to.

▶ **Do not ask for anything cooked rare: try and get the chef to crucify everything.** Heating food to a high level should kill most bacteria.

- **Always check the sell-by dates on any tins** bought, as some shops stock stuff for years.
- **Only use water from a sealed container** and always carry a means of purification. All water from a tap should be boiled and chemically treated. See *Making water safe* in *Chapter 12: Old skills revisited*, p285.
- **If you come down with watery diarrhoea,** increase your intake of water to avoid dehydration. Most cases will clear in three days with a light diet. Dysentery is a severe form of diarrhoea with blood and abdominal cramps. With rehydration it should resolve in a week. More serious cases may need antibiotics. Avoid passing it around – don't share cutlery or glassware, and be scrupulous about washing your hands every time you visit the toilet or at least use hand sanitizer gel. If you have to work, use an anti-diarrhoea medicine available from a pharmacy.

SCAMS AND STREET ROBBERIES: PREVENTION TACTICS

Scams abroad are so common that they've almost become part and parcel of going on holiday overseas. Apart from relieving you of your hard-earned cash, most are little more than annoying, but some can be a bit more disturbing. A little foreknowledge goes a long way – here's what to avoid.

The art of the street scam

Whenever you travel abroad as a tourist, you have to accept the fact that, to the local scammers, you're a legitimate target: naive, vulnerable and – compared to them – loaded. Don't announce your arrival with expensive designer clothing, flashy jewellery and a ton of valuable electrical and photographic equipment. Language barriers and cultural differences all make you the ideal prey but most scams are based around familiar themes like pickpocketing, diversion, begging or selling. To avoid falling prey, keep your wits about you and stay alert.

Street kid begging: Begging is a serious business in some countries, using children as cash collectors. I have seen many disturbing scenes of children with twisted or amputated limbs, deliberately maimed to extract money. My advice is not to encourage them or their adult abusers. There are plenty of registered charities who will take your money and put it to good use. Cross the road from these street beggars, don't make eye contact and they'll soon lose interest.

Fake police operate from airports and may try to escort you to a fake hotel, claiming it is for your safety. It's difficult not to feel intimidated by individuals dressed officially, but hold your nerve. Ask to see some ID or their official badges. If you're still in doubt, call the police directly and have them attend the scene.

Money-change scams: If you pay for something with a high-value note, take care – you may not receive the correct change back. Always say out loud the value of the note you've given, so they don't pretend it was one of smaller value. Learn to recognize the different denominations of money in the country and you'll also become aware of the more obvious counterfeit notes.

Pickpockets come in various guises. The best way not to fall prey to their tricks is to avoid getting distracted and to keep an eye, or better still your hand, on your valuables. Apart from the obvious ploys of bumping into you and relieving you of your wallet or purse as they pass, beware of **the handshake,** an overfriendly local who seems keen to make bodily contact, or **the distraction,** a staged fight or similar to divert attention while pickpockets steal your valuables.

Street robberies

Check out areas that you'll be visiting and, if you're in any doubt, stay out. Always try and travel as a group or team up with someone rather than moving around on your own, and if you're going to be drinking, try not to get completely wasted. Setting up a 'shark watch' is one way to protect your back (see *Keeping a lookout* in *Chapter 3: The social scene*, p73).

Be extra alert in well-known trouble spots. Research the potential dangers for your destination before you get there. In some countries, like Kenya or Honduras, a mugging can turn into a murder, whereas in Italy you're more likely just to have your bag snatched. Ideally, you should avoid any high-crime areas, but if you have to travel through them, never linger. Avoid places that are too far off the beaten track and look for areas that have a strong police presence or that are populated by plenty of people.

Blend in. If you look like a tourist, you look like a target. If you're in a dodgy area, keep your valuables hidden and try to merge into the local setting with your clothing, image and behaviour. Robbers and muggers will seize any chance, if you let them. A mugging is a mugging wherever you are in the world and the guidance remains the same – never label yourself as prey (see *Mugging* in *Chapter 2: Cutting about*, p34).

What to do if you get mugged
How to prevent the situation turning fatal. Your first instinct may be to fight back, but you should always weigh up the risks. If someone is pointing a gun at your head or a knife at your throat, don't risk your life for a material item that you can replace. In some parts of Latin America, muggers won't hesitate to shoot to get what they want (see *Avoiding a fight by spotting trouble before it arrives*, p216 and *The early stages: figuring out what an attacker wants* in *Chapter 9: Self-defence, SAS style*).

Report the incident to the local police and ensure that they provide you with a report, including details of any injuries you may have sustained. You'll need this when you file a claim through your travel insurance, and for financial compensation for any stolen goods. Keep all receipts, if you have to replace items before your claim is processed.

If you're injured, your travel insurance should cover in-patient hospital treatment. Keep all medical bills for the insurance company.

If your passport gets stolen or lost, inform the police and your embassy. At your embassy or consulate, ask them to bring up details of your passport and provide you with a stamped photocopy, which will assist when you're travelling through passport control and customs.

If your debit or credit cards are stolen, contact your bank to cancel them. If thieves have got your wallet or purse, they'll potentially have your home address and can use this together with the cards to make online purchases.

If you have no money, your bank might be able to make cash available to you at a local branch. Alternatively, contact your family to transfer money via mobile methods such as Barclay's Ping, o2 Wallet or Western Union for international money transfers within the hour. They charge commission but it's a lifesaver.

IF YOUR PHONE IS GONE

FIND SOMEWHERE with free internet access and make contact with friends and family to help you arrange another phone. They can also help if you need a quick loan or copies of essential documents. Most public libraries should have free access to computers and the internet; if not, use your police and embassy report to ask for help in a cafe.

GETTING AROUND ABROAD: HOW TO AVOID ROAD ACCIDENTS AND DODGY JOURNEYS

Road accidents

Over one million people are killed in road accidents around the world every year. It is without doubt one of the most dangerous aspects of travelling abroad. With all sorts of challenges out there, like dodgy road surfaces, hairpin bends and sharp cliffs, it's no wonder driving conditions are often lethal.

If you're travelling abroad and on foot, you need to be aware of the very different cultures. Making eye contact with drivers in Britain usually means the driver will slow down – not so, abroad. Be informed about each country's traffic culture if you want to stay standing. Check the Foreign & Commonwealth Office's Road Safety Overseas website: www.fcowidget.com. Here are some tips for staying safe on the roads.

Beware of poor road conditions and a lack of traffic enforcement in some countries, particularly Thailand. Drivers are unlikely to obey speed restrictions.

Avoid driving at night in Africa, if you can; it's just too dangerous. Most of the vehicles at that hour are unroadworthy with no working headlights or brake lights. Drivers and pedestrians are often drunk and there's a high risk of people wandering out into the road.

Watch out for 'Bosnian bikes': cars or trucks with only one headlight, especially when you're driving. Many countries do not have traffic police watching out for dangerous vehicles. A lorry or car travelling with only one headlight is a disaster waiting to happen – you might think it's a bike and completely underestimate its width, until it's too late.

Research your journey. Will it involve hairpin bends or a well-known accident spot? Try to avoid travel on any particularly dangerous roads. Try to travel in convoy if you're going on an organised trip.

Avoid being by the roadside after dark on foot. Just as in Britain, it puts you at risk of rapists, muggers and drunk and careless drivers.

Carjacking

See *How to prevent a carjacking* in *Chapter 2: Cutting about*, p40.

Taxis abroad

The safe use of taxis abroad requires you to be vigilant, but they can often be safer than public transport, especially at night. If you have to take one, follow these guidelines to help minimize any risks:

▶ **Always use a reputable company or one recommended by your hotel.** Licensed taxi ranks should be safe but you may get ripped off on the price. If you can, ask a local resident which firm they use. Be careful using any unlicensed taxi waiting near tourist spots.

▶ **Ask for the price of your journey first** and keep a tab on the route the driver is taking, if you know the way to your destination.

▶ **Use a GPS tracking app.** This will email or text your exact location to any of your chosen contacts if you fail to check in safely after a designated time.

▶ **Always wear your seat belt.** Many foreign drivers drive like they're on acid.

▶ **Keep your door locked and your window shut** if you're going through a rough area or feel uneasy.

▶ **Always sit in the rear,** where you can see the driver and where you're out of his reach. Make sure the doors open from the inside. Have your money ready when you arrive at your destination and do not hang around.

Public transport abroad

Not everyone can afford to take taxis and they're not always the best way to see a city, but using public transport in a foreign country can be a minefield for the unwary and naive visitor, who can quickly fall into the hands of every robber in town. Wise up and follow some basic rules and you too can enjoy travel like the locals.

Use trains with care. Criminal gangs do carry out organized robbery of passengers on trains, especially along tourist routes. Try and avoid travel at night. Look for a seat in a busy carriage in the middle of a train so that, when you arrive at your destination, you won't have to walk more than halfway down a potentially empty and badly lit platform. If possible, stay close to the emergency intercom.

If you have to travel on an overnight train, take care of your valuables. Lock down any luggage and secure it to anything fixed that you can find. Use every means available to secure your compartment. Some trains have a security device to be attached to the door handle.

Be alert to friendly strangers who offer you food or drink. Some gangs have been known to drug passengers this way and rob them later.

Watch out for criminal gangs operating on buses. Always try to travel with others. I personally prefer to sit at the back of a bus if there's a door there. I can watch who comes on and get off fast if trouble is afoot. If you can, travel on a first-class bus. These have a far lower incidence of crime than second and third-class buses, partly because security checks on passengers are carried out on boarding and because they use more secure toll roads.

Research your choice of bus. Never get on an overcrowded bus, make sure that it looks roadworthy and, if you can, choose a reputable vendor. Ask your tour guide or hotel reception staff to recommend some companies. If I don't know an area well, I'll often go to the British Airways desk at the airport and ask for their advice.

DRUGS: HOW TO AVOID BECOMING AN UNWITTING DRUG MULE

Every year, several thousand tons of drugs are trafficked across borders into countries around the world in an illicit multi-billion pound business. Most drugs travel via one of the established drug routes, but traffickers are finding new ways to get their drugs across borders, via the naive tourist. The unsuspecting traveller checks in at the airport and then, as their luggage is loaded on to the plane, a corrupt airport employee stashes a bag of cocaine in between the holidaymaker's clothes and tags the suitcase. At the other end of the journey, a baggage handler is waiting for the suitcase and its contents, but if they fail to spot it, the traveller is left explaining how a 200-gram pack of cocaine found its way into their swimwear.

How to avoid ending up in prison

Pregnant women and even children are perfect targets for smugglers looking to plant their drugs on an unwitting mule: they're much less likely to be subjected to X-ray or a search by customs and, in the case of children, far more willing to innocently agree to carry another person's bags through security.

Never agree to take luggage for anyone else, no matter who they are and refuse anyone who offers to carry yours. Women need to pay special attention. Be suspicious of new boyfriends that ask you to carry packages abroad for them or even to take their luggage. So many innocent travellers have been duped into trusting a stranger and agreeing to take their bag through check-in under their name or across border control. As always, trust no f***er – TNF – and tell them to get lost.

Secure your baggage. Many airports offer a baggage wrapping service which is quick and inexpensive. Not only does it protect your belongings, it also prevents any criminals from slipping illegal items, including drugs, into your bags without your knowledge.

EXTREME PUNISHMENT FOR DRUG CRIMES

MOST COUNTRIES have zero tolerance to drugs; some even have the death sentence, including Iran, Algeria, Thailand, Indonesia, Vietnam and Laos. For drug trafficking in Singapore and Malaysia, the death penalty is mandatory. Never knowingly transport drugs – the cost is just too high. Is a couple of grand really worth seven to thirty years in jail, or death?

I use zip ties – they're cheap and easy to use and very hard to replicate. Engrave your name on the back of the slide once it's done up and always keep spares.

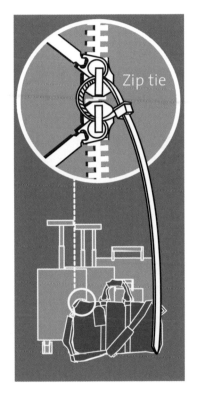

Zip tie

Look for signs of tampering. As your bag comes round the baggage carousel, have a good look at it before you lift it off. If you think that someone's been inside, leave it where it is and report it to the airport officials immediately.

If you get arrested abroad on drug charges

It's the worst-case scenario: someone has planted drugs on you and you find yourself up on a drug charge and thrown in a hellhole of a jail. What should you do?

Your first point of contact should be your country's embassy or nearest consulate, if you're not in the capital, or the High Commission, if you're British in a Commonwealth country. They should be able to contact your family and help them understand the legal system in the country where you're detained. Unfortunately, whether you're innocent or not, what they cannot do is get you out of jail.

For British citizens, Prisoners Abroad can provide support. Conditions in jails abroad are often extremely poor. Apart from the isolation from family and friends, prisoners are likely to face inadequate and inedible food, unclean water and overcrowded and unsanitary sleeping conditions. Prisoners Abroad is there to protect British prisoners' welfare, no matter where they are in the world. While they cannot help you get out of prison, they can provide grants to ensure prisoners have enough to eat and for medical care to manage conditions such as diabetes. Ask your embassy contact to put you in touch with the organization.

KIDNAP: HOW TO AVOID BEING SNATCHED AND WHAT TO DO IF YOU'RE ABDUCTED

Every year, thousands of kidnappings take place across the world. At one time it was solely for ransom; nowadays it often has more sinister motives, such as politics, crime, sex and religion. People once thought unlikely targets are now vulnerable to the world's kidnap gangs.

The kidnap hot spots around the world have changed too over the last ten years, as the global political and economic landscape changes. Alongside Latin America, some of the biggest hot spots today are Afghanistan, Pakistan and Iraq. Kidnapping has become big business.

Whether you're a tourist or a businessperson, educate yourself about the risks and avoidance tactics and, if you are unfortunate enough to become abducted, here's some advice to help you get out alive. See also *Siege* in *Chapter 8: Surviving GWOT*, p206.

How to avoid being kidnapped

You may not be able to predict a kidnapping, but you should be able to take steps to prevent one. If you have to visit countries where the risk of kidnap is high, here are my top tips on how to stay one step ahead of the kidnappers.

Maintain a low profile and avoid routine. When it comes to kidnappings, understated could keep you safe. Maintain a low-key appearance and behaviour: loud and flash only attracts individuals after your cash. Keep your social media profiles brief and your travel plans vague. Travel at different times of the day and via different routes – predictability can make you vulnerable. Avoid spending any length of time in risky destinations.

Be aware. Always know who is around you. Look for your escape routes wherever you go, whether you're in a restaurant, car park or office block. Do not expose yourself to danger by walking in dark, remote spots, at least not without an escort. Always have your mobile switched on and ready to hand.

What to do if someone tries to abduct you

Your best chance of escape is at the beginning of the abduction, when the kidnappers haven't yet got you in their control, but it can also be the most dangerous. Adrenaline levels will be running high and kidnappers likely to be at their most volatile. If you're in a public place where there are lots of people, it's worth making as much commotion as possible so that passers-by are aware that you are being abducted and will call the police.

KEEP PUBLIC

ONLY AGREE to a meeting in a public place where you are less likely to be abducted. Being taken to an unknown destination makes you vulnerable and separated from society and any assistance you may need.

If someone tries to bundle you into a vehicle, use your legs, body and arms to jam yourself across the doorway, holding on to the door or rim. Keep your head above the vehicle and shout and scream. If you get pushed in, try and open any door you can to get out. Check the ignition and remove any keys, or, if they're missing, jam anything you can find in the ignition switch to prevent a key being inserted, such as gum or a button off your shirt.

If you have a gun pointing at your head or a knife at your throat, and you're in a secluded area, it may be too risky to try and escape. If you're likely to be a ransom victim, remember that you are of value to the abductors only if you're alive, so the best chance of remaining safe may be passive cooperation. However, if your abductors are shouting Islamic statements like '*Allahu Akbar*' (God is great), you could be in serious trouble. At this point, you should look for a means of avoiding capture, as your chances of survival may be slim. See *If someone pulls a gun on you* on p178, below.

GET OUT OF TROUBLE – BIG PHIL'S TIPS

IF YOU'RE NOT under gun or knifepoint, and have considered that your best chance of survival is to escape, you may only get one chance – make it count. At the first sign of someone attempting to restrain you with rope or tape, forget any rules and do what it takes to stay alive. Most attackers want an easy target, so if you resist they may well decide they don't want the hassle and let you go. If you're grabbed by the arms, use your legs to kick back and aim for the shins, knees and groin. Don't be afraid to kick them in the most vulnerable places, especially the genitals. Use your fingers to poke them hard in the eyes and throat and bite them anywhere you can with your teeth. Aim to take a small bite which is more painful than a mouthful.

If you get the chance, attack and run. A kidnapper's speciality is keeping you hidden until someone pays up, it's not chasing you down. If you run, chances are that they won't come after you. Choose the opportune time to escape and act decisively. Use pepper spray and keys to attack. (See *Chapter 3: The Social Scene*, p70.) If the attack is sexually motivated and there is a crowd of people nearby, take your chances: fight and run. Shout instructions: 'Call the police! A man is attacking me!'

How to survive if you are kidnapped

See *Capture: how to survive being taken hostage* in *Chapter 8: Surviving GWOT*, p207.

MURDER: HOW TO HOLIDAY SAFELY IN DANGEROUS DESTINATIONS

One British tourist is murdered every week abroad – a small number considering how many tourists there are in total, and yet in some countries the risk of murder is high. To stay safe, always weigh up the pros and cons of your travel plans. A trip to northeast Honduras might make great sightseeing, but it's not much good if you end up being robbed and beaten to death. If you're travelling on business, you can't always be so choosy about your destination, but always go informed.

Before setting off, check the Foreign & Commonwealth Office website's recommendations under 'Safety and security' in your chosen destination. This provides information on serious crime risks like murder or kidnap, as well as any civil unrest or threat of terrorist attack. If you have to travel into zones that are classed as dangerous, the best you can do is be aware of the risks and take precautions. Here are some general tips for staying alive wherever you are:

If you're being robbed at knifepoint, don't just hand over your valuables. The chances are that you'll be killed anyway to avoid identification. Instead, throw your purse or jewellery as far away from you as possible. This forces the robber to move away to gather them, leaving you the opportunity to make a runner.

Don't hang around anywhere, even in your car. If you're being observed as a potential target, any downtime plays right into the hands of an attacker. They could be in beside you within seconds, and you'll be dead. Stay focused, check the car before you get in to make sure no one is waiting for you, then get in, lock the doors and get moving.

Don't be a sucker for a hard luck story; remember the rule: TNF. Be wary of individuals asking you for help and looking a bit pathetic. Many serial killers use this technique to draw unsuspecting and sympathetic women into their cars with horrendous consequences.

In well-known dangerous locations, keep to some simple rules. Avoid being out at night, especially on your own in isolated areas. Be extra vigilant when entering or leaving your hotel, restaurants, petrol stations, shops and your car at night; thieves often lie in wait for the unsuspecting. Always travel with all your doors locked, in case of roadside robberies. Take extra care on any form of public transport, especially in no-go zones where buses are the criminal fraternity's escort.

Pay the cash and take an official taxi. Unlicensed taxi drivers have been known to rob and assault passengers. Use only authorized, pre-paid taxis at airports. In cities, look for authorized cab ranks.

If someone pulls a gun on you, there's no way that you'll be able to outrun a bullet, but you may be able to react quicker than the attacker can pull the trigger. Look at the trigger finger and, if you can see it about to squeeze the trigger, run in the opposite direction to where the gun is pointed with all the speed you can muster, pushing off on the balls of your feet and sprinting. If they're right-handed and facing you, aim left (their right), aim right if they are left-handed. Run in a zigzag fashion: it's far harder for an attacker to hit a moving object (see *What to do if chased by a madman with a gun* in *Chapter 9: Self-defence, SAS style*, p233).

ESCAPE FROM
A BULLET

If the attacker is about to squeeze the trigger, run in the opposite direction to where the gun is pointed.

Run in a zigzag movement to make it harder for a bullet to hit you.

PIRACY: PRECAUTIONS AND WHAT TO DO IF YOU'RE ATTACKED

Yachting is a popular pursuit but in recent years it has also attracted the attention of pirates. Despite the relatively small number of incidents overall, occurrences can be common if you sail in dangerous waters. I've experienced pirates myself first-hand while protecting merchant ships, but on a yacht you're completely exposed and vulnerable.

Wherever you're sailing, do your research. Check all the intelligence you can on areas you'll be visiting. Read the piracy reports from the International Maritime Bureau's Piracy Reporting Centre and request safety information from your embassy. For US citizens, before you travel, register with the Smart Traveler Enrollment Program (STEP). This will enable you to obtain advice in any medical, financial or legal emergency when travelling abroad. It will also inform you of the potential dangers that you may incur on your trip.

Take out a kidnap and ransom insurance. Cases are often settled without payment but this can be useful to cover any financial loss.

Inform trusted authorities where you are going, with a rough course and timeline. Leave the same information with loved ones or reliable people, like your sailing club back home.

Stay away from known trouble spots. In remote places, you're more likely to be a target of criminals who could possibly rob you or worse. Never anchor yourself unless there are other boats around. If you are going to sail in dangerous waters, keep in touch with other yachts and sail with other vessels if possible. Flak jackets are a useful defence against gunfire.

Be wary of any small craft coming at you aggressively, or travelling on a parallel path. Small boats rarely come near yachts that are under sail unless they are planning to attack. Start moving away to confirm

PIRATE HOT SPOTS TO AVOID FOR YACHTS

IN MY EXPERIENCE, some of the worst areas for pirates are Somalia, West Africa, Venezuela and the Malacca Straits. In Venezuela, there have been several vicious attacks on private boats, with fatalities. While, in the Malacca Straits, although incidents have reduced in recent years, its location on one of the most important shipping trade routes in the world still makes it a prime target for pirates.

that you are being followed and then raise the alarm immediately. Start banging out Mayday distress calls. Leave your radio open.

Establish a place on board that would be secure in an attack and use it to protect yourself. Conceal a VHF transceiver out of sight, as pirates will destroy them once on board to avoid the alarm being raised.

If pirates hijack your yacht, fire a flare or drop a beacon in the water so that, if you do get sunk, the search-and-rescue teams have a starting point from where to search. Comply with the hijacker's demands rather than risk injury or worse.

WAR ZONE: CAUGHT UP IN CONFLICT AND CROSSFIRE, THE DOS AND DON'TS

We live in a volatile world where political and civil unrest can transform previously popular holiday destinations into rioting combat zones. Suddenly, your dreams of sand, sea and surf are torn apart by the most terrifying holiday nightmare. Alongside the violence, all kinds of panic can follow as people stockpile food and water and withdraw cash from banks. Even if you're not in the line of fire, then you might still be exposed to some serious stress and inconvenience.

Alternatively, you may have chosen such a 'high risk' destination as one of a growing number of war tourist adrenaline junkies.

THE TOP WAR-ZONE HOLIDAY HOT SPOTS

Cambodia's Killing Fields: Firing ranges and shooting animals for fun are all part of the experience, should you wish to participate.

Afghanistan's Bamyan district: A newly established tourism board claims to offer the best 'outback skiing' in the world. You can also see the mindlessly destroyed ancient Buddhas of Bamyan carved into the cliff.

Iraq's fourth-largest city, Erbil: Located in the region of Kurdistan, once a hot spot for terrorist attacks, this is now a cosmopolitan city and a popular tourist destination.

Sierra Leone's Freetown: After years of civil war, this location now offers luxury tours of the islands.

But beware, travel to dangerous zones has its consequences: aside from the risks presented by bullets, bombs and mines, some locals may see you as the enemy and treat you with hostility. It's at times like these that you need to know what to expect, how to prepare and how to survive. Having lived and fought in some of the world's toughest war zones, here is my honest advice to help you keep your head and ensure that you get out alive.

The dos and the don'ts: how to make it home alive

Before travelling, check the Foreign & Commonwealth Office's website for any trouble in your chosen destination. Use your social network to confirm. On arrival at your hotel, gauge the mood of the place. If you sense any kind of looming tension, start to make preparations and stock up on food – you may be held up in your hotel for some time or have to go on the run. Have an emergency pack ready that will keep you going for at least a few days.

Do your research. Whenever I travel to an unfamiliar destination, I spend time gathering all the background information I can find – the reasons behind a conflict and which factions are fighting and why. You never know when it might come in useful.

Insurance: Not every travel insurer will cover you and you may have to take out special risk insurance. Make sure that your policy includes acts of terrorism, war and dangerous countries.

Have a clear plan. Make sure that you know where you're going and plan ahead as to how you'll get there. Keep to official transport and find yourself a reliable local taxi service.

Flak jacket and helmets: If you're going to war-torn areas, make sure you wear protection. Flak jackets are heavy and can be a nuisance but, together with a helmet, it could save your life.

Do not photograph any military checkpoints, roadblocks or facilities without permission. Officials may get suspicious if they see photos being taken of sensitive areas and could think you're a journalist or spy. Some countries ban any photography of official buildings. You may also find that many dangerous war-torn areas do not welcome tourists.

Roadblocks: Be on the alert for these and try to stop to assess the situation before approaching – they may be a trap or, at the least, a way for corrupt individuals to extort money from you. If you are in any doubt, turn back. An ambush is likely to be positioned in such a way that you can't escape, so keep a lookout far in advance. If you do get trapped, keep your hands where they can be seen so that the other person doesn't think you're going to draw a weapon. Smile and be friendly. Stay in your vehicle and keep your doors and windows locked and closed. If you have women travelling with you, stay together. The checkpoint may have cut-offs: groups of people placed in a position to take on anyone trying to escape. Try and locate them as you approach so you at least know where they are if it all goes wrong.

THE EMERGENCY WAR-ZONE PACK

Collect non-perishable food and water: Anything that's light but nutritious: freeze-dried foods, dried fruits and biscuits. Add a little salt to your water as you drink. Especially in hot countries, you can sweat out pints and will lose vital sodium in the body – essential to the proper functioning of your heart, muscles and brain. Wherever you are, try and stay near to a source of water and top up whenever you can.

Combat zone essentials: A first-aid kit including iodine for purifying water, extra socks and a jumper or two, a battery-operated radio, a lighter and cigarettes for bartering. If the situation worsens, with civilians being murdered, you might want to consider securing a weapon. But keep it hidden to avoid becoming a target.

What to do if caught up in crossfire

If you think that there is the slightest risk that you may get caught up in a war zone, plan ahead before you travel. If you're a businessperson or employed in the media, charity sector or in an NGO, then you should be undertaking specific hostile training. If you're just a holidaymaker caught up in the middle of a conflict, follow my tips for staying alive.

Small arms: guns and bullets

Most weaponry used in outbreaks of civil unrest and war zones tends to be rifles and pistols. The trusty AK-47 is frequently used along with an M9 pistol, both of which can do serious damage.

If you are shot at, move like lightning. Don't just run in a straight line away from the gunfire. Go across the line of fire to force the shooter to keep refocusing their aim. Chop and change your path in a zigzag fashion. Hitting a target that's moving all over the place is a lot harder than one that's just running directly away from you.

You can tell how near a bullet is to you from its sound as it whizzes past. A distinctive crack, like a whip, means the bullet is too close for comfort. Listen for the thump of the weapon firing it to identify where the noise came from and head in another direction. If you hear a hissing or whining sound, the bullets are further away.

Find somewhere to take cover. If you are under continuous fire, your only choice is to take cover in a ditch, a building or behind solid rock. Don't choose walls and trees, as they offer little in the way of solid protection. A nine-millimetre pistol round will go through twelve layers of plasterboard, while the AK-47 can shoot bullets that will travel through solid concrete.

Don't be fooled into taking cover behind a vehicle. A pistol bullet can easily travel through the side of a car, while a rifle bullet will pass through its entire length. The engine is the only place unlikely to be penetrated by small arms fire. So if a car is your only cover, make sure that this stands between you and the shooter. The best use of a vehicle in crossfire is its ability to move fast and transport you out of a danger zone, so hit the gas and drive away from any shooting.

The big stuff: incoming mortar or artillery fire

Mortar weapons are the next step up from small arms: light and portable, they give a range of around six kilometres (three and a half miles) and are designed to propel grenades and bombs up in the air and land them directly on top of the target. Artillery ranges from light mobile weapons like Howitzers, which can fire a heavy shell over a long distance of up to thirteen kilometres (eight miles), to the kind of heavy artillery that looks like a tank, fires up to twenty-four kilometres (fifteen miles) and normally needs to be towed by a truck.

If there is incoming mortar or artillery fire, you'll hear a distant 'crump', indicating the weapon has released its shell, followed by an explosion as it detonates. After you hear the crump, you have a couple of seconds to take cover and should get under the most solid thing you can.

Try and keep a count of both the crumps and explosions. Even though you may not be able to see them, you should be able to tell roughly by sound how many shells have landed and roughly where, and if there are any blinds (unexploded ordnance). If the small bangs and big bangs don't match up, then you know that you need to be extra cautious when breaking cover, in case a shell goes off. If you see a blind or unexploded shell, get out of the line of sight. Unlike gunfire, this means move anywhere as far away as possible to take cover. Remember where it is and tell someone, if there are friendly forces trying to help. Do not go back and show them where it is.

Remember that these may just be the first few rounds of a series, while the gunner refines his aim. Don't wait until he finds his target.

If you are driving across open land, away from ready sources of cover, like buildings, and the explosions are close – fifty to one hundred metres – get out of the car and find somewhere solid to take shelter. A ditch is better than nowhere. Never lie under your vehicle, as that could be the target and, in any case, it would offer little protection: a mortar round will obliterate most vehicles and anyone nearby. If the explosions are some distance from you and not in your path, drive with speed and move out of the area quickly. If they are in your path, you need to find an alternative route or leave your vehicle and take cover.

How to avoid being blown up by a land mine

In many areas, land mines still remain active and it pays to have at least some knowledge of their dangers.

Anti-personnel mines and anti-tank mines: Anti-personnel mines are designed to maim rather than kill and will explode the minute you step on one. An anti-tank mine will only explode when a vehicle drives over it and will not normally explode if someone stands on top.

Recognizing where land mines are planted: Warning signs are often around, if you know what to look for. Derelict areas of

If you see a mine, stop and retrace your steps.

LAND MINES

untouched farmland, craters and dead animals are all giveaways. In locations where mines have been found, local people may have left warning signs, such as pieces of cloth or cans hanging from a fence. Check with residents. Also be aware that mines can move in the ground. In the Falklands, many of the minefields are buried in the top layer of peat that covers much of the island. As this shifts over time, so the mines sink, making detection and removal difficult.

Only walk on well-trodden footpaths and proper paved roads.
If the locals use a route regularly then it's more than likely safe, but don't trust the knowledge of every local resident. I once had to rescue a local woman who had walked straight into a minefield to pick a pretty flower, completely oblivious to the risks.

If you find yourself in a mined area, don't go any further.
Call for assistance or retrace your steps back to safety.

8 SURVIVING GWOT

IN THE WORLD OF THE GLOBAL WAR ON TERRORISM (GWOT), ANY CITY IN THE WORLD CAN BE TIPPED UPSIDE DOWN BY LUNCHTIME. HERE'S WHAT TO EXPECT AND WHAT YOU CAN DO TO SURVIVE.

'9/11 PUT WAR IN YOUR BACK GARDEN.' BIG PHIL CAMPION

THE GLOBAL WAR ON TERRORISM

Terrorist attacks: staying alert and recognizing suspicious activity

Bombing and suicide operations: spotting the bad guys and aiding your survival

Dirty bombs: signs to look out for and action you can take

Death in the air: what to do in the event of a chemical or biological attack

Hijacked: tactics for an aeroplane hijacking

Siege: hostage situations, escape and evasion, and Special-Forces rescue

IT'S MID-SUMMER IN LONDON and you're stuck in a sweltering hot tube train in the early-morning rush hour. For the last ten minutes, you've been trying to snooze but, with the champion snorer on your left and Mr Headphone Man on your right, it's proving difficult. As you shut your eyes once more, someone treads on your toes. You glance up to see a guy togged up to the nines in a thick padded jacket – the spitting image of the Michelin Man. He looks as out of place as a one-legged man at an arse-kicking contest. His eyes are darting everywhere, while his right fist is clenched around what looks like a small black tube with a wire running into his coat pocket. You're getting a very bad feeling about this guy. Is he a suicide bomber holding a detonator? As the train draws into the next station, you look around the packed carriage and wonder what should be your first move. Do you try to get the other passengers off the train without causing panic? Should you tackle the guy directly? Or do you pull the emergency handle and hope that the authorities come running?

BIG PHIL'S ADVICE: Spotting a terrorist isn't easy. We can all look at the guy huddled over his rucksack looking nervous and mistake him for a potential bomber, even though he may just be off for a job interview. If you genuinely think you have seen something or someone suspicious, you really do need to take action, but not the sort that sends your fellow passengers into a frenzied panic. Keep calm. Alert a station attendant at the next stop and get yourself out of the way. If you're sitting opposite someone and you clearly see them about to detonate explosives, you only have one option: get near enough to deliver a knock-out punch before they press the button.

Ever since 9/11 in 2001, the world has viewed terrorism in a whole new light. That an extremist group could defeat the security of one of the world's superpowers left many shocked and frightened. In Britain, we too were reminded that the threat of terrorism was here to stay, with our own dark day, 7/7, in 2005, and, along with it, the truth that the perpetrators were on our own doorstep.

Any one of us could get caught up in a terrorist incident and, although it's easy to think 'It will never happen to me', we all should take the time to be prepared. Stay alert and don't hesitate to report anything suspicious. It could save someone's life.

TERRORIST ATTACKS: STAYING ALERT AND RECOGNIZING SUSPICIOUS ACTIVITY

Intelligence services across the world are constantly monitoring the activities of a number of terrorist organizations, but sometimes even the most sophisticated surveillance can fail to detect an imminent attack. We can all do our bit by remaining alert and observant to everything around us. Unfortunately, the countless distractions of modern life mean our eye is often off the ball, allowing those with evil intent to get in through the back door. No method is perfect, but would-be terrorists do often give themselves away through tiny errors; so, for those sharp enough to pick up on the signs, the truth, as they say, is out there.

> If I saw something strange hanging out of a bin at the FA cup final, I would be more concerned than on an ordinary day.

The telltale signs of a terrorist

Absence of the normal; presence of the abnormal.

There is no prototype for a terrorist, only clues that, when put together, ring alarm bells. We were taught in the army to use the above principle when considering whether something was wrong.

I've listed some examples of suspicious behaviour below; if you can tick off three or four of these, then there might well be some foundation to your suspicions. But, while they could well indicate a potential terrorist, they might also highlight the innocent behaviour of your neighbours. So, before you pick up the phone to dial the Anti-Terrorist Hotline, use your common sense and give people the benefit of the doubt. However, if you spot anything that could be an immediate threat, such as an unattended package or bag or someone acting suspiciously, do not hesitate – call the police straight away.

The recce: Terrorists need to gather information about a potential target before an attack, so surveillance recces are common. Take note of strange vehicles parked in the same location on several occasions. If the owner or passengers are eyeing up places of interest for no apparent reason, it's worth logging some details: model, colour and registration number. If the same person is waiting in the vehicle each time, get a shot with your mobile phone. Pass this information on to the Anti-Terrorist Hotline or directly to your local police station.

An interest in official buildings: Be aware of individuals checking out official buildings or facilities. Watch to see if they are observing CCTV and other security devices. Observe anyone taking notes and sketching outlines, or anyone with blueprints and architect's drawings detailing the layout of the buildings. Keep an eye out for cameras or binoculars. CAUTION: They could be a surveyor or an estate agent, but they could also be planning an attack.

Abandoned vehicles in built-up areas: Report any suspicious vehicles to the police immediately, especially if smoke can be seen coming from the car. If delivery or rental vehicles are parked in unusual locations, such as in open spaces or outside derelict buildings, ask yourself, what are they doing?

Home-grown bombs: Bombs can be made with common items, including fertilizer and beauty products such as acetone (nail polish remover) and hydrogen peroxide (hair bleach). If anyone is purchasing large quantities of these items or gas cylinders it should raise a red flag. Be alert to odd pungent or fume-like smells or strange liquids coming from buildings – it could be the makings of a bomb. The homemade stuff smells like almonds – it's very distinctive.

Strange behaviour: Sometimes those up to no good will stick out like a sore thumb. It might be the way that they're dressed – winter clothing in summer – or that they're loitering near secure buildings. It could be something that you find out about an acquaintance that doesn't quite add up, such as a person who holds passports in different names for reasons that aren't clear, or who travels for extended periods and is vague about where they're going. It could even be someone who seems to own an inordinate amount of mobile phones – each of them pay-as-you-go. If in doubt, report your suspicions to the police.

BOMBING AND SUICIDE OPERATIONS: SPOTTING THE BAD GUYS AND AIDING YOUR SURVIVAL

Bombs are devastating. I spent several years serving with the British Army in Northern Ireland, so I know first-hand the damage they can inflict. Suicide bombers are equally lethal. In Israel, the victims who have survived being blown up carry with them a permanent reminder: nails lodged inside thighs, ball bearings in a skull, parts of a bomber's wristwatch lodged in a neck. All are the products of cheap-to-make and easy-to-implement homemade bombs, strapped to a bomber's body and designed to deliver a lethal explosion.

How to recognize a suicide bomber

There's no one sign that indicates a guilty person, they may not always look like a puppy next to a pile of their own mess, but several small clues together can build up a fairly accurate picture. The following combines my own knowledge with the advice given by intelligence officers who have spent years profiling suicide bombers.

Be aware of what's going on around you on public transport.
Keep a look out for passengers behaving oddly and any luggage or packages on the floor. If you spot one that appears to be unattended, don't be afraid to ask, 'Whose bag is this?', if no one comes forward, you need to act. Calmly state that the bag is unattended and suggest to other passengers that they leave the train or tube. If you can, wait until the train is in a station rather than a tunnel before pressing the emergency button, otherwise you will most likely be trapped.

Look for someone who is evidently nervous. They'll probably be avoiding eye contact, behaving awkwardly or licking their lips and sweating. Do they seem out of place? Are they carrying a package – most likely a backpack, luggage or briefcase – and are they walking forcefully to a specific area? Do they keep checking the package or looking at the exit?

Does the person look unusually padded? Perhaps they're wearing bulky clothes or a heavy raincoat, even in warm weather. Many homemade bombs will be packed with items like nails, screws, bolts and ball bearings, which will add bulk to the bomber.

Most suicide bombers are male, aged between twenty and thirty-five; some can be older and even female. Often suicide bombers will work in pairs.

If you think you have seen a suicide bomber
- ▶ **Don't approach them directly,** as they may get panicked into setting the bomb off immediately.
- ▶ **Avoid creating panic** among members of the public.
- ▶ **Move away** from them as far as possible – preferably out of the line of sight of any device; in other words, take cover.
- ▶ **Contact the police.**

The bombs

A homemade improvised explosive device (IED) carried by a suicide bomber or used by a car bomber is very different to a bomb used in war zones. The type of explosive used in warfare generates a major shockwave, but with the homemade bomb it is the contents – the shrapnel – and the way it's intended to explode that is more lethal. Suicide bombs are the ultimate anti-personnel device, designed to inflict the maximum damage after the bomb explodes. The shrapnel – ball bearings, nails or screws – will suddenly be launched in every direction: the equivalent of several hundred high-speed bullets.

Preventative measures

You can't live your life continually looking over your shoulder, but if the latest intelligence prompted a national warning about terrorist attacks, I'd most likely take the following precautions.

Avoid the obvious terrorist targets. Anywhere crowded is a potential bombing target: shops, train stations, airports, even sporting events or rock concerts. Try and avoid heavily congested areas – especially entrances and exits – and wait for a crowd to disperse before entering or leaving an area, if you can.

Although only 3% of all terrorist attacks around the world can be classified as suicide bombing attacks, they account for 48% of terrorism casualties.

Never sit or stand near areas that could turn into projectiles. Restaurants or cafes with huge glass windows, or shopping malls that are a mass of glass could all provide deadly flying weapons in a bomb attack. If you can, always look for areas that offer some protection or a shield, such as pillars and walls.

Surviving a bomb

If you can see or know where a device is, and have the time, try to get well out of the way before taking cover. If there's no time, get behind something so you're out of the line of sight of the device. If you receive only minimum warning of a bomb about to explode, you can enhance your survival chances with the following guidelines.

Lie low. Try to get as low to the ground as possible.

Don't run. Drop to the ground and try to lie on your side to minimize the surface area of your body exposed to the explosion. Use your upper arm to protect your face – especially the vulnerable eyes.

HOW TO
SURVIVE
A BOMB

Get low to the ground.
Lie on your side
to minimize
exposure and
use your arm to
protect your face.

After one bomb, expect another. Most bombers like to stage several bombings rather than just one. Immediately you hear or see the first blast or a flash and have hit the ground, stay there for a short while in case there are more on the way.

Try not to hold your breath. In any explosion, when the blast occurs followed by a shockwave, our natural reaction is to hold our breath but, in these circumstances, by doing so you create a pressurized balloon. As soon as the shockwave hits the body, the balloon – your lungs – will burst, causing internal bleeding. In less than ten minutes, you'll have drowned in your own blood. To stay alive, keep your mouth and air passages open. Lie on the ground and breathe in and out using small breaths. If the shockwave hits you doing this, you should avoid significant damage to your lungs.

Move away from any buildings. After a bomb, any kind of structure is likely to be unstable and liable to collapse; don't hang around to find out.

DIRTY BOMBS: SIGNS TO LOOK OUT FOR AND ACTION YOU CAN TAKE

As terrorists look for new ways to inflict harm, the use of radioactive material is a worrying menace. Current statistics show an increase in the number of thefts of radioactive materials from hospitals and laboratories, where security is minimal. According to figures from the Nuclear Threat Initiative (NTI), as the illegal trafficking of radioactive material continues, there is now clear evidence that it may be used in dirty bombs.

What is a dirty bomb?

A dirty bomb combines radioactive material with a traditional explosive, like TNT (trinitrotoluene), and it is often known as a radiological dispersion bomb. A 'dirty bomb' is not a 'nuclear bomb' and is far less harmful. A nuclear detonation would create a mega explosion that would blanket hundreds of square miles with debris and radioactive dust, whereas the radioactive material used in a dirty bomb would most likely cover only a few miles and hardly produce enough radiation to cause severe illness or death. Its aim is not so much to create physical harm, but to instil psychological terror among the population that could paralyse a city.

How to survive a dirty bomb

You cannot predict when or where a terrorist will attack or the type of radiation they'll use, but you can arm yourself with information. Radiation cannot be seen and, unless you have specialist equipment like a Geiger counter, you may not know that you've been exposed until it's too late. See *Lessening your exposure to radiation,* on p156, in *Chapter 6: Man-made disasters* for more detail, but the key thing is to create distance and density between you and the radioactive dust: if you can't escape upwind, take cover in a building, preferably a windowless basement. The combination of explosive material and radiation means that radioactive dust is likely to be released into the air, which, if inhaled, could cause serious damage. Extra precautions you should take include:

Wear a mask. Any type of mask should prevent you breathing in radioactive dust: even a damp piece of cloth or a shirt or blouse. None of these will protect against radiation, of course. The only effective shield against most types of radiation is a high density material like lead.

Seal up external doors and windows with duct tape inside your home or building. It won't stop radiation penetrating but it will protect you from further exposure to the dust.

If you've been contaminated by any radioactive dust, the majority will have landed on your clothing, so the quicker you can change, the better. See *If you've been exposed to radiation*, on p157, in *Chapter 6: Man-made Disasters.*

DEATH IN THE AIR: WHAT TO DO IN THE EVENT OF A CHEMICAL OR BIOLOGICAL ATTACK

The sarin gas attack in Toyko in 1995 by the religious sect, Aum Shinrikyo, was the first high-profile terrorist incident involving the use of a chemical agent. Chemical and biological weapons are quite different to conventional armaments, as they are invisible to the naked eye and rely on reactive properties to wreak havoc.

Designed to incapacitate individuals or pollute a location, each agent has its own unique action on the human body. Some chemicals, like sarin gas, are designed to kill rapidly by acting on the nervous system, and their presence can easily be detected by the rapid number of fatalities in the immediate vicinity. Biological agents include living organisms like anthrax, smallpox and ebola – some of the most destructive known to man. They tend to be slower to work but remain active for longer. Anthrax spores can survive for centuries in the soil, prolonging their deadly edge.

Producing and delivering chemical and biological weapons is an expensive and elaborate process and therefore not an ideal weapon for many terrorists. However, they could prove lethal if their supply ever got into the wrong hands.

Signs of a chemical or biological attack

Often the only signs of an incident are the victims. Look for a combination of the following.

Gas clouds: Gases and vapour are not normally visible to the eye, but a gas cloud may be present shortly after dispersal, if there is little circulating air. The gas usually enters the body via the respiratory system and can sometimes penetrate the eyes or skin. As the gas cloud falls to the ground, it can linger for several hours with high concentrations in contained locations, such as buildings or dense patches of trees. Look for a mass outbreak of victims suffering from nausea, respiratory problems, spasms or seizures, and confusion.

Liquids, vapours or powder: Look for droplets or fine powder on outside surfaces. Liquid contaminants usually resemble motor oil, but some can be hard to detect with the naked eye. Has there been any spraying in the area? If so, toxic vapours may be present and remain active for a week or more. For powder contaminants, look out for mail packages that contain white powder or that smell strange. These agents can be destroyed with standard chlorine bleach.

Observe any odd smells: Chemicals may smell of fresh cut grass or bitter almonds.

Insects and birds will normally fall from the sky. Pets, livestock and wild animals could appear to be dying in an airborne attack.

HIJACKED: TACTICS FOR AN AEROPLANE HIJACKING

Since 9/11, the incidents of air hijacks have dramatically reduced. Tighter security, better training of airport staff to profile potential attackers, and even increased public awareness have created a tougher and more resistant environment for terrorists to break through. But let's not lower our guard – hijackings do still occur. In the last few years alone, China has seen a sharp increase in aeroplane hijackings and, where once they were used solely for monetary ransom, now they have become yet another weapon in the terrorist's arsenal.

So what can you do in a hijack situation?

Finding a group of religious fundamentalists on board your flight, threatening to crash the plane, provides all the ingredients for sheer terror. However, if you can stay calm and think clearly, there are plenty of opportunities to take control in a hijack situation. Figure out what you're up against with the hijackers and try to assess the situation. What do they want? Is your life in danger? Is the aim to highlight a political cause? Is there a bomb on board, or is the plane to be used as a weapon in a suicide mission?

If there's no indication that the plane's likely to go down, your best bet for survival is to stay calm and follow the hijackers' instructions.

If you're being held for ransom then you have more time to escape.

The essential anti-hijack plan

If you're pretty sure that the hijackers are intent on murdering the lot of you, then you have no choice but to take action. If you've one foot in the grave and the other on a banana skin, it's time to act fast. One thing's for sure: to do nothing is to guarantee failure, as there are *no second chances*.

You and your fellow passengers must now attempt to overpower the terrorists and take control of the plane. Remember, there is strength in numbers. With more passengers than hijackers on board, it should be more than possible to overpower any threat, but that doesn't mean you need to try and rush your captors straight away.

Act the 'grey man'. The hijackers have the upper hand so, for now, don't act the hero and attempt any bravado – this is your time to blend in. Hijackers are likely to be nervous and trigger-happy, so unless you want to end up dead, toe the line and do exactly as you are instructed to by your captors. You can still be identifying weapons that might be available on an aircraft and thinking through your plan of attack. Only speak when spoken to. Some people, when they're nervous, sound as though they're talking in wet cement with a mouth full of marbles – keep your counsel and don't be tempted to join in.

Identify those who can help. If I was a hijacker, I would be weighing people up as soon as I got on the plane, as I would want to know who and where my biggest threats were. When I board a plane as a passenger, I do exactly the same: I scan the plane to see who is who and, although looks can be deceiving, I build up a half-decent picture in my mind as to who's likely to be an asset in a crisis and who isn't.

'It's not the size of the dog in the fight, but the size of the fight in the dog.' I'd be looking for someone who seemed fairly fit, anywhere between their late teens to middle age, rather than someone dribbling into their soup. If the cabin crew have allowed someone to take the exit seat next to the emergency door, it means they've agreed to open the doors in an emergency and so I know they're likely to be physically capable and up for it. You can profile people quite successfully, but you can also be quite surprised. This is one of the reasons why I'd reassess again, when things begin to turn noisy, and look at how people are reacting. You often find in circumstances like these that 'Mr Hard Man' suddenly becomes a cowering wreck.

A rolled up magazine can make a good weapon.

When an opportunity presents itself, strike and make it count.
You'll only get one chance, so, along with your fellow passengers,
come up with a plan and specify each person's role. Look for objects
that can be used as weapons. Pens and keys, a rolled-up glossy
magazine, hardback book, a laptop or even a pair of women's
high heels make good weapons, particularly when used to strike
vulnerable areas like the neck and groin.

**Throw an aeroplane blanket over a hijacker and temporarily
blind them.** This will allow other passengers to rugby-tackle them
to the ground. Belts are great for restraining or pulling someone
to the ground. Use the food cart to protect the cockpit or barricade
the hijackers in an area of the plane, like the back kitchen area.
Depending how many hijackers there are, you may only be able

Blind the attacker with a blanket.

Rugby tackle the attacker to the ground.

to barricade one or two in this manner. Alternatively, you may need to use the cart as a battering ram if the hijackers have locked themselves in the toilet or have already got access to the cockpit. Use whatever is available as weapons, such as fizzy-drink cans, either to throw at the attackers or to open and aim the pressurized fluid at them (see *Extreme self-defence: and improvised weapons* in *Chapter 9: Self-defence, SAS style*, p234).

REMEMBER:
Whatever you do needs to be done as aggressively and violently as possible before the terrorist has a chance to pilot the plane into the ground.

Aeroplane items gone bad

Planes carry all sorts of stuff that can be turned into improvised weapons. Here are a few ideas to get you started:

- **Hot water** for scalding.
- **Metal knives** from first class.
- **Oxygen canisters** heavy enough to be used as battering rams.
- **Cabinet doors** that can be used as shields to fend off or subdue hijackers.
- **Demonstration seat belts** used by the cabin crew in the emergency briefing make good swinging weapons by using the buckle to cosh people.
- **Tray tables and top locker doors** can be ripped off and used as shields against knives.
- **Stiletto heels** can make good stabbing tools.
- **Fire extinguishers** in operation are useful as a distraction.

Once the crew have been able to regain control of the aircraft it's vital to ensure any casualties are getting all the help they need; you may also have to deal with the dead. It's now that the cabin crew's training should kick in, but if they're too shaken or are the main casualties, you need to get to grips with the situation. Find out who has first-aid or medical training and, if necessary, who can fly a plane.

Work with the cabin crew to calm the situation down. The last thing you need is a plane-load of hysterical passengers while you're still up in the air.

Alert the authorities if there is nobody left who can fly the plane. Get in the cockpit, find the radio and make a Mayday call before receiving instructions from the nearest control tower on what to do next.

How to call for help on an aeroplane

If the pilot and co-pilot are both unconscious, and there's no one else to fly the plane, you must radio for help. The plane should be on a steady course on autopilot. Your first priority is not to panic and to make contact with air traffic control (ATC).

▶ **Position yourself in the seat and fasten the seat belt.** You should be sitting with the yoke (like a steering wheel) in front of you.

▶ **Find the PTT button ('press to talk') on the rear of the yoke.** TAKE CARE as the switch to turn off autopilot is also located here.

▶ **Alternatively, use the hand-held radio** normally located to the left of the pilot's seat, under the side window. It will work like a CB radio, so just push to talk and release to listen.

▶ **Press and hold either the PTT button, or push to talk on the hand-held radio, and say, 'MAYDAY, MAYDAY, MAYDAY.' State who you are and that you have been hijacked.** Remember to release the button to listen.

▶ **When you get a response from ATC,** state clearly what has happened. They will need to know that there is nobody in a position to fly the plane and will talk you through the procedure, including landing. As you look at the panel in front of you, state out loud the controls you see, touching each one as you go – this will help you remember their location.

▶ **If no one responds, check the radio frequency.** The radio should be located in the middle of the cockpit controls, near the throttle (manual levers). Ensure that it is set on the emergency frequency: 121.5 MHz.

▶ **If the plane is behaving erratically, autopilot may have been disengaged.** Check the button on the rear of the yoke, or ask ATC.

REMEMBER: You need to let the authorities know immediately once the plane is no longer under hijack. Some countries will deploy jets to bring down a plane rather than let it crash into a target and potentially kill thousands.

SIEGE: HOSTAGE SITUATIONS, ESCAPE AND EVASION, AND SPECIAL-FORCES RESCUE

For terrorists, hostage-taking is a profitable form of funding or negotiation, either to extort money or to secure the release of prisoners. Unlike kidnapping (see *Kidnap* in *Chapter 7: Away from home*, p174), the motivations of a hostage situation are usually political, social or religious. Many terrorist groups are young idealists with little experience of abduction. Highly wired, they're likely to be on edge from the initial abduction phase to the negotiation and the eventual release or rescue. Understand these phases and the likely conditions you could find yourself in, and you can aid your chances of survival.

The abduction

The two most dangerous stages in a hostage situation are right at the beginning and at the end. At these times, the abductors are nervous and the victims confused, meaning anything could happen.

If you're being held for financial gain then you're a prize to be bargained over and your captors will have a vested interest in keeping you alive.

HOLD IT TOGETHER MENTALLY

TRY TO KEEP A TRACK of the day and time through temperature change, bird song and traffic patterns. Keeping some form of daily routine is vital to your mental well-being and will stop you from becoming disorientated.

If you've been taken hostage to make a political statement then you still remain a prize, but may be used as leverage to obtain other goals, such as the release of political prisoners, or possibly as a human shield to protect your captors or sites from being attacked by security forces.

Don't fight back. In a one-on-one kidnapping, you might try to escape at this point, before the abductor has gained complete control, but in a hostage-taking situation, where there is normally more than one hostage-taker and victim, acting the hero could well lead to your death.

Capture: how to survive being taken hostage

No one knows how they'll react to being taken captive. Being imprisoned, with no personal freedom, and forced to sleep, eat and defecate in cramped, less than hygienic conditions can create severe psychological changes in a hostage.

Traumatized by a dramatic alteration in routine and lifestyle, one of the most common symptoms experienced by victims is confusion, followed by deep depression over the following weeks and months. A situation in which your captors decide your every move is one that can break the most hardened of individuals. If you can recognize the shock of the situation, and its effect on you, it's possible to learn to play the game and survive. Follow the captors' orders, but don't let your self-esteem or dignity be taken.

▶ **Stay calm.** Try not to let hysteria get the better of you. Captors will immediately label you as troublesome and are less likely to treat you well.

▶ **Eat** what you are given, to keep up your strength, even if you don't like the food.

▶ **Exercise when and where you can,** even if it's only basic things like press-ups or flexing exercises, to keep your muscles toned. Physical exercise can also help combat hunger.

▶ **Exaggerate any pain.** If you have to take beatings, try at all costs to protect your organs by curling into a ball and don't be afraid to yell.

▶ **Give respect to the captors' religion or beliefs,** but don't openly agree with their cause.

▶ **If you can, build up a rapport with your captors** by discussing universal subjects like hobbies or family. Your aim is to ensure that the captors see you as a human being, like themselves, which will lessen the chances that they'll be able to easily dispose of you. Avoid feeling too much empathy with your captors yourself, though, as it's all too easy to fall victim to 'capture-bonding' or the Stockholm syndrome.

► **Find purpose and score small victories.** Even being allowed to take your hands off your head could make you feel like you won the World Cup.

► **Make use of any newspapers or books you're given** and, once a rapport is made, try asking for other items to increase your personal comfort and keep your mind busy.

► **Get to know your fellow hostages** and support one another, if you are allowed to spend any time at all with them.

Negotiation

Every hostage situation has a purpose and, once the captors have secured their hostages, the deal-making begins. This is often a tense phase for the captors and the negotiators. Initially, both parties are likely to make exaggerated demands, but this is just part of the game: both sides need to feel that they've exhausted all options, without just settling for what's on the table. Procedure and protocol often mean that negotiation can be a drawn-out process, adding stress to the captors and hostages. Hopes of a release can be raised, only to vanish at the last minute because the negotiations have failed. Captors may, in turn, be frustrated and take it out on the hostages. Rest assured, though, that there will be highly trained negotiators working for your release. Remaining calm and patient can aid your survival chances greatly.

Those negotiating with the captors will first aim to secure the release of women and the vulnerable. Any captives released early could provide valuable intelligence about the inner workings of the hostage group to the authorities trying to secure your safety.

CAPTORS OFTEN MOVE their hostages to a remote location to remove the chance of escape – this could occur several times during your abduction. You may be drugged and disorientated, but try and clear your head and focus on what's going on around you. It can help you build up a picture of what's happening and remove the fear of the unknown, as well as occupying your mind. Things to be aware of:

▸ **Are there outside noises** which sound familiar, or smells? Listen for the captors' conversations; try and define each captor's personality and their accents. Who is the leader and do they maintain strict control over the other captors? Are some more willing to talk – could you build up a rapport with them?

▸ **Look for any patterns** in their behaviour that might aid your escape or buy you time. Will they let you go to the toilet on your own? If you ask for a drink or something to eat, are you more likely to get a boot to the head? Do they have an organized rota during the day and night, and for meal times? What time do they change over? Are there periods when there doesn't appear to be anyone guarding you? Does anything trigger aggressive or passive behaviour in them?

▸ **Do not be tempted** to make or keep notes: if found, they could endanger your life.

▸ **Be careful** what you ask your captors and don't come across as too keen to know what's going on. Observe covertly so that you can remain 'the grey man'.

Escape and evasion: how to break out

As one of a group of hostages, the chances are that you may well be able to overpower your captors and escape, but the situation is laced with danger, so take care to consider all your options before taking action. Try and assess how valuable or expendable you are to your captors. Carefully discuss a potential plan with your fellow hostages and make sure that each person knows their role. To escape safely, you're going to need to choose your moment carefully, catching the abductors when they are at their most vulnerable. A good time would be when they've not slept for hours and are unlikely to be alert. If you see an opportunity such as an open window or door and you think you can escape, take it and aim for the nearest person or place that won't compromise you: a local shopkeeper or a policeman. If you're somewhere remote or in a foreign country, you'll need to work out who is likely to be friendly and who isn't.

Fighting back

If people are being killed and there are firearms involved, you need to get out and that may mean using one of the captor's weapons – most likely a gun. Some inexperienced captors may leave a weapon lying around, or you may have to choose your moment to attack and take the weapon.

If you've never used a firearm before, you should know how to get it into action. Otherwise, it just becomes a club. In the movies, you always hear the term 'lock and load', which makes me cringe because it's the wrong way around. If you're under threat, here's an idiot's guide to using a firearm. Note, this is for that last-ditch attempt when your life is on the line and there is no rescue attempt underway. Otherwise, leave it to the experts.

ANY ATTEMPT TO ESCAPE MUST BE CARRIED OUT WITH ONE HUNDRED PER CENT CONVICTION

ONCE YOU'VE FORMED A PLAN with your fellow captives, you have to see it through. This is no time for niceties; it's literally life or death, so summon all your energies and aggression and fight as if your life depends on it – because it probably does. See *Extreme self-defence* in *Chapter 9: Self-defence, SAS style (p234)*.

How to use a gun

▶ **Check to see if the weapon is already loaded** by ejecting the magazine. There should be a release button near the trigger. (See illustration for pistol and rifle.)

▶ **If the gun is not loaded,** find some ammunition and insert. The pointed ends of the bullets should be facing forward. Once full, reinsert the magazine and push upwards until it clicks into place.

▶ **Prepare the gun to fire.** This is called 'cocking the weapon'. On a pistol, it will usually be the top slide which is pulled back – this will load the bullet, ready to be fired. On a rifle, there will be a cocking handle or lever (see illustration). Use your non-dominant hand to do this and keep your index finger above the trigger housing.

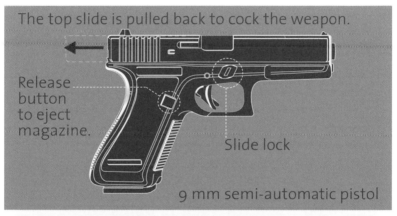

The top slide is pulled back to cock the weapon.

Release button to eject magazine.

Slide lock

9 mm semi-automatic pistol

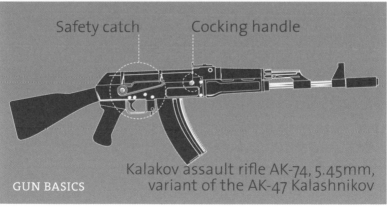

Safety catch   Cocking handle

Kalakov assault rifle AK-74, 5.45mm, variant of the AK-47 Kalashnikov

GUN BASICS

- **Ensure any safety device/catch is off.** This is normally situated within reach of the trigger, towards the back of the gun (see illustration).
- **Hold the gun with your dominant hand:** your right hand, if you're right-handed. If you want to use your other hand for support, do so, but most modern pistols have little recoil. Always keep your finger off the trigger until you have your target in your sight.
- **Try and imagine a straight line** from you, along the weapon and through the target. You'll have more success at hitting someone if you **aim at their torso** – even then, it's not easy.
- **Squeeze,** but don't snatch the trigger.
- **If nothing happens,** you've either got no ammunition or you need to cock the gun.
- **Don't worry** about replacing the safety catch – if you don't pull the trigger, it won't go bang.
- **Never point the weapon or pull the trigger at anything other than the intended target.** When you are not firing, run your finger along the trigger housing and keep the gun aimed downward until you are ready to shoot.
- **If the rescue forces arrive,** make sure that you discard the weapon like a hot potato to avoid a blue on blue: friendly fire.

What to do when the men in black come to bust you out

If all negotiations have failed, Special Forces may well enter the scene to rescue captives. Although you might think, 'Great! We're saved!' this is one of the most dangerous moments in a hostage situation. Captors can easily become trigger-happy as they're taken by surprise and are confronted with the prospect of their prize negotiation tool being snatched away from them. If the men in black do come to get you out, here are a few simple rules that you must follow.

YOU MAY WELL BE TREATED LIKE A TERRORIST

SPECIAL FORCES need to make sure that everything is under control before they let anyone go, so you could be searched or removed from the scene by force.
Do not resist. Follow all instructions to the letter.

When it turns noisy and you hear gunfire, hit the floor with your hands on your head and wait until someone comes and gets you. Don't hide in a cupboard – stay where you can be seen. You have less chance of being hit in crossfire if you're on the floor and you haven't got a weapon.

Don't go rushing forward. At this stage, the rescuers will not be sure who is a hostage and who is a captor and everyone will be high on adrenaline. Follow instructions carefully and expect to be treated temporarily as one of the guilty until the rescuers can differentiate between captors and hostages.

9 SELF-DEFENCE, SAS STYLE

SOMETIMES THERE JUST ISN'T ANY WAY TO TALK OR NEGOTIATE YOUR WAY OUT OF TROUBLE. WHEN YOUR BACK IS UP AGAINST A WALL, WHAT YOU REALLY NEED ARE SOME OF THE SAS'S BEST TECHNIQUES.

'BETTER TO BE JUDGED BY TWELVE THAN CARRIED BY SIX.'
TRADITIONAL SAYING

THE ART OF SELF-DEFENCE: PREVENTION IS ALWAYS BETTER THAN CURE

Pull your punches: how to avoid a fight and talk your way out of trouble

On the defensive: getting out of trouble, quick and easy

Striking back: when there's no way out

Getting the f* out:** escape and evasion with the bad guys on your heels

Extreme self-defence: improvised weapons

SCENARIO

YOUR BOSS HAS LOANED YOU his Jaguar F-type to collect his wife from the airport. You've got an hour to kill before you're due to pick her up, so you drive to see your mates to show off the motor. It's in a dicey part of town, but it is broad daylight so you don't anticipate any hassle. You spend half an hour with your mates and then decide to head for the airport. As you knock off the alarm on the remote, a guy steps out of nowhere, hoodie drawn tight around his head. He's waving a knife in your direction and signalling for you to hand over the car keys. Do you attempt to get in the car and drive off quick? Should you throw him the keys and reduce any risk of injury, or do you decide to tackle him with the only items you've got to hand: a bottle of water and a glossy magazine?

BIG PHIL'S ADVICE: Never put yourself in a position where you could get hurt. If there's an easy way out, take it. There's rarely a good enough reason for being a dead hero or even a badly bruised one. If avoiding confrontation fails, you can always try negotiation, but if the choice comes down to a material possession, like a car, or your life – throw them the keys and save you and your family a whole lot of heartache or worse.

Whether you're defending your home from burglars, protecting yourself and your loved one from a drunken crowd or attempting to escape from a mugger, self-defence is an invaluable asset to have when you're cornered. An instructor once told me the best way to avoid being punched was to get out of the way – real self-defence is the art of avoiding conflict. But what happens when things turn really noisy and you've nowhere left to run?

If there's no chance of escape, you've gotta FIGHT, FIGHT, FIGHT!

PULL YOUR PUNCHES: HOW TO AVOID A FIGHT AND TALK YOUR WAY OUT OF TROUBLE

Managing any kind of fracas requires the essentials of observation and the ability to spot trouble brewing – that way you can either move away or defuse the situation before it escalates into a full-blown brawl. The first thing I do when I enter a building is look for the nearest exit routes because I never know when I might need them. If you've missed your chance to walk away, don't forget that it is still possible to talk your way out of trouble. Employ words wisely and they can enable you to take control of most situations.

Avoiding a fight by spotting trouble before it arrives

Prior to every mugging, stabbing or beating, an assailant's intentions will be written all over his or her body. Observed accurately, body language can provide a heads-up on any number of dangerous circumstances, allowing you to make a speedy exit. To de-escalate a situation, you need to know what's coming your way. Here are my top tips for what to look out for.

> You can easily get drawn into other people's crap if your head is up your arse.

The eyes: If you're suddenly aware of someone burning holes in you with their gaze – be prepared. Narrowed eyes and a fixated, dagger-like stare can indicate you've become a target. Excessive blinking and dilated pupils can also indicate stress. Your first move should be to create some space between you and them and be prepared to make a speedy exit. Look for where their eyes make contact – this could be where they'll strike first.

The face: Faces often reveal a person's inner thoughts. In the animal kingdom, teeth bared and eyes narrowed often indicates aggression, and it's likewise in humans. If the jaw appears clenched and there's a grimace instead of a smile, your opponent is getting ready for a fight. Bulging head and neck veins mean they're preparing to throw a punch. Interestingly, as our temper rages, the blood flow either makes us red in the face or a deathly pale, as the blood rushes to the organs, ready for action.

The mouth: At the very moment when you are going to be hit, the assailant's mouth will clench. It's a natural defence for him or her, in case you strike straight back, and is a dead giveaway that events have TURNED NOISY.

The voice: Someone about to attack is more likely to begin by muttering as a sign of annoyance before launching into shouting or verbal abuse. Any alteration in pitch or delivery, accompanied by hand gesticulations, should alert you to an imminent attack.

The body: When someone is about to undertake an attack, their body prepares them. Adrenaline starts to flow, the heart beats faster and breathing deepens. Look for hands that are clenched with knuckles visible: the mind is thinking 'fight'. Observe the body stance: moving to face you side on, like a boxer, means they're preparing to lurch forward with a right or left hook. Movement in the head and arms like a nodding dog signifies, 'Come on, I'm ready for you,' while folded arms and a stiff body may say, 'I'm not easily frightened.'

Routine can bring you trouble

Studies show that many violent attacks, like rape, are premeditated. The perpetrator is familiar with the victim's everyday habits: the same bus each morning to work, a regular Monday-night exercise class, or a shortcut home through the park. Routine allows an attacker to plan whatever crime they have in mind, leaving the victim unwitting prey. But we don't have to leave the house each morning at the same time or follow the same route home. If you think you're being watched or followed,

Try and make your lifestyle as unpredictable as possible and avoid routine like the plague.

do something about it. If we vary our schedule, we become a moving target, and one that's not half as easy to track or attack.

How to talk your way out of trouble

Not all violence starts with an immediate physical attack, some incidents build up from a heated argument or intimidation. Where there's time to talk, you can de-escalate a situation and leave before knives are drawn or fists start to fly. Clearly this won't work in an attempted mugging, but knowing how to defuse a volatile situation with words and attitude can be a powerful tool.

Don't be afraid to apologize. If you're in a situation where you've caused offence to someone, a simple sorry can sometimes be enough to avoid a fight. Act sincere and back off – whatever it takes to calm the situation down.

Keep calm and confident. To take the heat out of a situation, make sure you don't add to the flames. If you can feel your heart pumping faster than normal, breathe deeply and slowly. Keep your body and face relaxed and tone of voice calm. Confidence can give the impression of strength, without a muscle in sight.

Avoid aggression. Avoid shouting, raising your voice, intimidating eye contact or sudden moves that are likely to antagonize an aggressor. Keep all exit routes clear for you and for them. Be gentle but stay firm and never turn your back on a potential attacker.

Never show your fear. It's easy to say, hard to do. Try to keep your voice steady and low – a shrill tone will only reveal your nerves. Stay silent rather than jabbering: silence can be the great disarmer in the initial stages of an attack.

Show respect for yourself. Never plead as a victim – you immediately make yourself vulnerable and more likely to be attacked. Show yourself as a human being and treat them likewise.

Use distraction. Attackers often expect fear and aggression. If you can offer up the opposite, it may defuse a situation. Try and make others aware of what is happening, especially if they look the sort that will help. They may well assist or their added presence may be enough to get the attacker to back down.

ON THE DEFENSIVE: GETTING OUT OF TROUBLE, QUICK AND EASY

There comes a time when all the verbal negotiation in the world won't make a would-be assailant back off. This is when you have to think smart and prepare to physically defend yourself.

The early stages: figuring out what an attacker wants

Do you know what the attacker wants? The degree of violence used in an attack is usually dictated by its purpose. A mugger intent on stealing your valuables may only need to push you sideways to grab a handbag but, if they want a wallet or smartphone inside your pocket, they may well threaten you with a knife. A rapist, unfortunately, has quite different intentions and his first goal will be to restrain you in some way. Understand the motivation and you can respond accordingly.

Remember that your behaviour can affect an attacker's behaviour. In any confrontation, never assume anything until you have the evidence to back it up. Someone may not be out to attack you, and yet the wrong reaction from you could initiate a fight. If you feel uncomfortable in any situation, the best thing to do is move away: the longer you stick around, the greater the chance of something untoward happening.

Some situations can escalate into violence because an individual's attitude or approach has been misread.

The art of creating space

In any violent confrontation, your attacker is going to try and control the situation by trapping you in some way. Do not concede power by allowing them to dictate.

Make noise and lots of it. Raise the alarm by attracting attention from bystanders and, hopefully, you'll scare off any would-be assailants and make your escape.

Make sure the attacker is never close enough to touch you with their hand, foot or weapon. Keep a full circle of space around you at all times. Move sideways, not backwards. Your ultimate aim is to get out of the way and to avoid any contact. The minute your space is invaded, you're likely to get hit.

If you're pinned against the wall by several individuals, use lateral movement to escape. Take one person by the shoulder, arm or chin and move either to the left or right. The forward momentum of your attackers will cause them to topple in on top of one another as you slide out to the side.

Turn your body so that your side, and not your front, is facing the attacker, and keep moving. This position creates distance, enabling agility and the ability to move away from a punch.

BIG PHIL'S **REAL LIFE TALES**

I WAS ONCE HIRED to look after a journalist and, while he was doing his bit in a scrapyard arguing with a very suspect woman who was threatening all sorts, a huge skinhead approached me. I was all but ready to let him have it when he asked me if the place sold tyres. That's all he wanted. If I had reacted or become too aggressive early on, this could have kicked off badly.

Hands off: how to get them off your back

If you've tried to talk someone out of violence and attempted to make your escape but still haven't managed to lose them, chances are by now physical contact has been made. Don't be too concerned. Most attacks start with a grab and there are plenty of ways of turning this to your advantage.

First things first, try and relax and don't be predictable. Anger and fear is what your attacker is both expecting and hoping for, as it makes you easy to control. Take a breath, drop your shoulders, remain calm and act confidently. Once the attacker can see that you're not frightened, you may well have unnerved him enough to be able to end the attack then and there.

A word of warning: learn a technique and learn it well. If you're grabbed, you can use several techniques to free yourself (see below) but, as with any self-defence move, take the time to practise until the move becomes automatic. In the heat of the moment, you won't have time to remember a grip, let alone use it.

Don't be afraid to use any part of your body as a weapon. Kick, punch, elbow, bite or headbutt – forget the niceties when your life is at stake. Attack the soft parts of the body which have no muscle: eyes, throat, genitals and knees. The swifter and more violent you can be, the more chance of pulling it off. There's certainly no need for a two-hour Hollywood-style punch-up. Wherever you decide to attack, hit hard and fast and get out before they can hit you back.

How to escape from different grab holds

Delivered without hesitation, these techniques can get you out of trouble quickly.

One-handed wrist grab: An attacker will often grab your wrist to prevent you from lashing out or to force you to go with them. The weakest point on the hand is the fleshy part between thumb and forefinger. Tighten your arm and rotate your wrist towards the attackers thumb, and pull down and out. If need be, hold the attacker's arm while you do so. Once you are free, continue to move in the direction you freed yourself.

Dig your fingers into the fleshy part of the hand which has hold of you and give it a damned good squeeze.

Two-handed wrist grab: If an attacker grabs your wrist with a two-handed grip, use your free hand to reach through the attacker's arms and grab your trapped hand and pull back sharply.

ONE-HANDED WRIST GRAB

TWO-HANDED WRIST GRAB

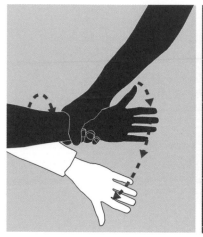 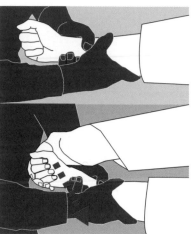

Waist grab: If you're grabbed from behind around the middle of your body, your best defence is to lash out with whatever you have free. Stamp behind on their foot – not the toes, but the middle part where it hurts the most. Kick the shins by kicking forward and back with your heel and, if you can, reach your heel into the groin area. If your arms are free, use your elbow to aim for the stomach area just beneath the ribs. You may be in a position to deliver quite a substantial blow with your head. You need to be hitting the nose and, if you feel any lessening of the attacker's grip, keep going as violently as you can until you are free.

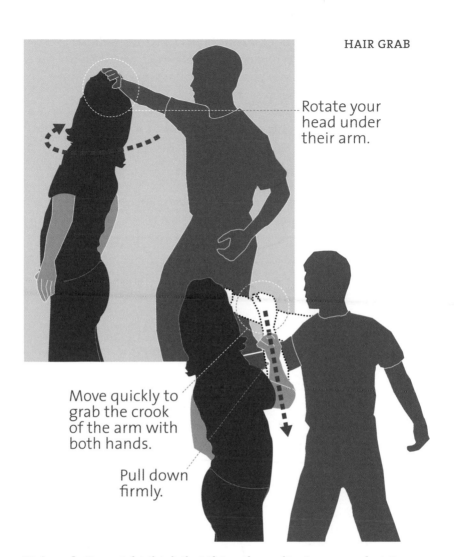

Rotate your head under their arm.

Move quickly to grab the crook of the arm with both hands.

Pull down firmly.

Hair grab: You might think that this only applies to women but it can also be used on men with short hair. Figure out which hand the attacker is using and then step towards that side of their body. Rotate your head under their arm so that their wrist twists with your head and you come up on the other side. As you stand up, move quickly to grab the crook of the arm to get leverage and pull down firmly.

How to escape from different types of strangleholds

This is one of the most dangerous situations to encounter: act quickly to avoid injury or potential strangulation.

The ligature: If someone loops any form of ligature around your neck from behind, quickly take your thumb and stick it down the back of your neck where there's a gap, slide your thumb around to the front to create space and then use both hands to pull it away from your throat.

Front neck choke: Push two fingers straight into their trachea – cavity in the neck – and they'll soon release. Alternatively, a thumb stab to the eye or a grab of the genitals can be enough, but it has to be done aggressively and without mercy.

One-arm rear neck hold: Grab the attacker's arm to stop them tightening their grip around your neck. Get your chin down to stop them pulling you back and choking off your windpipe. Bend over

ONE-ARM REAR NECK HOLD

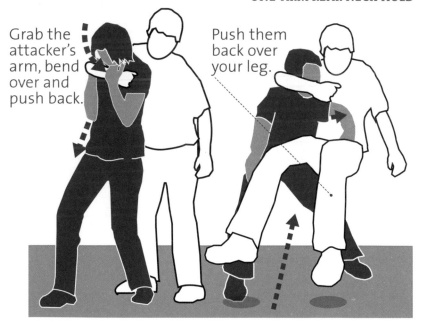

Grab the attacker's arm, bend over and push back.

Push them back over your leg.

and push back with your hips and then, with the nearest leg to their body, move your leg behind their hip. Using your arm and elbow against their chest, push and sweep them back over your leg until they're on the ground.

Two-arm neck hold or rear naked choke: Sometimes an attacker will hold one arm around your neck and the other behind your head in a tight neck lock. Get your chin down to stop them squeezing your windpipe and choking you. With both hands, reach up and peel their fingers and hand off your head. Grab a finger and pull down hard to your left with your right hand, if it is the attacker's left hand (and vice versa, if it is their right), taking your opponent off balance. Follow through by using your left hand on top of your right and continue pulling down until your opponent is on the floor.

TWO-ARM NECK HOLD

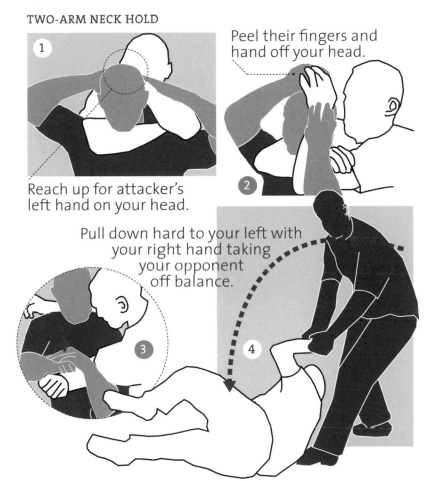

1

Peel their fingers and hand off your head.

2

Reach up for attacker's left hand on your head.

Pull down hard to your left with your right hand taking your opponent off balance.

3

4

Escaping restraints

If someone tries to tie your hands together, never cross them. Instead, keep them side by side and a little apart, although not so much that the attacker spots your tactic. The art of escape is to leave room for manoeuvre.

If someone tries to tie you up around the chest, it's the same idea: take a deep breath to expand your ribcage as much as possible. Once the tie is made and you exhale, there should be room to wriggle out later on.

STRIKING BACK: WHEN THERE'S NO WAY OUT

Hand-to-hand combat can help you to disarm, deflect, defend, restrain and attack. Just don't expect to become an expert overnight – moves need to be learnt and practised to be of any use in a real situation. My advice is to master two or three techniques, add in a decent blow and your chances of getting away from any assailant are greatly enhanced.

Don't forget to be realistic: attacking someone who's built like a giant when you're only five foot five is never going to have a happy ending unless you know where to strike and you strike hard. Weigh up each situation and be prepared, even if it's just mentally, and you should survive to see another day.

Most people couldn't go two rounds with a revolving door. If you're not in training, keep in mind that you need to get it done with speed and get out of the way.

Your body parts as weapons

Each part of your body can make a useful weapon. Use them wisely and accurately and you may find that they're all you need to stop an attacker in their tracks.

▶ **The heel palm:** Use the heel of your palm to strike under the chin or chest.

▶ **The head:** A headbutt can deliver a weighty blow to a nose, eye socket or anywhere on the face.

▶ **The side palm:** Attack with the side of your palm on the side of a neck or in a chopping motion to the windpipe. With the thumb on top, you can bring it up vertically and slice it into the groin.

▶ **The hammer fist:** A closed fist makes a useful hammer.

▶ **The elbow:** Bony, sharp and strong, this makes a good attacking tool and can be used in all directions to strike the attacker wherever they are.

▶ **The knee:** Used with momentum, this is a strong and powerful weapon.

▶ **The forearm:** The inner blade-like part is good to chop at an attacker's throat or to block and push away the incoming attack of a punch.

▶ **Fingers and thumbs:** These can go into small holes, like eye sockets and under the chin, and can be used in a downwards motion to rip off an ear with only 25 lbs of pressure.

▶ **The toe:** In a good boot or shoe, a toe can be brought straight into a shin or the groin area. REMEMBER: unless you are a ninja, only kick what you can reach comfortably with your feet.

▶ **The heel:** Especially for girls with high heels, use to bring back into a shin or to stamp on someone. The average-sized woman can deliver 300 lbs of downwards pressure through a heel by just standing on it.

Preparing to attack

Every violent situation is likely to be different. The best fighters are those who practise and they're also the ones who've gone over every possible scenario in their mind. Do your homework: ask yourself what you'd do if a mugger came at you from behind, or you woke to find a man in your bedroom with a knife. It's not nice to have to imagine such circumstances but it can help you to prepare.

How to deal with a headbutt: A headbutt coming your way can seriously disorientate you if it's delivered correctly. As your attacker comes in, immediately place your palms on the front of their head, dropping your chin to make it more likely they'll hit your forehead. If you don't have time, just drop your head slightly to ensure they don't get you in the face and they may well come off worse. If you can manage to turn their head away by pushing it, then this may buy you enough time to get away.

BLOCKING A HEADBUTT

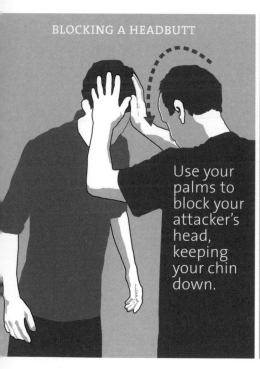

Use your palms to block your attacker's head, keeping your chin down.

Push their head away to create distance.

HOW TO BLOCK A PUNCH

Block their wrist and forearm and push away to the side.

Knee them in their stomach.

Deliver several heel strikes to the underneath of their chin.

How to block a punch aimed at your face: Use your forearm on the same side as the punch to block their wrist and forearm and push away to the side. Use the palm of your other hand to deliver several heel strikes to the underneath of their chin. Use the full weight of your body – including hips and legs – to provide more power and follow through. Reach around the neck with this hand and pull the whole head down leaving the attacker perfectly positioned for your knee in their stomach.

How to escape when the attacker has you pinned on the floor:
If the attacker is on top of you, use your feet to kick and push them away. Aim anywhere that you can: head, chest or groin. If they are holding your wrists, take them off balance by stretching your arms out to the side and then sliding one hand back. At the same time, bring your knees in tight against their buttocks, lift your hips off the floor and, with your arms, thrust them up and over to the side. This should leave you well positioned to knee them in the groin.

HOW TO ESCAPE WHEN THE ATTACKER HAS YOU PINNED TO THE FLOOR

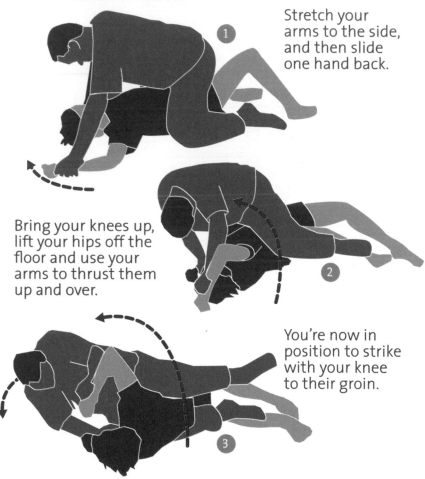

Stretch your arms to the side, and then slide one hand back.

Bring your knees up, lift your hips off the floor and use your arms to thrust them up and over.

You're now in position to strike with your knee to their groin.

THE TARGET AREAS TO STRIKE

REMEMBER: You must only do what you believe is necessary in the heat of the moment. Do not use force that a reasonable person would consider excessive, especially to areas such as the eyes and throat.

The parts of the human body that are most vulnerable are those that have little muscle or bone to protect them. You should employ a level of force, sufficient only to effect your defence.

The eyes: A two-fingered poke to the eyes or a two-thumb screw can temporarily blind someone and, if delivered hard enough, may do permanent damage. The aim is to stop them in their tracks so that you can escape. No more, no less.

The nose: A punch to the nose, especially if it draws blood, will bring tears to an attacker's eyes and stop their attack for the time being.

The throat: A strike here can kill, so be careful. A two-finger prong to the trachea (the hollow in the neck) should be enough to stop anyone immediately.

The groin: For men, especially, it's a highly sensitive area but may not be disabling enough to stop someone in their tracks, so always follow up with a strike to another area.

The knees: A boot to the side of the knee will disable most; any more and it could cripple.

The shins: A firm kick to the shin can be highly painful and is an attractive target if you're wearing decent shoes. Strike hard and fast and repeatedly until you can make your escape. You can veil your intentions by raising your hands to cause distraction while you carry out the deed to the shin.

The feet: The middle part of the foot is full of small bones and nerves – a quick stamp here can stop someone instantly.

GETTING THE F*** OUT: ESCAPE AND EVASION WITH THE BAD GUYS ON YOUR HEELS

In any threatening situation, your best option is only to engage in confrontation when there's no other choice. To walk away or, better still, run might seem the coward's choice but, believe me, when it comes to protecting yourself, it should be your first choice. But once you're on the run, what do you do to escape safely and what happens if your attacker comes after you?

How to go on the run and stay safe

You've spotted your exit and taken to your heels. Now what? Initially, you want to run as fast as you can to create distance, but only until you can find cover or safety. Depending on your level of fitness, you may not be able to run far before you're exhausted, so pace yourself. After 200 yards or so, take a quick look over your shoulder to see if your attacker is following you – there's no point running flat out to the point of exhaustion: you'll have no strength to fight back if your attacker catches you.

Create as much devastation and mayhem as you can by pulling over bins, smashing windows and setting off car alarms to hopefully get people up and involved. The more distraction there is from you, the more likely the attacker will be deterred. You can always pay for a window later.

As you're running, think about where you can go to be safe. Is there somewhere nearby that can provide a hiding place, or a crowd of people you can ask for help? Depending on how well you know the area, keep your eyes peeled to avoid any dead ends and choose routes that are easy to run. If your chosen destination is a long way off, you need to pace yourself and try to find somewhere to take a breather.

If your attacker is still in pursuit, but clearly slowing, speed up. The more distance between you, the better your hope of losing your attacker altogether. Some attackers may well give up at this stage or at the least their stamina levels will have been exhausted.

Create obstacles for your attacker. Throw anything you can find: a tree branch, a rock, even rolling a public rubbish-bin or a parking bollard can hamper their movement and slow them down, giving you enough time to escape.

The more barriers you can create between you and them, the better.

Attract attention, if near a public area. Move to where there are people and, if possible, where it's brightly lit and make lots of noise. Some people won't respond to 'Help!' but they may well on hearing 'Fire!'

What to do if chased by a madman with a gun. One can only hope that you're never in this situation, but, if you find yourself the wrong side of a gun, don't lose hope. Most handguns are difficult to shoot accurately beyond a metre (three feet), especially if the target is moving. Only twenty-four per cent of specially trained police officers and four per cent of criminals actually hit their target within one to three metres (three to nine feet). If you're going to run, never run in a straight line – always zigzag. A moving target is hard to hit and one running all over the place, even harder.

CHANCES OF BEING HIT BY A BULLET

US DEPARTMENT OF JUSTICE statistics reveal the following:

12%	6%	3%
There is a twelve per cent chance an abductor will shoot you in a populated area.	If you are being shot at, there is a six per cent chance of being hit by a bullet.	And a three per cent chance that that bullet will result in your fatality.

EXTREME SELF-DEFENCE: IMPROVISED WEAPONS

If you're tempted to carry a weapon as a means of self-defence, be careful: carrying any implement with the intention of using it to injure is illegal in most countries, even in the name of self-defence. It also puts you at high risk of injury. Many knife-wound victims are often injured with their own blade when an attacker seizes the weapon and strikes out. However, that doesn't mean that you can't defend yourself. With a little ingenuity and imagination, you'll find that there are numerous everyday objects all around that can be turned into handy improvised weapons. Remember, though, if you're going to pick up any kind of weapon, you have to be prepared to use it or the chances are that it will be used against you instead.

Everyday items gone bad

I bet you if I entered your home I could find enough ordinary household items to stock up my very own arsenal. Most people only think of guns and knives as weapons, but they're often not the best choice if you're aiming for self-defence. Look around your home, or when you're next out and about, and you'll find a surprising number of ordinary items that can be used. When you utilize a homemade weapon, your aim is to try and do one (or more) of three things:

- **Puncture:** Stab a hole in someone.
- **Slash:** Cut them open.
- **Crash:** Hit them hard enough to make them stop.

THE ONLY TRUE FORM OF RESTRAINT IS WHEN AN ATTACKER CEASES TO BE A THREAT

ALWAYS WEIGH UP your odds of delivering enough violence to make things stop. If it is you or them, then you really need to take it to the extreme until you are out of danger.

The weapons in your home

In your own home you'll most likely be defending yourself against a burglar or possibly a rapist, so the objective is to hurt them enough that they'll leave.

▶ **Hardback books, chairs, laptops, lamps:** Anything that has weight and can be thrown will make a useful weapon.

▶ **Coins, cans of fizzy drink or food:** Smaller, weighty objects like these can travel like a projectile.

▶ **Hairspray, nail polish remover, furniture polish, fizzy drinks:** Use these as a temporary method of affecting your attacker's vision; some need to be shaken and opened at the attacker.

▶ **A powerful-beam torch:** I always keep one of these by my bed at night. A full-beam light, shone directly into an intruder's eyes, can temporarily blind and instantly stun – offering you a chance to make the first move. It also makes a useful striking device.

▶ **Glass of water or hot drink:** Either of these drinks thrown straight into an attacker's face can provide a quick and simple distraction, giving you time to get away.

▶ **The kitchen cupboard:** Not literally, but any of its contents will do. Pots and pans can make for an effective strike. A coffee mug swung into any vulnerable area of the body – face, groin or collarbone – can disable or slow down an attacker. The weight of it alone can do some serious damage.

Out and about weaponry

When you start to analyse what we carry around with us every day, it's amazing how many of these items make useful weapons.

▶ **Hairbrush, perfume spray, steel-ended comb:** Inside a woman's handbag you'll never be short of an item or two to use as a weapon. The sharp edges of a hairbrush can cause a lot of pain. A perfume spray to the eyes and the steel end of a comb targeted at a fleshy part of the body can help ward off an attacker. Just remember, only use reasonable force.

▶ **Loose change:** As any footballer who's been on the receiving end will know, a coin to the head hurts. Just like a small stone, a coin is hard and can travel a good distance, making it a useful projectile. Easy to carry and reach in an emergency, you can use them one at a time or grab a bunch of loose change and throw it hard at your attacker. The surprise and the pain could well give you enough time to make your escape.

▸ **The pen:** A ballpoint or a fountain pen can be deadly if thrust into any of the soft parts of the body, such as the eyes or throat, but can make an equally effective defensive weapon. Forced down hard into the back of someone's hand, a leg or even the sensitive groin, these make nifty weapons.

▸ **The umbrella:** The most versatile improvised weapon is an umbrella. Choose the long version with a pointed end, if you can, but even the small hand-sized ones have their use. The best part about a long umbrella is that it can keep you at some distance from your attacker, blocking their moves and keeping them at bay, while extending your reach. Use the pointed end to strike or stab and the full length to swipe.

▸ **Hot coffee, bottled water or canned drinks:** Most of us will have one of these during the morning rush hour into work. A scalding hot drink can do enormous damage to an attacker;

SHIELDS

NOT EVERY ITEM needs to be used to attack. A shield is just as important – to protect yourself against an attacker's knife or punches, or to work as a distraction. Wherever you are, look for a large item that can create a barrier between you and them: chairs, tables, public rubbish bins and mobile placards can all create obstacles that will slow an attacker down. If an attacker is within striking distance, you might need to use a more mobile shield: a backpack, briefcase, suitcase or handbag can all make good defence material. And don't forget soft sheilds, like a coat or blanket, which, when thrown over an attacker, can temporarily blind them and offer you the chance to escape, or an opportunity to wrestle them to the floor.

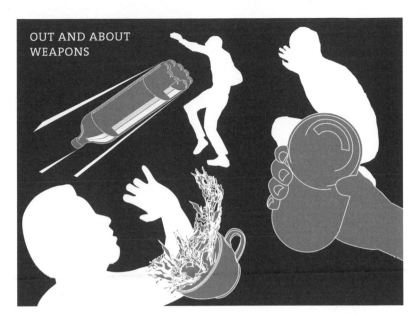

likewise, a full plastic bottle, or even a canned drink, thrown like a missile. All of these offer up the element of surprise and distraction and, in the case of a hot coffee, a nasty burn. While a bottle and a canned drink make good weapons of force, scrunch the can up and you now have a sharp-edged tool.

▶ **Keys:** In a bunch, these can make a very fine knuckle duster. Interlace each key in between your fingers and use them as an effective stabbing tool that will have most attackers on the run (see illustration, on p70).

▶ **Magazines:** Everywhere you go, there is usually a magazine or two going free: on public transport, in hotel receptions or on aeroplanes, advertising in-flight goods. Rolled up in the right way, any shiny magazine makes a useful tool either to bludgeon or stab someone, or roll it up and fold it into two to create a blunt but heavier object. See *How to roll a glossy magazine into a weapon* in *Chapter 8: Surviving GWOT*.

10 THE BARE ESSENTIALS

ELITE SOLDIERS ALWAYS CARRY AN EMERGENCY DRESSING TAPED TO THEIR PERSON AS THEY GO INTO BATTLE: THAT WAY, IF THEY GET WOUNDED, THEY CAN TREAT THEMSELVES. HERE'S A GUIDE TO SAVING YOUR OWN LIFE, THOSE OF LOVED ONES AND FRIENDS, AND EVEN STRANGERS YOU MEET ALONG THE WAY.

FIRST AID: THE ESSENTIAL LIFESAVER

How to save a life: symptoms and treatment for life and death conditions

Medical emergencies: practical solutions, any time, any place

Improvisation: using everyday household items to fix your body

SCENARIO

YOU'VE AGREED to accompany your fiancée and her parents for a Sunday morning stroll through the New Forest. It's a lovely spring day, the bluebell flowers are blooming and the birds are in full song – what could possibly go wrong? As you get into the forest, you suddenly realize just how muddy it is underfoot and curse the fact that you didn't bring your wellies. You're just about to tell your mother-in-law-to-be that she should watch her step when, suddenly, in front of your eyes, she slips, bangs her head on a broken tree branch and is lying unconscious in the squelchy mud. Your fiancée has started to scream and her dad's begun an impromptu coughing fit. It's now up to you to do the heroic thing and administer first aid, but where do you begin?

BIG PHIL'S ADVICE: Even a little first-aid knowledge can be a lifesaver. In those essential first few minutes after a trauma, you can make the difference between life and death. First aid isn't designed to be a replacement for the medics – your aim is to buy someone enough time until the experts are able to take charge. In any medical emergency, there are three vital signs you need to confirm in a person:

▶ **Airway?** Can they talk to you? If not, open their airway, Place one hand on their forehead and with two fingers under their chin, gently tilt the head back.
▶ **Breathing?** Place your cheek close to their mouth and listen for breathing. Are the stomach and chest rising and falling?
▶ **Circulation?** If they're not breathing call for help and then start chest compressions (see *Essential emergency treatments*, p244).

Each year, in Britain alone, nearly three million people go to hospital with injuries that could have been helped by first aid. In a crisis, we rely on the emergency services to reach us, but, in reality, they may fail to arrive in time to deliver the help we need. Fifty-five per cent of road accidents result in death within the first few minutes after a crash. Eighty-five per cent of the victims could be saved if first aid was given immediately.

The fear of making a mistake stops most people from doing what is necessary. Learning to provide basic first aid is not complex; anyone can do it with some simple know-how and practice.

To do nothing is to fail, the consequences of which could be death.

HOW TO SAVE A LIFE: SYMPTOMS AND TREATMENT FOR LIFE AND DEATH CONDITIONS

As a father of two kids of my own, three stepchildren and four step-grandchildren, I can tell you that a medical emergency can happen at any time and usually when you least expect it. I have experienced my daughter choke on a husk of grass, my son pile over and faint after hitting his spine, and my stepson break his arm when I was away, meaning I had to give instructions to my partner, Wendy, over the telephone.

First aid is one of the most essential life skills anyone can learn. It's not designed to be a cure, but it is intended to buy the patient time, and time can be the critical line between life and death. Knowing what to do until proper help arrives really can save a life. When you've got the luxury of the NHS and a paramedic on call, you think you'll never need it, but in a medical emergency it's often the speed of response that matters most, not the medical expertise that you receive too late in the day.

Recognizing the signs of a medical emergency

Strokes, heart attacks and choking are the sort of common medical crises that could happen to any of us, and yet it's a sad fact that seventy per cent of the population wouldn't recognize the symptoms of these killer conditions, let alone know how to respond with the correct emergency care.

The following aims to help you identify four of the major causes of death. It describes the typical symptoms that warrant calling for emergency help, and shows you what you can do in those first few vital minutes of a medical crisis before the paramedics arrive.

WARNING: If anyone you know or meet has a sudden onset of one or more of the following, call the emergency services immediately. Each of these symptoms can indicate a serious, life-threatening medical condition that requires expert medical treatment. Your aim is to keep the casualty alive until that help arrives.

A heart attack occurs when the supply of blood to the heart is blocked by a blood clot

Symptoms: Possible signs of a HEART ATTACK include:

▶ Crushing, tightening pain in the chest, which spreads to the left arm.

▶ Pain in between the shoulder blades, back or jaw, especially if it's accompanied by nausea.

▶ Dizziness, weakness and shortness of breath.

▶ Women tend to experience fatigue, breathing difficulty and pain in their jaw or neck before chest pain.

What to do:

▶ Call the emergency services.

▶ Check breathing and pulse.

▶ If the person is conscious, place in half-sitting position; use pillows, cushions or anything soft and padded to support their head, shoulders and under their knees.

▶ If the casualty is unconscious, lay them flat and loosen clothing at the neck, chest and waist. If they are not breathing, start chest compressions (see *Essential emergency treatments*, p244).

Choking is caused by an object stuck in the throat or windpipe, blocking the flow of air

Symptoms:

▸ Hard coughing, gagging and gasping for air.

▸ If the casualty cannot breathe, cough or speak and is turning blue, there is a serious obstruction that requires immediate attention.

THE HEIMLICH
MANOEUVRE

What to do:

▸ Remove any obvious obstruction in the mouth and call the emergency services.

▸ Give up to five back blows using the heel of one hand in between the casualty's shoulder blades.

▸ If that fails, try the abdominal thrusts known as the Heimlich manoeuvre (see illustration).

• Stand behind the casualty and wrap your arms around them.

• Make a fist with one hand, place this just above the casualty's belly button and just below the breastbone.

• Wrap your other hand around this, ensuring your thumb is kept clear of the casualty's ribcage.

• With both hands, use quick thrusts pulling in and upwards.

▸ Perform the Heimlich manoeuvre five times and then follow with five more back blows, in total, for three cycles or until the obstruction is removed.

When my daughter choked and was turning blue, I tipped her upside down and hit her back. It hurt her, but the husk of grass flew out and she was breathing again.

A stroke is caused either by a blood clot that forms in a brain artery, or a weakened blood vessel that bursts
Symptoms:
- ▶ Face drooping.
- ▶ Arm weakness.
- ▶ Speech difficulty.
- ▶ Remember FAST: Time to call 999.

A simple test you can use on yourself is to push your tongue into your teeth. If your tongue feels lopsided then you may be having a stroke. Also, a severe burning pain in your head at the front could be an indication.

What to do:
- ▶ Call the emergency services.
- ▶ If the casualty is conscious, support their head and shoulders with pillows so that they are sitting slightly raised.

Shock occurs when insufficient blood flow causes vital organs, like the brain and heart, to fail. It normally accompanies trauma or illness
Symptoms:
- ▶ Skin that feels cold and clammy to the touch and has a grey pallor.
- ▶ Shallow breathing and gasping for air.
- ▶ Dizziness.
- ▶ Anxiety or restlessness.
- ▶ Loss of consciousness.

What to do:
- ▶ Call the emergency services.
- ▶ Raise legs above heart level to return blood flow to the organs.
- ▶ Loosen any tight clothing but keep them warm and reassure and comfort them.
- ▶ Treat with CPR if they lose consciousness (see *Essential emergency treatments*, p244).

Essential emergency treatments

Before conducting any first aid, always ensure that you will not become a casualty yourself and that the casualty is not at risk of further harm. If you can, call for help first and then attend to the individual.

If someone's breath and heart have stopped, use cardiopulmonary resuscitation (CPR)

CPR = chest compressions + mouth-to-mouth resuscitation

Chest compressions (hands-only CPR): This can be used on its own when there is no breath or heartbeat, such as in a cardiac arrest, electrocution or suffocation.

▶ Open the casualty's airway and check their breathing. Gently tilt their head back with your fingers underneath their chin and listen and look for breaths.

▶ If there is no breath, place the heel of your hand in the middle of their chest, fingers outstretched and lifted away from the chest. Place your other hand exactly on top and interlock your fingers.

▶ Press firmly down for five to six centimetres (two inches) and release.

▶ Repeat at a rate of 100–120 per minute until they recover or an ambulance arrives.

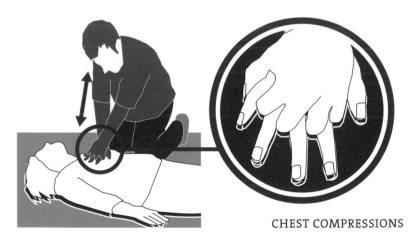

CHEST COMPRESSIONS

For children, use only one hand for compressions.

Mouth-to-mouth resuscitation (rescue breaths): This can be used with chest compressions for near-drowning or for resuscitating children. Give two breaths for every thirty chest compressions.

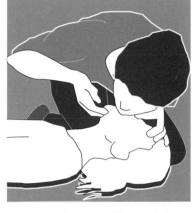

MOUTH-TO-MOUTH
RESUSCITATION

▶ Close the casualty's nose with your fingers, inhale, cover their mouth with yours, and blow in with a strong breath for approximately one second (think 'one thousand'). Watch for the chest to rise.

▶ Remove your mouth and let the chest fall.

▶ Repeat once more, before doing another thirty chest compressions. Continue until they recover or an ambulance arrives.

For children, the preferred method is to place your mouth over their nose and mouth as a better seal can be achieved. Give two quick, shallow breaths. Check to see if there are signs of life before commencing chest compressions.

Mouth-to-nose resuscitation: This is equally as effective on an adult as mouth-to-mouth, especially if the mouth is injured or cannot be opened.

Where someone is unconscious but breathing, use the recovery position

This is useful even if you're in doubt over a person's state of consciousness, as it makes monitoring their situation easier (see illustration, p60).

- Turn them gently on to one side.
- Ensure their airway is open by lifting their chin.
- Place their upper hand under their lower cheek to support their head.
- Place the upper leg at a right angle and the underneath one stretched out to make sure that they cannot roll forwards or backwards.

If someone is bleeding severely, use pressure and elevation.
Direct pressure:
- If any object is embedded in the wound, such as a knife, do not pull out, as it could be stemming the flow of blood.
- Apply pressure either side of any object or directly over an open wound with a clean, absorbent material – a towel will do, if nothing else. Keep the pressure for ten to twenty minutes or until the bleeding stops (see illustration).
- If a limb is bleeding and the bone is not broken, raise and support the limb above the level of the heart to reduce blood loss.
- If the bleeding has stopped, use a clean absorbent dressing and bandage tightly.

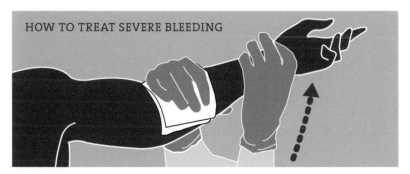

HOW TO TREAT SEVERE BLEEDING

Pressure points:
- If a wound continues to bleed heavily after direct pressure, try applying pressure with your fingers to the nearest arterial point to the wound, to slow the blood flow.
- Locate the correct point (see illustration) and apply pressure just above the injured area, where there is a joint. If it's a leg

wound then apply pressure to the femoral artery, positioned in the crease of the groin.

▶ A femoral bleed can drain you in minutes. In some larger people you may need to use your heel to keep it shut, but be careful to avoid the wound itself.

Elevation: Keep a limb elevated to let the blood return to the heart and slow blood loss by reducing blood pressure. It won't stop a serious bleed, but should be used in conjunction with other methods.

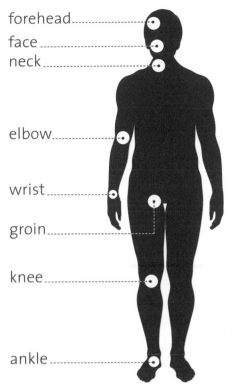

forehead
face
neck
elbow
wrist
groin
knee
ankle

ARTERIAL POINTS

MEDICAL EMERGENCIES: PRACTICAL SOLUTIONS, ANY TIME, ANY PLACE

A medical emergency can happen to any of us at any time, turning our lives upside down without warning. We might get bashed over the head by a mugger, suffer from smoke inhalation in a house fire, or get bitten by a dog on the way home. Any one of these incidents would warrant a trip to the doctor, but what happens if you're miles away from home with no mobile coverage? What exactly are you supposed to do?

Firstly, don't panic. With some basic first-aid knowledge and access to ordinary everyday items, you can sort yourself or a loved one out in no time, at least until the emergency services arrive.

Bangs on the head

It's a winter's morning and you're jogging down the high street with your best mate when he slips on the ice and cracks his head. He's seeing stars and has double vision; he can't walk in a straight line and feels sick.

First aid for concussion:

▸ Call the emergency services.

▸ Apply a bag of frozen peas or a damp cloth to the head injury to reduce pain and swelling. If the person gets sleepy, let them rest, but wake them every fifteen minutes for the first two hours to ensure that they're still conscious, can answer questions and respond to touch or pain (pinch the skin if necessary). Continue this every thirty minutes for the next two hours.

Scalds from boiling water

It's been a long day at work and all you want is a cup of tea and a rest. You're just about to pour the boiling water, when your cat leaps out of nowhere and lands on your head. All you can see is a fuzz of fur as boiling hot water seeps through your thick denim jeans. With a strong burning sensation, you whisk them off to see a red, blistering thigh.

First aid for scalds and burns:

▸ If the skin is blistering, seek medical care.

▸ If clothes are not stuck to the skin, remove them.

▸ Cool the area immediately with cold water for ten to twenty minutes.

▸ Use a single layer of cling film to cover the burn and protect it without sticking.

▸ For feet or hands, use a clean, clear plastic bag and tie to keep the air and risk of infection out.

▸ Keep the rest of the body warm.

▸ Do not use ice or grease on a burn or scald. Ice will cause a dramatic temperature change in the skin and cause more damage. Grease will trap the heat in the burn, which will slow the healing process and cause more pain.

Smoke from a fire

You forgot to get some new batteries for the smoke alarm in your parent's country cottage and have spent the last hour putting out a fire caused by your drunken mate's cigarette. Everyone is coughing and choking, their saliva has turned a nasty shade of grey, and they're all finding it hard to talk as their chests tighten.

First aid for smoke inhalation:

- ▶ Call the emergency services.
- ▶ Immediately move yourself and those affected away from the smoke into clean air to help replenish oxygen levels.
- ▶ Sit everyone down.
- ▶ If individuals are coughing up sputum or vomiting, prevent them from lying down.
- ▶ If anyone's breathing stops, administer CPR (see *Essential emergency treatments*, p244).

Crack . . . What's broken?

Your son is sprinting towards the goal when the giant from the other team delivers a sliding tackle straight into his legs. One of his limbs is visibly out of place and misshapen, he's unable to move without extreme pain, and there's swelling, bruising and numbness.

First aid for a broken bone:

- ▶ Call the emergency services.
- ▶ If medical care is likely to be delayed, make the patient comfortable and wrap a rolled blanket or pillow around the limb to provide support and prevent movement (see *The improvised medical kit: splint*, p255).
- ▶ Tie securely with bandages, but take care that they do not reduce blood flow or affect the nerve supply (see illustration).

HOW TO APPLY A SPLINT

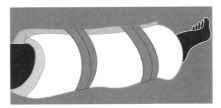

Sprains and strains

It was only a ten-second chase after the dog, but then something went pop in the back of your thigh and you fell and twisted your wrist. Both are now swollen, bruised and painful.

A sprain is when excessive force is applied to a joint; a strain when the muscles are stretched beyond their limit. **Sprains** can occur in the ligaments around the wrist, thumb, knee and ankle. **Strains** tend to occur in muscle fibres, like the hamstring, calf, quadriceps, groin and lower back.

First aid for sprains and strains:

 ▸ Remove anything that may restrict blood flow, such as shoes and tight clothing (unless outdoors).
 ▸ RICE stands for rest, ice, compress and elevation:
  • **Rest** the injured part of the body.
  • Wrap **ice** in a damp towel and apply for fifteen minutes every two to three hours. Continue for the first two to three days.
  • **Compress** using a support elastic bandage or secure a crepe bandage to support the affected area.
  • Keep the limb or joint **elevated.**

Extreme cold

Your friend has persuaded you to go hiking with him up Snowdonia and stupidly he forgot his hat. After constantly shivering for some time, he now seems to be having difficulty coordinating his limbs and is slurring his words.

First aid for hypothermia:

 ▸ Call the emergency services.
 ▸ Move the affected person somewhere warm immediately – even the warmth from a body hug can do the trick.
 ▸ Remove any wet clothing. Use a blanket, hat, coat, scarf and gloves to help restore heat, protecting the head and torso first before the extremities.
 ▸ If they can swallow, provide warm drinks (not alcohol) and high-energy food – anything with fat and sugar.

▶ Do not place them in a hot bath, as this can cause a dangerous drop in blood pressure, which could lead to death.

First aid for frost-nip:
▶ Look for red skin that turns an unnatural pale white colour, especially around the nose and ears, as well as numb fingers and toes.
▶ Move inside or add more clothing layers to the body, including gloves, scarf and hat.

First aid for frostbite:
▶ Call the emergency services.
▶ Look for swelling of the skin and blisters that are coloured red. Apply warm cloths to the affected areas, or place hands and feet in warm water – not hot.
▶ If the affected area begins to feel hard and frozen, and medical care is not immediately available, move somewhere warm, remove cold, wet clothing and wrap in warm blankets.
▶ Thaw hands and feet in water that is at body temperature or just slightly higher and keep the temperature consistent for thirty minutes to thaw fully.
▶ Amputation may be necessary if the frostbite reaches the deep layers of the muscles and bones.

Extreme heat

It's a scorcher of a day, so you and the wife head off for the beach. Unfortunately, on your way there, your car's air conditioning packs up and the electric windows jam. All you can do is sweat and sweat, so much so that your wife nearly passes out. She says she feels dizzy and tired, her heart is beating fast and she appears confused.

First aid for heat exhaustion:
▶ Other signs to look for include cool, clammy skin, fainting, vomiting and thirst.
▶ Place them in a cool environment and provide plenty of water.
▶ If they have muscle cramps, they may be salt depleted. Use a

specially prepared supplement drink that contains the essential salts of potassium, sodium, magnesium and calcium. Most sports drinks are unsuitable as they do not contain magnesium.

First aid for heat stroke:
▶ Call the emergency services if they have additional signs such as a body temperature of forty-one degrees Celsius, nausea, rapid breathing, hot, dry skin and confusion.
▶ Move the person somewhere cool.
▶ Remove as much clothing as possible and use an ice pack or damp towels on key areas, such as armpits, groin and the neck, to cool the skin until their temperature falls.
▶ If the person is still conscious, provide cool water, which should be sipped. Do not give ice as this can cause shock.
▶ If the person has lost consciousness, treat with CPR (see *Essential emergency treatments*, p244).

Drowning

Your best mate can't swim, so when he fell in the swimming pool, you feared the worst. As you pull him out, his lips are already turning blue, his stomach is distended and he feels cold and clammy.

First aid for drowning:
▶ Only enter the water to rescue someone if it is safe to do so and a person is unconscious.
▶ Once they are out of the water and on the ground, turn the casualty's head to one side to drain any water or debris from their mouth and nose.
▶ Check to see if the casualty is breathing.
▶ If not, start CPR by giving thirty chest compressions and two rescue breaths (see *Essential emergency treatments*, p244).
▶ Call the emergency services.

Dog or human bites

You knew that you should never have petted the cute girl's dog. Now you've got two huge bleeding fang holes in your hand.

First aid for dog or human bites:
- ▶ Wash the wound with soap and water and cover with a sterile dressing.
- ▶ If the wound is deep, it may require stitches.
- ▶ Get a tetanus jab and/or a rabies vaccination if there is any potential risk of either.

Insect stings

You never did like insects, so it was just your luck to have a huge bee sting you smack on the nose while you were trimming the roses. You can now feel your face swelling and your chest wheezing, alongside a red, raised rash on your face.

First aid for stings:
- ▶ Aim to remove the poison sack from a bee sting as soon as possible. Scrape it off with a credit card, rather than pulling, to avoid releasing more poison into the blood stream.
- ▶ For all stings, wash the area with cold water and treat with ice wrapped in fabric for twenty minutes.
- ▶ If you suddenly have difficulty breathing or a swelling in your throat, you may be suffering from a severe allergic reaction (anaphylactic shock), which needs emergency treatment – call the emergency services. An antihistamine may help until you receive medical assistance.

Drink and drug overdoses

You're invited to an all-weekend party and it isn't long before the drugs start getting passed around. You decline, of course, but your mate doesn't and he's soon staggering across the dance floor, the worse for wear. He's sweating buckets and is clearly hallucinating as he throws punches into thin air before slumping in a heap at your feet.

First aid for drink and drug overdoses:
- ▶ Call the emergency services.
- ▶ If the casualty is conscious and sitting up, loosen their clothing, keep them warm and remain calm around them.

- ► Collect any drugs, pill bottles or even vomit to assist paramedics and hospital staff to identify the drug taken.
- ► DO NOT put them under a cold shower, give them coffee or walk them around.
- ► If they're unconscious but breathing, place them in the recovery position (see illustration, p60). If they have stopped breathing, administer CPR (see *Essential emergency treatments*, p244).

IMPROVISATION: USING EVERYDAY HOUSEHOLD ITEMS TO FIX YOUR BODY

You're at home in the middle of the night, heating up some jumbo pizzas in the oven. As you pull them out with just a tea towel, the telephone rings. You leap to answer it and, in so doing, manage to singe the entire length of your arm on the oven rack. At 11.50 p.m. on a Friday night, you can't bear to join the inhabitants of your local A&E, but what can you use to treat your red, raw and now blistering arm?

Not every medical emergency requires a professional first-aid kit or even any kind of medical supplies. Most first-aid problems can be treated effectively with some simple household items that even the most unprepared of us are likely to keep in stock. So next time you burn your arm or nearly slice your finger off with a carving knife, open your kitchen cupboards and become your own medic.

The improvised medical kit
Burn dressing: cling film
- ► Cool the area as quickly as possible with cold running water for ten minutes.
- ► If you're not near to a tap, try any cold, clean fluid, such as a beer, milk or orange juice.
- ► Cover with something that won't stick, to protect it from infection. Cling film is ideal, but, if you haven't got that, try a freezer or food bag (empty and clean).

▶ Wrap it around and tie, and you have a homemade burns dressing. Seek emergency help if the burn covers a large, deep area.

▶ **Do not apply any cream, unless it is specifically for burns: any oil will only accelerate the cooking effect of the burn.**

Splint: cardboard box, rolled-up newspaper or a blanket

▶ Improvised splints can be made from all types of material, even a cardboard box. Flatten it and fold it into three sections so that the broken leg or arm sits in the middle with the two outer sections either side; tape into place. Ensure the splint provides support above and beyond the area that is broken. A rolled blanket or newspaper can make good alternatives.

▶ If more support is needed, tie the casualty's feet and ankles together with a thin towel and do the same with the knees: the idea is to reduce movement to the limb and thus avoid the risk of further damage.

Stop bleeding: towels, T-shirts or pillow cases

You don't always need a pristine gauze pad to stem bleeding. As long as it's clean, anything will do: a towel, pillow case, tea towel, T-shirt – even your hand. Apply firm pressure for at least ten minutes to slow, and hopefully stop, the flow of blood. Always keep bleeding limbs elevated.

Hypoglycaemia (low blood sugar): chocolate and fizzy drinks

If your diabetic friend is feeling faint, they may have missed a meal. To raise their blood sugar levels in an emergency, find something sweet like a fizzy drink (not diet), some sugar cubes, orange juice, honey, jam or even chocolate. If they're unconscious, rub a small amount of jam or honey on their gums, which should return them to consciousness.

Bandages: stockings, a pair of tights or a scarf

Use nylons or a shemagh scarf as a bandage for broken bones, ligament strains and muscle sprains.

11 BIG PHIL'S LOCKER

TO STAY ONE STEP AHEAD IN A DISASTER SITUATION, IT'S VITAL THAT YOU CREATE YOUR OWN SURVIVAL KIT. HERE'S A GUIDE TO THE ESSENTIALS THAT YOU'LL NEED, WHEREVER YOU ARE.

SURVIVAL BEGINS WITH THE KIT YOU CARRY

The emergency survival kit: what to include in a grab-and-run situation at home

The car survival kit: what to take in case you get stranded on the road

The travel survival kit: the essentials in case things go wrong

Survival choices: essential kit and improvisations

IT'S BEEN A BAKING HOT SUMMER and now it's raining. The weather forecast predicts it could be torrential – wetter than a sock in a puddle. You go to bed hoping that everything will have calmed down by morning, but at 4 a.m. you're woken by the sound of rushing water. Outside, the main road has been transformed into a fast-flowing river and your downstairs living quarters are now a giant paddling pool with bits of furniture floating freestyle. It's predicted to last all week and, with no power or drinking water, you've been left high and dry, or rather high and wet. You've got some food in the freezer, a few canned items in the larder and a pack of bottled water. What else can you salvage that will help you survive the next few days? And what are the essential items that every good emergency kit should contain?

BIG PHIL'S ADVICE: You can never predict every disaster but what you can do is be prepared. An emergency survival kit – I call it my 'grab sack' – is your means for getting by. It should contain enough of the essential items that will help you stay alive until you can be rescued. There are three elements to survival, without which you won't last very long: shelter, water and food.

Whether you're traipsing through an exotic jungle, spending a week going native in the Scottish highlands or just surviving a natural disaster in your own home town, without a good survival kit you won't last two minutes. The best kits don't have to weigh a ton or have you walking around with a machete hanging off your belt, but they do need to include the essentials.

The following insights and advice are built upon years of travelling halfway across the world to exotic, war-torn, dangerous and unpredictable destinations. It will give you the know-how to create a basic kit that will keep you going in an emergency, and help you gear up for a scheduled trip, whether near to home, or abroad. Most of all, it will ensure that, no matter what unforeseen adventure you encounter – you'll be prepared.

THE EMERGENCY SURVIVAL KIT: WHAT TO INCLUDE IN A GRAB-AND-RUN SITUATION AT HOME

In an emergency, some of us can pack a bag in a flash and be gone, but when you've got an entourage of kids and all the responsibility that goes with that, any kind of trip or journey is nothing short of an expedition. If you want to be ready to go at a moment's notice, the best thing you can have is a pre-prepared emergency kit. This means you'll have a guaranteed supply of food and water, items to keep you warm and dry and essential medications – everything you and your family need to survive for a few days, until help arrives. Whenever I'm at home, my grab sack is always packed and waiting for me in my downstairs loo. This bag never changes and goes all around the world with me. Everyone should have a grab sack ready to go, or at least a box of basics. Tuck it away in a storeroom, or even the cupboard beneath your kitchen sink, where it's within easy reach should the unexpected happen. See also *Survival choices*, on p267, for more details about each element of kit.

The basic kit for emergencies

A kit for an emergency situation at home requires all the basic items your household uses on a daily basis – it's about survival, not luxuries. You'll also need to get by without essential utilities, such as electricity, gas, running water, toilet facilities and telephones.

It doesn't need to be fancy, it's unlikely to cost the earth and it should be customised to suit you. As no one can predict what sort of crisis they'll encounter, you have to consider all the possibilities and prepare accordingly. Most of the smaller items should fit inside a lightweight backpack or sports bag. If you're packing for a family, you'll probably need several. The bulkier items, like bottled water, should be kept nearby in a box. Here's what a good basic emergency kit should include:

Food and water: If you're under lockdown at home or have been evacuated, chances are that resources will be limited. Stock up on bottled water: three gallons of water (13.5 litres or 24 pints) will provide enough drinking water to last one person for three days. It sounds a lot, but you can always use any spare to prepare food and clean your teeth. Non-perishable food is essential: freeze-dried, canned meals, dried fruits, biscuits, cereals and dried milk. Keep at least three to five days' supply hidden away for when things go pear-shaped. If you want to be able to heat food at home or on the road, consider a small camping cooker.

Warmth: Think about how you'll cope if all the utilities, like gas and electricity, go off and how you can stay warm and dry if you have to fend for yourself outdoors. Consider a small back-up generator for the home or some other means of heating and cooking. A good lighter and matches are handy too.

Shelter: If you end up having to create your own shelter outdoors, you'll need something to protect you from the elements. Choose materials that are lightweight and easy to pack; go for a tent, bivvy bag (one-man tent) or, my preference, a collapsible festival tent. I keep one in my grab sack and one in the car. It's small, flat and sits in the boot under a mat.

Sleeping materials: You'll need lightweight and easily folded sleeping bags or a warm blanket for each person, plus a roll-up mat for a bit of padding underneath. Blow-up pillows are handy and small – just don't forget a pump.

Clothing and footwear: Everyone should have a complete change of clothing, including underwear, shoes and socks, a long-sleeved top and a fleece jacket or similar. Natural fibres are best for insulation and will allow the skin to breathe. Sports fabrics that allow perspiration to dry quickly are great but expensive. Don't forget gloves, scarves and hats if you live in colder climes.

First aid, medicines and sanitary items: Make a kit customized to the needs of you and your family, especially if you require prescription medicine. Include soap and toothpaste and add extras like painkillers, flu remedies and diarrhoea medicine.

Light: A sturdy, battery-powered or wind-up torch is essential for any emergency. I always have my trusty SureFire torch in my kit. Your other choice is a couple of headlamps with enough extra batteries to keep them going, or a solar charger. Candles, tea lights or camp lights can offer more overall light, but make sure that they don't cause a fire.

Toilet facilities: If you've got no running water, heavy-duty garden bags and a bucket will suffice. Line the bucket and use some cat litter in between each visit to keep the smell down. Regardless of where you're going to crap, at least pack toilet paper so you have something to wipe your arse on. It's no good using your sock if you're going to have to walk anywhere.

Essential utensils: Cutlery and a mug for tea won't take up much room but will provide a few creature comforts, and don't forget a can opener for your non-perishables and a bottle opener for your beer. A good sterilizing fluid diluted to the correct strength of two capfuls (thirty millilitres) to five litres of water is a useful addition. You can use it to sterilize baby's bottles and their toys. It will also help clean surface areas to make them safe for food preparation.

Cash: In a power outage or any calamity, everything will go down, including the ATMs. Keep a small amount of cash in your property, especially if you receive warning of a pending natural disaster.

Phone charger: I guarantee this is the one thing you'll forget to take on the day of the race. Get yourself a solar-powered one, stick it in your grab sack or emergency box and you'll be connected – unless the networks go down.

THE CAR SURVIVAL KIT: WHAT TO TAKE IN CASE YOU GET STRANDED ON THE ROAD

Most of us rely on our cars like we do our limbs. But venture away from the cities and, when things go wrong, as they often do, you could find yourself stranded in the middle of nowhere with a satnav that's useless and a mobile that can't get a signal. It's at times like these that you will thank yourself for packing a bag of goodies and tucking it away inside your car.

Every car should carry a basic emergency survival kit. Alongside the usual essentials, such as a red warning triangle, a de-icer, shovel and a high-visibility vest, a true vehicle-based emergency kit is one that will take care of your needs as well as your car's. Remember to update it as and when the weather changes or if you decide to travel somewhere remote. Once it turns winter, I add in the snow chains, the shovel and a few blankets; come summer, I'm thinking about a means of keeping cool and hydrated. See also *Survival choices*, on p267, below for more details about each element of kit.

You might think it's an extra addition that you can do without, but, trust me – it will not only take the hassle out of coping with the unexpected, it could well save your life.

The essentials for travelling in your car

Assess the weather conditions you're likely to experience on your journey and ask yourself how you'll achieve a good supply of the survival basics: shelter, water and food. On top of these three, you'll need to consider how you'll

REMEMBER: Before you set off on a journey, consider how you'll provide yourself with the three essentials of survival: shelter, water and food.

stay warm (or cool), whether the type of food you've got will ensure your survival and whether the water supply is going to be safe and within easy reach.

Can you survive with some water-sterilizing tablets and a river or stream? Bottled water during freezing conditions can easily freeze up and burst, unless it's protected from the cold. In the hot weather, you run the risk of water getting heated, a breeding ground for bacteria and a perfect recipe for a nasty stomach bug.

Ensure that you have all the necessities, like sleeping bags and appropriate clothing for the season. In a car, there are also some additional things to consider, like whether you intend to stay inside your car or take your chances and find shelter elsewhere. Either way, it's a case of considering all of the circumstances that you could find yourself facing and building your preparations around them.

Staying inside the car

If you do break down, or get stranded in freezing or sweltering conditions, you must decide where is best – inside the car or outside. But if you stay inside, pay attention to these points:

If you're low on petrol and have no reserves, you'll have to conserve the petrol at all costs. Use any blankets and huddle together for warmth; or drink fluids to keep cool and erect shades over the windows.

If you have a full tank and are only a few miles away from civilization, then you can afford to run the engine and use the heater or air conditioning. Run the engine for fifteen minutes and then break for twenty minutes before restarting. This should ensure you stay comfortable but conserve petrol.

Make sure that the exhaust/tailpipe is clear of snow and debris as you could end up inhaling toxic fumes.

Open the windows every now and again to keep a supply of fresh air circulating.

Avoid using the radio continuously; check weather and traffic alerts only when the engine is running.

The essentials for your car (winter = W)

- **Petrol or diesel:** you may need to keep the car running to stay warm, so always carry an extra five litres.
- **Red warning triangle** in case you break down.
- **Tow rope.**
- **High-visibility jacket** so you can be seen in the dark.
- **Fire extinguisher** – expensive but worth including.
- **Spare parts:** fuses for electrics; spare bulbs for headlights, brake lights etc.
- **Jump leads.**
- **Headlight adapters** if driving on the other side of the road.
- **Anti-freeze gear:** windscreen wash; de-icer/scraper; key lock heater; lighter. **W**
- **Rock salt** or even cat litter to aid grip on icy roads. **W**
- **Snow chains and shovel** (folding or normal). **W**

The essentials for you (summer = S; winter = W)

- **Food:** self-heating ready-to-eat meals, protein bars, dried fruit and cereal snacks.
- **Water bottles** (think about weather conditions and take appropriate containers to protect the plastic bottles from melting in the summer and freezing in the winter).
- **Blanket** (heat reflecting).
- **Bivvy bag** or festival tent; rain coat/poncho as shelter.
- **First-aid kit.**
- **Mobile phone** and phone charger car adaptor.
- **Compass and map.**
- **Rope or parachute cord,** in case you need to make shelter or be towed.
- **Snow grips** for shoes. **W**
- **Sunshield** for the windscreen and side windows. **S**
- **Torch.**
- **Umbrella.**

THE TRAVEL SURVIVAL KIT: THE ESSENTIALS IN CASE THINGS GO WRONG

Travel can either be a pleasure or a nightmare. Whether you're on holiday, travelling for work or even a gap-year student, there's invariably a mishap or disaster waiting to happen, and always when you least expect it. A different language, a new culture and an unusual cuisine can all offer tantalizing delights or a headache and a dodgy tummy.

SURVIVE BY POINTING

POINT IT: Traveller's language kit, is a book with photos of everyday items across a variety of categories, from food to shopping and transport. There's even a photo of a loo roll.

Packing to travel abroad

If you're travelling abroad, even minor emergencies can come to seem like disasters. However, you can take the sting out of the unexpected by packing a few items that should keep you out of serious mischief. One essential for any trip abroad is an appropriate first-aid kit. A holiday in Thailand requires a very different range of medication to one in Italy. You then need to consider which items airport security will let you take on board and what you will have to check into the hold. Every trip is different and you need to build your kit around what you're most likely to need, usually items that will assist in locating help and ensuring survival. See also *Survival choices* on p267 for more details about each element of kit.

I write kit lists and pack according to where I'm going and why. I lay it all out on my bed and I check it before I put it away. It sounds simple and it is.

I plan trips like military operations, maybe not as intense, but the methodology has been drummed into me over the years. It's no good wishing you'd remembered a certain piece of kit when you're halfway across the English Channel, heading east.

I adopt a three-tiered packing system: the absolute essentials, which never leave my side, the stuff which I wouldn't want to lose, and everything else – the spare stuff I'm not going back for.

Absolute essentials

These are the items I keep on my person at all times, mostly in a waterproof pouch.

ID, cash, travel docs: Passport and photocopies plus some spare passport photos. Cash in different denominations, split across bags. Credit card, plus a spare, and travel tickets and reference numbers.

Communication: Mobile or smartphone, which I've backed up on iCloud, and my UTAG ICE memory stick.

Vital extras: A good-quality analogue watch, a pen and my shemagh. I sometimes keep my SureFire torch on my person, too.

Items which I would not want to lose

These are kept in my grab sack and taken as hand luggage. Remember, it has to fit in an overhead locker, so be realistic about what you include.

Food and water: Dried packet food and a few protein bars. Remember to keep them in date. A water sterilizer or iodine tablets, that can also double up as infection prevention.

Shelter and warmth: A small sleeping bag or blanket, and a bivvy bag that is tiny but effective and will protect you from the elements. A few garden bin bags can also be useful as a sunshade, a DIY rain suit, or an emergency toilet.

Clothing: I always pack a lightweight set of clothes, including footwear, as well as normal clothing.

Fire: Common lighters and one book of non-strike or safety matches are allowed on board most planes, one per passenger.

Medication/first aid/sundries: If you're on medication, don't forget to stock up to cover the length of your entire trip, plus an extra week or so, and keep the boxes to prove what they are in case customs ask. For first aid, don't forget the basics: bandages, plasters, painkillers and diarrhoea tablets. Toilet paper and some antibacterial hand gel or wipes also make handy additions.

Communication, navigation and signalling: My Silva compass, my iPad or laptop, all my chargers, including a solar-powered one, and a satellite phone. I also include a small handheld GPS, a spare mobile phone and a small mirror for signalling.

Lighting: A good torch with a strong beam has many uses in addition to vital light. My SureFire Defender makes a good self-defence tool, either to temporarily blind someone with its beam or as a defensive weapon. I also take an LED headlamp.

Personal protection: Alarms or a pepper spray are useful, but beware, as these are illegal in certain countries. **NOTE: Not allowed in hand luggage.**

Multi-tool kit: This saves space and has all the extras you might need, including two knives, pliers, wire cutters, screwdrivers and a saw. **NOTE: Not allowed in hand luggage.**

Extras: A roll of duct tape as an all-round fixer, a sewing kit for rips and tears, a pair of sunglasses and another set of photocopies backing up all your important documentation.

Everything else

Packed in the hold is all my spare clothing and whatever else I need for the trip, whether it's skiing, climbing, working or just lounging on a beach.

And God forbid that I turn up in Ibiza without my favourite thong.

SURVIVAL CHOICES: ESSENTIAL KIT AND IMPROVISATIONS

Creating your emergency survival kit should not be tackled half-heartedly. Remember: this is your lifeline out of whatever hellhole you're in. There's some amazing kit out there for every scenario imaginable, but, unless you want to cart it all around in a removal truck, you can't take everything. So what should you choose as a bare minimum and what can you improvise along the way?

The following outlines my personal thoughts on what will get the job done with ease; the total lifesavers, and where you can improvise by making the most of what's around you.

A kit for task

Your kit is vital to your survival. Make sure that it covers all the bases.

Navigation

As statistics reveal, a lack of navigational skills can cost you dearly: sixty per cent of under-twenty-fives rely entirely on their satnavs, but, when they fail, you're in big trouble.

Map: Unlike a satnav, a good map is unlikely to lead you into a field of sheep when you were hoping to visit your Aunt Ivy for her birthday. If you want to navigate your way across hills and valleys and locate your nearest water source in a disaster, then you need an ordnance survey map, available in paper form or digitally for smartphones and tablets. If you're going on a long car journey or just trying to get around town then a road map or an A–Z will allow you to use shortcuts with a minimum of fuss.

Compass: Look for one that can be read easily and is accurate, stable and fast. My own favourite is the Silva, which is filled with liquid, making for easier reading and protecting the needle. If you're plotting a bearing on a map, you need a baseplate compass, and, if you don't mind an extra bit of weight and a slightly higher price, get one that has a mirror. This will allow you to view the compass dial and your aligned target at the same time, making it far better for accurate bearings, plus you can use the mirror for signalling.

Watch: The most useful watch is one with an analogue display. Using the hands of the watch and the sun, you can easily have a useable compass, (see *Navigation* in *Chapter 12: Old skills revisited*, p290). For me, reliability and precision timekeeping is crucial, so I want a watch that isn't going to lose power in the middle of a disaster, therefore, I always carry a back-up battery.

Nature: Learn how to use cardinal directions using stars and the sun so that, if everything goes pear-shaped, you've still got a means to get your bearings (see *Navigation: Old skills revisited*, in *chapter 12*, p290).

Signalling

These are vital for when you need help.

Whistles: Look for one that's tough, loud and shrill. It should reach around 105 decibels – loud enough to attract someone's attention – and be easy to blow, even if you have asthma. Heavy-duty plastic is better than metal, unless you don't mind your lips sticking to the metal in the freezing cold.

Signal mirror: Alongside the whistle, a signal mirror is the other essential item for any kind of survival, whether you're on a plane or a boat, hiking or travelling within deep woodland. Look for something that's unbreakable, resistant to scratches and, if you can afford a little extra, one that is made of high-quality glass – its reflectivity will be higher and your signal brighter.

Flashlights/torches: LED lights are better for their bright light, durability and the length of time batteries will last. Around 210 lumens will light up an open field, a dark street or your entire bedroom. My favourite is the SureFire Defender – its bright beam is second to none and it's always in my grab sack or on my person. It can be operated with one hand by depressing the button on top, or kept on constant beam by twisting the end. Directed at someone's face, you can temporarily incapacitate them with its bright light. It can also be used as a close-quarter self-defence weapon – its nasty serrated ends making it an ideal striking device. The SureFire is one hundred per cent legal to carry on planes and I've taken mine on every flight I've been on for the last ten years.

Personal beacon locators: If you're travelling by sea or on land and your smartphone moves out of range, these can be used to alert the rescue services by forwarding your exact location in an emergency. Some models are linked with a worldwide dedicated search-and-rescue satellite network, ensuring speedy rescue.

Communication

When you're in a desperate situation, sending a message to the outside world is a top priority. Simple tools, like your smartphone, can surprisingly offer just as much help as the many gadgets out there that cost serious money.

Social media: Twitter, Facebook and SMS texts are now some of the best tools to have in any kind of emergency or survival situation. When the 3G4G network is down and you can't make calls, send an SMS text that doesn't rely on the newer technology. You can even send an SMS to your Twitter and Facebook accounts, giving you access to family and friends – and, crucially, rescue teams that can get you out of trouble.

Satellite phone: If you're likely to be out of range or are in a complete lockdown situation following a terrorist attack or disaster, these should still be working and can connect you to the emergency services super-quick. They're not cheap but can be hired and, if you're going off the beaten track and cannot guarantee a network, they can be a lifesaver.

Radio scanner: In any disaster, natural or man-made, situational awareness is priceless. A scanner will enable you to stay right on the front line of events as they unfold, accessing fire, police and paramedic radios and receiving notification of road blockages and imminent disasters. Download one of the many apps now available for your smartphone and receive live audio from around 4,000 emergency-service radios. The apps can be used abroad but major coverage is currently limited to radios located in the US and Australia.

Clothing

There's no special secret or art to what to wear – it's just about getting the basics right. I have five rules: stay warm (or cool), stay dry, keep your feet safe and snug, cover your head and protect your hands. You can waste a lot of money on specialist outdoor clothing, but layering simple items will give you all the flexibility you need. I'll add more layers if I want to warm up and remove some to cool down (for more tips, see *The big freeze and the scorching heat: Natural disasters,* in *Chapter 5*, p120). What I've listed below are some basic guidelines for what you need to consider, depending on your destination. If I'm doing any travelling that has potential for drama, such as long drives into the wilderness or flights over the middle of nowhere, I'm always going to prepare for the worst.

One thing's for sure: I definitely won't be taking the 1700 to Paris dressed like Crocodile Dundee.

Underwear: This is your inner layer and should fit well enough so that it can absorb sweat but not be so tight that it's uncomfortable. Take care that the material does not cause itching. Vests are good in hot and cold weather and don't forget long johns in winter.

Shirt: My choice is light, breathable and long-sleeved, which gives me the option to roll the sleeves up. They have multiple pockets for storing important stuff, and also a hidden pocket where I keep some rolled-up cash. There's also enough room for maps, a mobile phone or airline tickets.

Jumpers: To minimize space, you need a fabric that will fold down flat. It needs to provide warmth and yet also have the ability to dry quickly. The good old-fashioned fleece still offers a lot of versatility in all weathers. Make sure that you get one with a zip at the neck so that you don't overheat.

Trousers: My personal choice is combat trousers. They're loosely cut, allowing for a full range of movement, and the bottom half of the legs zip off, so I can wear them as shorts. When the leg parts aren't being worn, they can be used for a number of things: stuffed with leaves or newspaper, they make a good pillow; in the event of a broken leg, you could fit them over both legs as the start of a good splint; tied at the bottom, they'll make a handy container, or, filled with sand, a useful water filter; and, if someone kicks off on a plane, they'll even make a temporary pair of handcuffs.

Belt: I use a military-style belt with a plastic rolling buckle. Other than holding up my trousers, I've used mine for many things: a dog leash, a restraint, a spare seat belt or extension, a load strap and spare strap when my luggage handle broke, a splint strap, a sling and a tourniquet.

Money belt: For me, the dodgier the place, the more likely I am to wear this. Good for spare cash, travel tickets and your passport.

Jacket/coat: I always take a jacket, even if it's only a lightweight one in the heat. In the hot desert, where temperatures soar in the daytime and plummet at night, this extra layer of clothing is vital. You don't have to spend a lot. My favourite jacket has a waterproof Goretex outer shell and a warm fleece inner layer that's removable.

Hat: Always carry a hat. In the cold, it's like putting a lid on top of a flask of tea. In the heat, a wide-brim waterproof hat is invaluable. Alternatively, a baseball cap worn back to front will protect the neck from the sun. The shemagh scarf, a favourite of mine, will protect you from the sun and sand, and also offer you extra warmth at night.

Gloves: I like to have what I call an inner 'touch' glove and an outer glove. The outer will keep the inner dry and take the wet, while the inner can be used for tasks that require some ability to feel, such as putting tent pegs into the ground. Lightweight leather gloves are useful to protect your hands if you're using tools.

Socks: These need to fit neatly but allow the feet to breathe. Wool and cotton are good fabrics, just make sure the material doesn't cause irritation.

Footwear: My favourite is a military desert-style boot because they don't look out of place travelling, but other boots are equally as good. Look for something that's sturdy enough to support your ankles, that doesn't allow your foot to slide around when you walk, but isn't so tight that you get blisters. The sole should have a good grip so that you can go across rocky ground without slipping. Just make sure that they're well broken in before you travel.

If you're in a sticky situation, I know I'd rather have some sturdy boots than a pair of Christian Louboutin.

HOW TO CREATE A PRUSIK KNOT

TAKE A PIECE OF CORD and form into a loop. Pass the loop under a line of rope and over and pull through. Do this three or four times, pulling downwards to maintain the tension on the cord. When you're finished pull the knot tight.

Shoelaces: In a survival situation, a spare pair of laces is invaluable. Join together and tie each end around a tree trunk to hang your tarp or poncho over. Sticks can substitute for tent pegs to secure each of the four points in the ground. Tied into a Prusik knot (a symmetrical slide-and-grip knot, see box), they can help in climbing up a slippery slope or shifting heavy kit.

Warmth and shelter

Choose something light enough to transport and that's suited to your anticipated needs. In an emergency, you need to use what's around you.

Bivvy bag: These are light, transportable sacks with a hood which you close over your head for warmth. Best for dry weather, they can be a little too snug and sweaty for some, although choose a breathable fabric and the problem of condensation is minimal. They can also be used as an extra layer to waterproof your sleeping bag. Alternatively, use as a rope to climb down a slippery slope or, in an emergency, I might turn it into a leg splint, rolled up lengthways and placed in between the legs before taping them together.

Sleeping bag: Before you buy, know your journey and destination. What sort of climate are you likely to encounter? Are you going to need serious warmth sleeping outside on a mountaineering trip or just some basic bedding on a road journey? Buy according to need.

Tarpaulin/basha: A large, flat sheet of camouflage-colour canvas or any waterproof material, like polyethylene, can be used to erect a roof for shelter. You can buy one for next to nothing in a general DIY store or online. Most come with eyelets or loops for rigging up with cord or tent pegs. Alternatively, drape over a tree branch and anchor with stones.

Poncho: I prefer a military-style poncho to a tarp because it has so many different uses. In its original form, it works like a blanket-style raincoat, or I can use it like a tarp as a sun shade or a waterproof shelter. If I make a tie at each end, I can even turn it into a hammock, or, in a medical emergency, it will work as a stretcher. The choices are limitless.

The improvised shelter: If you don't have any of the above, look for something that can keep the elements off you. Fallen trees, a hole in the ground, house debris or a sheet of metal can all offer some means of cover. Even a black rubbish bag and two tree branches can be used to erect a temporary shelter that will keep the rain out.

Waterproof matches and lighters: I always carry a lighter so that I've got some means of generating fire for warmth and cooking. Also worth purchasing from any camping shop is a ferro rod – they're not expensive but will give off a stream of sparks, even in the pouring rain. Matches, unless they're waterproof, must be kept dry, as they're useless when wet. Alternatively, I use my compass as a magnifying glass and let the sun's rays do the rest (see *How to make a fire* in *Chapter 12: Old skills revisited*, p282).

Tools

My personal preference is to carry a good-quality multi-function tool kit rather than separate items. It's compact, light and provides me with a tool for all my needs: everything from a blade to a bottle opener. I'll also improvise items, depending on what's around me.

A compact disc (CD): I often carry one of these which, if broken, will give me a good blade in an emergency. Alternatively, a twisted piece of metal, a broken piece of glass, even a shard of hard plastic can work well. In essence, if it's sharp and it cuts you, chances are that you can use it as a blade.

A drink can: Use the underneath of the can to reflect and concentrate the sun's rays to create a flame with some tinder – a bit of fluff off your jumper or sock will do. The ring pull can be fashioned into a fish hook and used with a pair of laces as a fishing line, and the top of the can, removed, will work as a blade.

A smartphone: Apart from the obvious ability to communicate, the light from these can serve as a good signalling device.

A credit or debit card: Most of us will have one of these and they make very good car de-icers and a nifty blade.

Thermal mug: I like to have a good cup of tea wherever I go, so my mug goes with me. Strung over a naked flame, you can use it to heat the water and soup as well.

Grab sack

If you shift about a lot, it's going to get used time and time again. I have had three over the years: a Berghouse civvy day sack-that went everywhere with me during my military days, a black rucksack that seemed to be owned by every civvy that travelled to Iraq, and my third grab sack – a Blackhawk hydration sack. All three have served me extremely well and been a part of my life. I've been sad to say goodbye when each of them eventually wore out.

The sack: This should be sturdy but lightweight and comfortable. It should be of a decent size, but small enough to fit in the overhead locker of a plane, when full. The arm straps must be strong, adjustable and comfy. Check that it has decent-sized compartments: two on the exterior is more than enough for any man or woman for the odd item, like a pen or torch, or even a spare pair of socks.

Carabiner snap hook: Used to secure my sack close to me; if someone wants to make off with it while I'm asleep, they're in for a big shock. The carabiner has a multitude of other uses: an emergency glass or windscreen breaker, a knuckleduster, a clamp or pulley, a tourniquet tightener, a climbing aid and a means of securing other items to your body. Used with the belt, it can act as a makeshift seat belt and I even use it to suspend my thermo mug over a fire.

I am anal about my grab sack: probably the best habit I picked up from the military.

12 OLD SKILLS REVISITED

OUTDOOR SURVIVAL REMAINS AS MUCH OF A CHALLENGE AS IT EVER WAS. EVEN A SHORT HIKE IN THE HILLS CAN TURN TO RAT SHIT WITH THE WEATHER LEAVING YOU FURTHER BEHIND THAN A SNAKE'S ARSE. HERE'S HOW, WITH A LITTLE KNOWLEDGE, YOU CAN TURN YOUR SURROUNDINGS TO YOUR ADVANTAGE.

'ASSUMPTION IS THE MOTHER OF ALL F***-UPS.' UNKNOWN

SURVIVAL IS ALL ABOUT THE BASICS

Shelter and fire: the essentials for survival
Water collection: means and methods
Food sourcing: the art of scavenging and survival
Navigation: the bare essentials
Signalling and search-and-rescue: how to alert others to your whereabouts

IT'S YOUR BEST MATE Dave's thirtieth-birthday celebrations and you've agreed to join him and a few friends on a holiday in Brazil. Sun, sea, sand and good old jungle survival is what Dave said. You're not quite sure what 'survival' means, since Dave is hard pushed to change a plug, but it's a holiday, so you're game. The flight from Rio de Janeiro to Manaus is smooth and, as the pilot comes in to land, you catch sight of the vast dense greenery of the rainforest. Suddenly, without warning, the aeroplane veers off to the right and rolls out of control. When you regain consciousness, you find yourself, your mates and other passengers still seated in the tail end of the plane, now on the floor of the dark, dank forest. Do you stay with the aircraft and trust the emergency services will find you? Set off in the hope of finding help, and some food and water, on the way? Or should you grab everything on the plane, including all there is to eat and drink, and whatever stuff you can find to make shelter?

BIG PHIL'S ADVICE: Survival is about doing whatever it takes to get you through the next hour, day or week until help arrives. If I'd just survived a plane crash, the first thing I'd do is figure out what was left in the wreckage that I could use to survive. Could the fuselage make a temporary shelter, with cushions and blankets to keep me warm? Did any of the food and water supplies survive the crash and, if so, how long are they likely to last? Failing all of this, I'd be looking for a way to signal for help and then I'd be on foot, searching for any sign of man-made existence that could possibly help me get out of there and home in one piece.

You've done all you can to prepare. You've packed your emergency survival kit and even bought a state-of-the-art personal beacon. Now you're off and ready to face the world, confident that you're prepared for anything that comes your way – but are you? Suppose the emergency is in your very own home, cutting you off from vital resources – what would you do then?

Becoming a master of a whole range of complicated survival techniques is all very well if you're planning on spending two weeks living in some remote cave. But for the average person stuck in the middle of a disaster, the only thing of concern is how they're going to feed themselves and how they're going to keep warm. In those situations, the last thing you'll have time for is thinking about which type of flower leaf might save your life.

Having spent years on the streets, living as a runaway, and later working in the most dangerous war zones, I've become skilled at making the most of what's around me. From an early age, I learnt to scavenge: taking clothes off washing lines to stay warm and rooting through dustbins for my next meal. I even discovered where I could get a choice smoke from all the discarded cigarettes outside bus stops, phone boxes and shop entrances. To me, survival is all about being a good opportunist. Here is my guide to basic survival skills, SAS style.

SHELTER AND FIRE: THE ESSENTIALS FOR SURVIVAL

Shelter: an absolute essential for survival

Without warmth and protection from the elements, you'll die – it's that simple. Shelter, more than food and water, should be your number-one priority. In a remote area, with little clothing and no warmth, you will need to find somewhere that will keep you warm and dry. Wear as many layers as you can and always try to avoid the rain: a wet body makes a cold one, and that can be a deadly combination. In every location, you can normally find something that will provide you with insulation. Think about the homeless and how they use cardboard boxes to shut out the chill of a winter's day, how the odd newspaper can make for a nifty blanket, or how stuffing a rubbish bag with leaves could perform the same job as a sleeping bag. Here are some essentials when you're considering shelter.

Try to be realistic: it's not going to be the Ritz, but as long as you get out of the rain, wind or snow and stay warm, that's all you need. Whether you're considering the remains of an air-crash site, a partially collapsed building, an upturned boat or a derailed train carriage, your priority is to locate somewhere that will protect you from the elements and then make the necessary adjustments to make it as comfortable as possible until help arrives.

Before you settle on a location, conduct a 360-degree check of any site that you intend to use, especially collapsed buildings. Earthquakes often have second tremors, so avoid any unstable structures. Look out for anything that's hanging over you or that looks unsafe. If in doubt, stay out. There's no point surviving a plane crash only to die in a landslide.

Shelter in extreme disaster situations

Even in places where you might think you'll be safe, things can go wrong on a biblical scale and at lightning speed. Think of the floods in America or the earthquakes in Japan, China and Pakistan. Knowing where to look when the infrastructure has been altered could save your life. Keep it simple and get out quickly with what you can find. Avoid other parties, who may be looting and generally disturbing the area, by scavenging in pairs: one to keep a lookout while the other does the business. As they say, safety in numbers.

> You don't want to head straight from surviving an earthquake to getting killed by looters.

Plane crash: If the fuselage is still intact, and you've checked that you're not near the fuel tank, you could make your shelter there.

The inner foam of seats will provide insulation and the cushions will raise you off the ground and protect you from the cold.

Natural disasters: Anything lightweight and waterproof can be the start of a shelter, if you're outside. Aim for rubbish tips, recycling banks and shops that may be prepared to let you have waste packaging that can provide insulation to trap body warmth. Items to look for include large cardboard boxes, bubble wrap, polystyrene and newspaper. Use the larger items and cover with black rubbish bags to produce an efficient waterproof shelter.

Stranded in a remote location: If your car has broken down in the middle of nowhere, your best bet is to remain inside until the rescue services arrive. If you have no means of immediate shelter, look for cover. A derelict barn or even a pigsty would keep the rain and wind off your back. Again, make the most of what's around you.

Improvised shelters

If you're nearer home and, for whatever reason, are facing a night or two on the streets, here are some suggestions that could offer you a roof over your head. Only use when you've exhausted all other options, including staying with relatives and friends, emergency shelters and the like.

Car: If you have a car, sleep in it. Some countries do not allow it but, if you've nowhere else, it is an option. Stay in areas that are reasonably well lit and avoid dark alleys – you're only asking for trouble, if you stop near them.

Train stations and bus depots: Open into the night and usually with waiting rooms; if you don't look like a complete hobo, you should be able to get away with at least an hour or two here, and the CCTV should deter any untoward events.

I regularly used to sleep on sidelined trains around Southampton. They were fairly easy to access.

GET OUT OF TROUBLE – BIG PHIL'S TIPS

I DON'T CONDONE breaking the law, but if you're facing a life-or-death situation then you may need to turn to other means of finding shelter. These are to be used as a last resort only.

Boats and marinas: When we were kids, we slept on some of the best yachts in the Solent. They were warm and dry, with toilets, showers and fresh water too.

Ghost gates: Public libraries, museums, pubs, clubs and large shops are all options if you can remain there after they close. Beware of sensors.

Derelict buildings: These can also offer some refuge, but you need to watch out for any dangerous equipment or unsound structures.

Boiler rooms in large buildings: Accessible with a bit of effort.

Underground car parks: Not as warm, but still some form of shelter, if you're desperate.

Making your home safe and warm in a disaster

In a natural disaster, it may be that your home is damaged and you're without gas or electricity to provide heating, but you still have some cover over your head.

Move your family into one room. Insulating a small area will be far easier than a whole house. Use resources around the home: utilize sofas, mattresses, seat cushions, curtains, sleeping bags, blankets, pillows and rugs.

Temporarily repair any damaged windows by sealing them with plastic sheets or bin bags and tape. Prior to a storm, you should board them up with wood, if you have time.

If your home is uninhabitable and you cannot remain inside or you are being evacuated, take what you can from the surrounding debris that may be used to good effect, such as blankets, sleeping bags and anything that can keep you warm.

See also *Floods* in *Chapter 5: Natural disasters*, p118.

Fire: a fundamental of survival

If you're in a situation where you're likely to be cut off from civilization with no means of warmth or shelter, then building a fire may just keep you alive. To create fire, you need several elements: a **spark** to ignite a flame, **tinder** to burn, proper **kindling** to get it started and some **air** and **fuel** to keep it going.

How to make a fire

▶ **Before you start a fire,** check that you're not under anything that could catch light, such as trees, or near any dry bushes or grass.

▶ **Prepare your space,** clearing ground of debris and encircling the area with stones, to avoid the fire spreading.

▶ **Ignite your tinder.** Lay small kindling – twigs and thin branches – in a tepee type shape on top, but make sure there is room between each branch so that the air can circulate.

▶ **Add thicker sticks** on top, still aiming to maintain air circulation.

▶ **Once the fire is established,** alternate the sticks in a criss-cross fashion to help the fire last.

HOW TO MAKE A FIRE

Ignition

Rubbing two sticks together is all very well, but, unless you're a skilled survivalist, the only thing you're likely to create is sawdust. Always carry more than one means to start a fire. Aim to create an intense heat or sparks that will result a flame.

> **Lighter:** Choose one with a flint and wick system, for all weathers.

> **Magnifying glass:** I use my compass glass but you can also use the lens of a pair of binoculars or a camera. Hold the glass in front of the sun until you see a small bright spot. Angle it at some tinder (fluff from your pocket is ideal) and you should eventually get a flame.

> **Fizzy drink can:** Polish up the bottom of the can and hold it facing the sun. Aim the reflected beam of light on to your tinder until it begins to burn. Gently blow on it to encourage a flame.

IGNITION

> **Ferrocerium or ferro rod:** Widely available and sold for purpose, this is a man-made metallic material that will give off a large number of sparks, even in the pouring rain, when scraped against a rough surface.

Tinder

Choose something small that will burn quickly and easily. I'll use anything that I can lay my hands on: the lining of a jacket, the stuffing from a cushion or the inner foam from a car or plane.

> **Cotton wool balls smeared with petroleum jelly or lip balm:** Burns quickly.

> **Dry grass, straw, silver birch bark:** Dry, light and thin, it will catch alight instantly.

> **Lint:** The fluff inside the waste drawer of your washer or drier, and even in your pocket.

Kindling

To keep the flame alive, start small and build your way up.

- ▶ **Twigs, small sticks, dried leaves, grass, bark and pine needles:** Dry and small.
- ▶ **Crisps:** Cooked in oil, ultra-thin potato or corn crisps make good fuel for any fire.
- ▶ **Newspaper:** Several newspapers rolled into a long sausage. This will burn slowly and allow more time for tree branches (fuel) to catch fire.

Fuel

To make a longer-lasting fire, choose bulky material.

- ▶ **Dry standing sticks and branches:** Lay in a criss-cross fashion.
- ▶ **Large branches/insides of dead tree trunks:** Add once your fire is burning strongly.
- ▶ **Bunches of dry grasses:** Useful to keep a fire burning when there's no other fuel.

WATER COLLECTION: MEANS AND METHODS

It could happen to anyone: your car breaks down in the middle of nowhere and suddenly you're stranded without food or water. All you can do is hope that you can find some resources, but where? With a little knowledge, streams and rivers, snow and rain can become a supply of drinking water. A safer means, however, might be to keep a stash of bottled water at home and in your car and replace the bottles with fresh ones before the use-by date.

On average, we all lose between two and three litres of water daily. If you're in a situation where water is limited, sensibly ration what you've got, but not to the extent that your health suffers. Keep all exertion and activity to a minimum to limit perspiration and, if you can, travel during the cooler times of the day. Don't eat a meal without drinking some water, though, as the body needs water to digest. And forget about imbibing your urine – it's two per cent salt and, unless you can purify it, you will only become more dehydrated.

Be aware of the signs of dehydration
▸ **Five per cent loss of your body fluids** causes thirst, sleepiness and weakness.
▸ **Ten to fifteen per cent loss** causes muscles to tighten, diminished vision, skin to wrinkle, painful urination, pins and needles in the limbs and deafness.
▸ **Any loss over fifteen per cent** is usually fatal.

Finding a natural water source
▸ **Always treat** any natural source of water by boiling or sterilizing. No outside source is safe. See *Making water safe,* below.
▸ **Head downhill** – water will always gravitate towards low-lying ground.
▸ **Look for grazing animals** and grain-eating birds – especially at morning and dusk when they'll gravitate towards water.
▸ **The cleanest water** is from a rapidly flowing source, like a stream or river. Moving water dilutes and breaks up pollutants quicker than standing water.
▸ **Avoid lakes and ponds.** Stagnant water provides a perfect breeding ground for all kinds of bacteria and parasites.

Making water safe: sterilization and purification

Boiling water will kill most types of the microorganisms that cause disease. Chemicals such as iodine and chlorine aren't as effective as boiling for this purpose, but they do allow you to keep water safe for twenty-four hours, if it is stored correctly inside a food-grade plastic bottle or glass container with a screw-on cap.

Boiling water
Remove larger debris and sediment by filtering it through a clean shirt or cloth. Find a container that will withstand heat: an aluminium tin can or a ceramic bowl both work well. Heat the water over a fire until it boils and continue for **at least three minutes.**

Chemical treatment of water

Chemical treatment of water is more effective, particularly against Giardia (a microscopic parasite that causes an intestinal infection), if the water is preheated to at least twenty-one degrees Celsius (sixty-eight degrees Fanhrenheit). Stir all chemically treated water well, then leave for **at least thirty minutes** before consuming. This allows the chemicals time to work.

▸ **Water purification tablets:** Available from chemists and supermarkets, these will kill microorganisms such as cholera, typhoid and dysentery.

▸ **Household bleach:** Use only regular bleach – no scent, no cleaners. Add eight drops or an eighth of a teaspoon to one gallon of water.

▸ **Sterilizing fluid (sodium hypochlorite):** Dilute two capfuls (thirty millilitres) to five litres of water. Can kill bacteria, fungi and viruses.

REMEMBER: Do not continue using iodine-treated water for more than a few weeks, especially if you are having treatment for your thyroid or are pregnant, as it can stimulate the thyroid gland.

▸ **Iodine:** Iodine is more effective than bleach in making Giardia inactive. Use liquid two per cent tincture of iodine and add five drops per litre of clear water or ten drops per litre of cloudy water.

FOOD SOURCING: THE ART OF SCAVENGING AND SURVIVAL

Natural disasters like hurricanes, earthquakes and snowstorms can often separate us from vital sources of food and water. One of the best preventions is to stockpile food and water at home, in case of emergency. If you're away from home, learn to make the most of everything around you. Even in the worst disasters there are usually enough resources to keep you going. Survival, in this instance, is about making yourself aware, using what's available and keeping your eyes open for any opportunities of a free meal. Here are my tips for what to do when the food runs out.

Making what you have got last

If you haven't stocked up, you're going to have to try and make do with what you've got and not waste anything. If you've got no power for the fridge or freezer, depending on the temperature, most foods will keep, if stored correctly. The only exception is meat, fish and dairy.

Fridge first: Perishables like meat, fish and most dairy will only last a few days without chilling, so try and eat these first. Eggs and hard cheese can last for a week. Fruit and veg need to be stored somewhere cool, dry and dark, and will keep for many weeks. Cooking meat will give you a few extra days of shelf life.

Freezer: Most freezers will keep food frozen for longer without power if the food is packed closely together. Once food is thawed, you must eat it within a few days, less if you are unable to keep it below four and a half degrees Celsius (forty degrees Fahrenheit).

Store cupboard: Dried food, freeze-dried food and anything canned should be fine for many months – eat these last. Tinned fish, like tuna, mackerel and salmon, and meats, including chicken and ham, will provide protein, and don't forget about peanut butters and canned beans, which also make a good source of protein.

Finding food for free

In a disaster, scavenging is survival. Whether you've plunged to the ground in a plane crash, or run aground at sea, the chances are that you could well find yourself surrounded by a good supply of food in the wreckage, without having to trek off into the wilds. In any emergency, always utilize what's nearest at hand.

Free foods are available in the wild. Fruits, vegetables, nuts and even weeds – they're all for the taking, but knowing what's safe can be difficult, so stick to the basic rules below and always use the 'taste test'.

The food-waste bin

Some might turn their nose up at rifling through rubbish bins and waiting for restaurants to dump their unused food, but, if you're desperate, there's no shame in using food that's only going to waste. Each day, supermarkets throw away thousands of pounds of food as rubbish, just because it's out of date. Bread, milk, fruit, yogurts and convenience food, like packet soup, are all available. It may not be one hundred per cent legal, but it is one solution, if you're in the middle of an emergency without food or money.

Do your homework: Work your way around the stores and restaurants to find out when they place their food out and which are the best spots. Some bin their food on a certain day of the week, others may try to deter scavengers by covering the food with a blue dye.

Discover the quietest time to forage: Be aware of CCTV, and respect the homeless, who may need the food more than you. When you're approaching, grab what you can and then make a swift exit – you can sort out what you do and don't consider safe at home.

Frozen food stores are a great start because food is far less likely to have begun to decompose.

Finding food in the wild: the rules

There's little point in trying to teach you how to recognize every fungus that's safe to eat on the planet, because, unless you have a PhD in botany, you'll be unlikely to remember any of them. That said, there may well come a time when you find yourself left with nothing but the wilderness.

▶ **Always do the 'taste test' first** (see box) – never start gorging on any food.
▶ **If you have any reaction,** such as a swollen tongue, difficulty breathing or a rash, discard immediately.

- **Avoid anything brightly coloured** – it's usually a warning by nature.
- **If you can cook it, do it to the max.** Better to eat burnt food than suffer a burning belly.
- **Any bugs you find can be fried,** but, if you're going to eat raw, carry out the 'taste test' and don't eat too many in one hit.
- **Avoid eating the stems of plants with a milky sap,** such as dandelions. The leaves and flowers of this plant are fine, though.
- **Stay clear of any shiny leaves.**
- **Look out for plants with thorns.** Some, but by no means all, of the berries on these plants can be safe to eat, so use the, 'taste test' again.
- **Avoid any berries that are white or yellow.**
- **Fungi are tricky.** Many are edible but others are deadly. Unless you're absolutely one hundred per cent certain, don't risk it.

THE 'TASTE TEST'

THE KEY RULES to remember:

1 Identify an item to eat, such as a plant.
2 Rub it on the back of your hand or your wrist and then leave it a good half-hour. Make sure that you crush the plant to release all of its juice.
3 If you have no reaction on your skin, rub some on the corner of your lip or hold it against your lip for five minutes. Do not put it in your mouth at this stage.
4 If you're still okay, try some on your tongue – but don't chew – and wait another fifteen minutes.
5 If there's no reaction, chew and hold in your mouth, but don't swallow. Again, leave for fifteen minutes, then swallow.
6 If after several hours you've had no reaction, you can eat sparingly, but cook it, if possible. After eight hours with no reaction, you can presume it's safe to eat.

NAVIGATION: THE BARE ESSENTIALS

It's a fact that, each year, hiking groups get lost and disorientated because they don't know how to navigate and haven't planned ahead. Once you're lost, there's a serious risk of exhaustion, which can lead to dehydration, hypothermia or death. Navigation is both a skill and an art, that needs to be learnt and practised. Unlike cities full of landmarks and street signs, in rural areas, featureless fields, moors and forests dominate, making it difficult to get your bearings. If you're serious about navigating, sign up to a course that will teach you properly how to use a map and a compass. Here's what to do if you find yourself stranded without a compass or a map – my 'bare essentials' navigation.

Most mountain rescue incidents are caused by poor navigational skills, an inability to read the terrain and inappropriate navigational equipment.

Improvisations on a compass

Using the sun in daytime (north of the tropics)

If it's sunny and you have a watch with hands, or even if you have a pen and paper to draw one (and you know the time), you can always locate south. Aim the hour hand of the watch at the sun. From the centre of the watch, draw an imaginary line to where twelve o'clock sits on the watch's face. You now have a segment from the hour hand to twelve o'clock. Divide this segment into two equal parts and you'll find that the line bisecting the two parts points south.

For south of the tropics, point twelve o'clock at the sun. North bisects the angle between twelve o'clock and the hour hand.

Using the moon and stars at night

At night, you can use the moon during its crescent phase – the stage between a new moon and a full moon. Draw an imaginary line from the point of each side of the crescent and continue down until it reaches the earth. The point at the bottom signals south.

USING A WATCH AS A COMPASS

By looking at the stars, you can use the movement of the earth to help you determine which direction you're facing. Fix your eyes on two distant points, such as two trees, or find two sticks, one slightly longer than the other. Insert the sticks upright in the ground, the longer one a metre (three feet) in front of the first. Line up any star with the tops of the sticks or trees and wait until it appears to have moved.

- ► If the star moves to the left, then you're facing north.
- ► If the star moves to the right, then you're facing south.
- ► If the star rises upwards, then you're facing east.
- ► If the star moves downwards, then you're facing west.

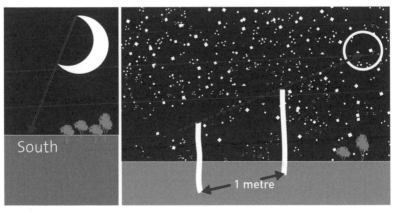

USING THE MOON AND STARS

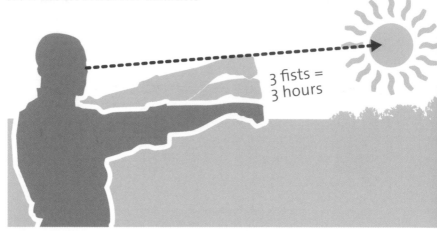

3 fists =
3 hours

Knowing how much daylight you have left

If you're in any kind of emergency situation, it's useful to know how much daylight you have left. Here's one method which works using your fist:

▶ Locate the sun's position in the sky and face towards it.

▶ Hold one arm out straight in front of you and make a fist in the direction of the sun, but lining the base of your wrist with the horizon.

▶ Make a fist with your other hand and place this fist over the first. Move the first fist up on top of the second and continue until you reach the sun. Each fist equals one hour, so, if you counted three, you have three hours until sundown.

MAKING A TRAIL MAP

TAKE A PEN AND NOTEPAD to make a trail map, noting down the terrain, any landmarks or anything unusual that you would recognize again: ponds, odd-shaped trees, logs or rocks. This can help you retrace your steps, if you get lost.

Navigating when you're lost: pacing

So many people go round in circles when they're lost on foot, especially in the wilderness, where there are few landmarks. This method will enable you to search in all four directions and hopefully find help along the way.

▶ Before you get into a situation, find out how many normal paces you take to cover one hundred metres (one pace is a double step: left and right). For me, it is around sixty-two. Use a football pitch and count your paces from one goal to the other.

▶ From your starting point, choose a direction and walk 400 metres, counting your paces as you go. For me, that would be 248. If you're going uphill, you'll shorten your pace, downhill it will lengthen.

▶ Look for any signs of a path or road, agricultural land, or a house – even a fence – that could lead you to help.

▶ Return to your starting point by counting your steps back and then do the same in the other three directions, until you find assistance.

SIGNALLING AND SEARCH-AND-RESCUE: HOW TO ALERT OTHERS TO YOUR WHEREABOUTS

In an ideal world, we'd all have personal locator beacons alerting the nearest search-and-rescue team as soon as we were in trouble, but in reality it's often the case that disasters happen when we're least prepared. That's when improvisation becomes our best friend. Before any journey, ensure that you have a friend or family member primed to request help if you don't arrive or call as planned. Remember, time is the enemy in any survival situation: the longer it takes to alert people to your situation, the lower your chances of survival.

The art of signalling

There are three types of signalling device. Each have their place and you can never have too many, as long as they achieve the desired result of someone coming to rescue you.

Automatic signalling devices

These include devices that will transmit your details to the rescue services, usually for a minimum of twenty-four hours, some infinitely until turned off.

Personal beacon locator: Connected to a network of satellites across the world, once activated, they send out a distress signal transmitting exactly where you are to search-and-rescue control stations who operate twenty-four seven. Always ensure that the device is vertical and there is nothing around you to block the signal. Face south, if you can, to enable a quick transmission to the satellites.

Manual signalling devices

These include signals that rely on the survivor operating them, but they usually have an infinite length of life, so can be used again and again.

Whistle: A whistle uses a lot less energy than yelling for help and produces a loud, penetrating sound which travels further, especially in windy conditions. If you're in trouble, give six good blasts of a whistle and wait one minute before repeating. Continue until someone finds you.

The recognized international distress calls are based on groups of six in the UK and Europe, and three in the US.

Torch/flashlight: Deliver the traditional SOS signal by turning it on and off to give three short bursts of light, followed by three long bursts of light, followed by three short bursts of light.

Brightly coloured clothing: If you can find a clearing and have enough clothing for the task, lay them out to spell 'SOS'.

Mirror: Use any shiny reflective surface, like metallic sunglasses, jewellery or a belt buckle. Aim for high ground and, when you see an aircraft, hold the mirror towards the sun and tilt it so that you

HOW TO USE A SIGNAL MIRROR

get a beam of light reflecting off it. With your other hand, separate
your forefinger and second finger to shape a V (the sign for help)
and aim towards the aircraft with the beam of light through your
fingers. Be careful not to flash the mirror for more than a few
seconds at a time, as it could temporarily blind the pilot.

Short-lived devices

These are the least effective of all the types of signals because
they rely on rescuers being in the right place at the right time and
actually seeing the signal.

Fire: Darkness is one of the best times to light a fire for signalling
purposes. Find a clearing that can be easily seen from the sky. If
in snow, you may have to clear an area. Ideally, build three fires,
either in a triangle (the international distress signal) or in a straight
line with approximately twenty metres (six feet) between them.
Alternatively, you could burn a tree, but be careful that it is isolated in
case others nearby catch light and the whole forest goes up in smoke.

Smoke: In daylight, smoke is more effective than fire. Try and aim for
three areas of smoke. Coloured smoke is more easily seen. Green leaves
or some water will produce white smoke, pine branches will give off
thick smoke, while oil-soaked rags or rubber will produce black smoke.

APPENDIX

The statistics included in this book have been sourced from official research, studies and government based data publically available. The original sources are listed below.

1 KING OF YOUR CASTLE

▶ Office for National Statistics, Crime Statistics: Nature of Crime tables 2012/13, burglary.
▶ Office for National Statistics, Crime Survey for England and Wales: Items stolen in incidents of burglary with entry, 2011/12.
▶ Credit Industry Fraud Avoidance System, Fraudscape, 5 March 2013.
▶ FEMA 'Ready' Campaign, Home Fires, December 2011.

2 CUTTING ABOUT

▶ Office for National Statistics, Crime Statistics, Focus on: Violent Crime and Sexual Offences, 2011/12.
▶ Office for National Statistics, Crime in England and Wales 2009/10, mugging.
▶ NHS Health and Social Care Information Centre, Hospital Episode Statistics for Admitted Patient Care, April 2012.
▶ Office for National Statistics, Crime Survey for England and Wales, property crime, 2011/12.
▶ Office for National Statistics, Crime in England and Wales, year ending March 2013, offences involving knives and sharp instruments.

3 THE SOCIAL SCENE

▶ BC Welsh, DP Farrington. Effects of Improved Street Lighting on Crime: a systematic review. Home Office Research, Development and Statistics Directorate, August 2002.

4 THE CYBER SCENE

▶ Office for National Statistics, Internet Access – Households and Individuals, 2012.
▶ OFCOM, A Nation Addicted to Smartphones. http://consumers. ofcom.org.uk/2011/08/a-nation-addicted-to-smartphones/
▶ The Pew Research Center's Internet & American Life Project, August 5, 2013, 72% of Online Adults are Social Networking Users.
▶ Facebook, 699 million daily active users on average in June 2013. http://newsroom.fb.com/Key-Facts
▶ MT Whitty, T Buchanan(2012). The Online Romance Scam: A Serious Cybercrime. CyberPsychology, Behaviour and Social Networking, 15 (3), 181–183.
▶ OFCOM Consumer research, October 2012.
▶ National Fraud Authority, Annual Fraud Indicator, March 2012.
▶ iSAFE survey, 2004.

5 NATURAL DISASTERS

- ▶ Munich Reinsurance Company, Natural catastrophes worldwide, 2012.
- ▶ General Assembly Economic and Social Council report, June 2012–May 2013.
- ▶ Centre for Research on the Epidemiology of Disasters (CRED), Annual Disaster Statistical Review, 2012.
- ▶ EM-DAT: The OFDA/CRED International Disaster Database – www.emdat.be – Université Catholique de Louvain, Brussels, Belgium.

6 MAN-MADE DISASTERS

- ▶ World Health Organization, Road Traffic Accidents, Fact sheet Number 358, March 2013.
- ▶ Department for Transport, Reported Road Casualties in Great Britain: 2011, Contributory factors to reported road accidents. Table RAS50001.
- ▶ MJ Kallan, Dr Durbin, KB Arbogast, Seating patterns and corresponding risk of injury among 0–3-year-old children in child safety seats, Center for Clinical Epidemiology and Biostatistics, University of Pennsylvania School of Medicine. Pediatrics, May 2008.
- ▶ International Civil Aviation Organization (ICAO), 2012 Safety Report, Worldwide traffic volume: 2005–2011 scheduled commercial flights.
- ▶ International Civil Aviation Organization (ICAO), 2013 Safety Report, Accident Records: 2006–2012 scheduled commercial flights.
- ▶ Galea, Prof Ed. An analysis of the seating charts of more than 100 plane crashes. University of Greenwich, November 2011.

7 AWAY FROM HOME

- ▶ Foreign and Commonwealth Office, British behaviour abroad report, 2013.
- ▶ World Health Organization, Road Traffic Accidents, Fact sheet Number 358, March 2013.

8 SURVIVING GWOT

- ▶ Pape, R.A. (2003), The Strategic Logic of Suicide Terrorism, American Political Science Review 97, 343–361.

10 BARE ESSENTIALS

- ▶ British Red Cross, First Aid for All, 2013.
- ▶ European Transport Safety Council. Reducing the severity of road injuries through post impact care. Brussels 1999.

INDEX

Page numbers in italics denote an illustration

A

ABC check, first aid 239
abduction 174–177,
 206–213
aggressive driving 42–44
air conditioners 125, 157
airway, breathing,
 circulation (ABC) 239
alarms
 cars 40
 home security 23
 personal 34, 266
alcohol *see also*
 drunkenness
 accident statistics 58
 date rape 65–66
 moderation while
  travelling 141, 144
 pacing yourself 60, 72
 poisoning 60
alerting others of
 problems *see* raising an
 alarm
alertness 16–17, 31–32, 35
anaphylactic shock 128,
 253
animals *see* dogs; wildlife
avalanches 99, 100–105

B

banking online *86*, 89–90
bartering 287
bees 127, 253
bicycles 27, 45–47
bin bags as emergency
 kit 265
bins
 as burglary access
  tools 25
 food scavenging 288
bites
 first aid 39, 252–253
 statistics 37
bleeding 243–244, 246–
 247, 255
body language
 confidence 32, 35, 36,
  218, 221
 hitchhiking 50
 on the street 32, 35, 36

suspicious behaviour
 193, 216–217
bombs 191–192, 193–194,
 196–197
brace position *145*
bridge collapses 155
broken bones 154, 249
buddy system 73–74
building collapses 152–
 154, 196
burglary *see also* intruders
 access points 22, 25
 being a potential target
  15, 27
 confirming a break-in
  20–21
 deterrents 14
 in the garden 26
 rogue traders 16–17
 signs of 14
 statistics 13, 15, 26
 stolen items list 21, 26
burns 248, 254–255
buses 47–48, 171

C

carabiner snap hooks 143,
 275
cardiopulmonary
 resuscitation (CPR)
 244–246
car-jacking 40–42, 178, 215
cars *see also* driving
 abandoned vehicles
  191
 alarms 40
 being stranded 262, 280
 bridge collapses 155
 crime statistics 39
 defensive driving 40,
  44
 drink-driving 61
 escape from drowning
  137–140
 passengers 134–135
 petrol conservation 262
 road accidents 135–137,
  168–169
 security 39
 survival kit 123, 136,
  261–263
 theft 39–40
 water escape 119
cash *see* money
CCTV 14, 25, 47, 72, 288
chest compressions
 244–245

children
 begging 166
 chest compressions
  245
 child seats 135
 choking 242
 cyberbullying 93–94,
  95
 as drug mules 172
 mouth-to-mouth
  resuscitation 246
 online security 78
 protection from online
  predators 95
choking 224–225, 242
civil unrest 53–55
cling film as burn dressing
 254–255
clothing
 abroad 164
 avoid attention 34, 36,
  55, 165, 167
 cyclists 45
 emergency kit 260,
  270–273
 heatwaves 126–127
 hitchhiking 48
 layering 120–121, 270,
  278
 motorbike gear 45
 signalling 294
 snow protection 122
 suspicious behaviour
  192, 193
 travel kit 266
 war zones 183
cold weather 120–124
communications *see also*
 phones; social media
 calming dogs 37
 travel kit 265, 266,
  269–270
compasses 268
computers *see* online
 security
concussion 248
cooking emergency
 supplies 259, 260, 275
CPR (cardiopulmonary
 resuscitation) 244–246
credit cards
 checking for fraud 89
 as emergency tools 275
 online security 90–91,
  92
 travelling 163, 168
 virtual 91

credit reports 88–89
crime evidence
  burglary 20–21, 23
  cyberbullying 94
  date rape 67–68
  drink spiking 64
  muggings 167
  robberies 51, 52
crowd control 54–55
cyberbullying 93–94, 95
cyclists 45–47

D
date rape 63, 65–68
dating
  meeting safely 82–83
  online 77, 80–84
  responsibly 67
  scams 83–84
daylight, calculating how
  much is left 292
dead locks 23
dehydration 285
diabetes 153, 255
disasters
  food sourcing 286–289
  shelter 151, 152, 279–
    280, 281
  statistics 99–100
distraction burglars 16–17
dogs
  aggressive behaviour
    37–39
  bite first aid 39, 252–253
  as burglary deterrents
    14
doors
  building collapses 152
  earthquakes 112
  locks 22–23
  preventing entry 16–17
  signs of burglary 14
  storm protection 107
doorstep burglars 16–17
drink cans as tools 274,
  283
drink-driving 58, 61
drinks see also water
  abroad 165
  emergency supplies
    259, 262, 263, 275
  spiking 57, 58–59,
    63–65
  water sterilization 260,
    265, 285–286
  weapons improvisation
    235, 236–237

drive-pass recce 20
driving see also cars
  emergency stops 133
  in floods 119
  roadblocks 183
  safely 132–134
  skidding 123–124
  in snow 123–124
  in tornadoes 107, 108
drowning
  escaping from
    submerged car
    138–140
  first aid 245, 252
  shipwrecks 142
drugs
  addicts 61–62
  avoid being a drug
    mule 171–174
  drink spiking 57, 58–59,
    63–65
  overdoses 62 63,
    253–254
drunkenness
  avoiding others 59
  protecting friends
    59–60
  sobering up 71
  violence 57
dust devils 108
dustbins see bins
dysentery 165

E
earthquakes 110–113, 279
eBay 92
ecstasy 63
electricity supply 107,
  122, 259
emails see also online
  security
  attachments 85
  phishing 87–88, 90, 97
  public computer access
    87
  scams 96
emergency survival kit see
  survival kit
escape routes
  abduction 209–210
  avalanches 102, 103
  building collapses 152
  defensive driving 44
  fire at home 27, 28
  hitchhiking 50
  plane crashes 144, 146,
    149

public places 52, 216, 233
self-defence 232–233
shipwrecks 130,
  140–141
on the street 31, 36
train crashes 150, 151
tsunamis 115
violent crime 176, 220
volcanoes 117
evidence of crimes see
  crime evidence
eyes, UV protection 122
eyesight checks 134

F
Facebook see social media
fake emergencies 17
Ferro Rod 274, 283
fire
  emergency signalling
    295
  forest fires 126, 127
  at home 27–29
  plane crashes 146, 147
  rescuing others 28, 29
  survival 28
  train crashes 151
fire blankets 29
fire extinguishers 29
fire lighting
  emergency kit 266, 274
  technique 282–284
first aid see also medical
  kits
  anaphylactic shock
    253–254
  bites 39, 252–253
  bleeding 243–244,
    246–247, 255
  broken bones 154, 249
  burns 248, 254–255
  cardiopulmonary
    resuscitation (CPR)
    244–246
  children 242
  choking 242
  concussion 248
  drowning 245, 252
  drug overdoses
    253–254
  frostbite 251
  head injuries 248
  heart attacks 241
  heat exhaustion 251
  heat stroke 252
  hypoglycaemia 255
  hypothermia 250

insect stings 253
jellyfish stings 128
mouth-to-mouth
  resuscitation 245
recovery position 59,
  60, 246
shock 243
smoke inhalation 249
splints *249*, 255, 273
sprains and strains 250
stroke 242–243
vital signs check (ABC)
  239
floods 118–120
food
  abroad 164–165
  as alcohol protection 72
  emergency supplies
    122, 184, 259, 262, 263,
    265
  hangover cures 72–73
  at home after disasters
    286
  as kindling 284
  scavenging 278,
    287–289
  storage 286
  taste test 289
  wild 287, 288–289
footwear
  cold weather 121–122
  heels 36, 70, 227
  practicality 272
foreign languages 264
forest fires *126*, 127
fraud, online shopping 89,
  90–92
friends as protectors 73–75
frostbite 121, 251

G
gangs 31–34
garden security 25–27
GBH (liquid ecstasy) 66
Giardia 286
global war on terrorism
  (GWOT) *see* terrorism
gloves 121–122, 272
grab sack 258, 265, 275
graffiti as burglar's code
  15
grey man 52, 201, 209
gun crime 52–53, 176,
  178–179, 233 *see also* war
  zones
gun use 211–212
GWOT *see* terrorism

H
hangover cures 72–73
hats 121, 126, 272
head injuries 248
heart attacks 153, 241
heat exhaustion 125, 251
heat stroke 125, 252
heating in emergencies
  see warmth in
  emergencies
heatwaves 125–127
Heimlich manoeuvre 242
helmets 45, 55
hijacking 42, 200–205
hitchhiking 48–50
holidays, not advertising
  you are away 27, 79
home security *see also*
  intruders
  alarms 23
  assessment 22
  CCTV 23
  earthquakes 113
  fire escape plans 27, 28
  fire-fighting 28
  floods 118–119
  hurricanes 106
  lighting 23, *24*
  locks 22–23
  preserving evidence 21
  preventing entry 15,
    16–17, 22, 25
  radiation exposure 156,
    157, 197
  signs you are away 15
  suspect visitors 15,
    16–17, 25
  timer switches 23
  valuables 15, 17
  valuables recording
    20–21
  weapons improvisation
    235
hostage situations
  206–213
hotels 54, 163–164
hurricanes 105–107
hyperventilation 153
hypoglycaemia 255
hypothermia 250, 275

I
identification
  back up 161
  check suspected
    visitors 17
  child safety 94

travel essentials 161, 265
identity theft
  abroad 168
  online risks 79, 81,
    84–89
  shredding personal
    documents 25
  statistics 84, 87
immobilizers 40
insect stings 253
insurance
  home security
    requirements 22
  travelling 162, 167–168,
    180, 183
  valuables identification
    20–21, 26–27
internet security *see*
  online security
intruders 13, 18, 19, 20
  see also burglary; home
  security
iodine 286

K
ketamine 63
kettling 54
keys
  cars 40
  safe place in the home
    17, 22
  spare sets 22, 68
  as weapons 70, 237
kidnap 174–177
kindling 284
knots, prusik 272

L
ladders for fire escape 27
land mines 186–187
landslides 109–110
lighting
  basic emergency kit
    260
  daylight-sensitive low-
    energy 23
  motion-sensor 14, 23, *24*
  streets at night 35, 36,
    68, 71
  travel kit 266
locks 22–23
luggage security 163, 171,
  172–173

M
magazines as weapons
  202, 237

magnifying glass as fire starter 283
malware 79, 96
maps 267
mayday calls 205
medical kits
  home emergencies 260
  improvisation 254–255, 271, 273
  travelling 162, 184, 264
memory sticks 161, 265
mirrors as signal devices 268, 294–295
mobile phones *see* phones
money
  basic emergency kit 260
  emergency spare cash 55, 68, 70
  mugger's wallet 35
  online payments 85, 89–90
  travelling 162–163, 166, 168, 265
  weapons improvisation 235–236
money belts 271
motion-sensor lights 14, 23, 24
motorbikes 45–47
mountains
  avalanches 100–105
  volcanoes 116–117
mouth-to-mouth resuscitation 245–246
mouth-to-nose resuscitation 246
muggings 31, 34–36, 167–168, 219
murder avoidance 177–179

N
navigation
  emergency kit 266, 267–268
  techniques 290–293
netspeak 95
night time
  navigation 290, 291
  signalling 295
  street safety 35, 36–37, 61, 68, 178
  telling others your plans 37, 68, 70
  travelling 48, 68, 169, 171

nightlife *see also* drugs; drunkenness
  buddy system 73–74
  choosing safe places 68–69, 71–72
  flashpoints 71
  getting home safely 68
  'shark watch' 58, 75
nuclear power disasters 155–157

O
online security *see also* emails; social media
  banking 86, 89–90
  computer security 79, 85, 86, 89, 96
  cyberbullying 93–94, 95
  dating 77, 80–84
  identity theft prevention 79, 81, 84–89
  parental controls 78
  passwords 86, 90, 91
  payment safety checks 85
  protection from predators 95
  scams 83–84, 96–97
  shopping 90–92
  WiFi risks 90
opportunist crime 14–15
outdoor survival skills *see also* fire lighting
  basic rules 277
  food sourcing 286–289
  forest fires 126, 127
  heatwaves 126–127
  navigation 290–293
  plane crashes 149, 277
  shelter 278–280
  signalling 293–295
  water collection 284–286

P
pacing 293
paedophiles 95
passports *see* identification
passwords 86, 90, 91
pedestrians *see* street safety
personal alarms 34, 266
personal beacon locators 269, 294

phishing 87–88, 90, 97
phones *see also* social media
  apps safety 96–97
  back up 265
  chargers 261, 263
  cyberbullying 94
  earthquake predictors 111
  emergency contacts speed dial 37, 49
  filming crimes 42
  muggings 35
  radio scanner apps 270
  satellite 269–270
  security software 90
  as signalling devices 275
  spare sets 55
  survival kit 261, 263, 265
  theft 168
  use in emergencies 153, 269
pickpockets 35, 166
piracy 180–181
plane crashes 143–149, 277, 280
police tactics 53–54
power supply 107, 122, 259
pressure points, bleeding first aid 246–247
public transport
  abroad 170–171
  crashes 150–151
  safety 47–48, 178
pubs, choosing safe ones 68–69

R
radiation exposure 156–157, 197
raising an alarm
  abduction 175
  aeroplane hijacking 205
  intruders 18
  piracy 181
  on public transport 47–48
  social media 269
  on the street 33–34, 36, 232, 233
  text messages 269
  violent crime 53, 219, 220
rape, self-defence 67, 177, 231
recovery position 59, 60, 246

rescue breaths 245–246
rescuing others
    collapsed buildings 154
    fire *28*, 29
riots 53–55
road accident statistics
    132, 133, 168, 240
road rage 42–44
roadblocks 183
robberies 51–52, 166–167,
    178
rogue traders 16–17
Rohypnol (Roofies) 66
routine varying 175,
    217–218

S
saliva test for orientation
    153
satellite phones 269–270
scalding 248
scams
    online 83–84, 96–97
    phishing 87–88, 90
    rogue traders 16–17
    travelling 160, 165–166
scavenging 278, 279,
    287–289
search and rescue
    networks 269, 294
seating choices 74, 144, 151,
    170, 171
security *see* home
    security; online security
self-defence *see also* body
    language
    avoiding violence 33,
        216–219
    basic rules 215, 221, 226
    blocking punches 229
    creating space 220
    dogs 38
    escape from holds
        221–226, 230
    escape routes 232–233
    head-butts 228
    hijacking 201–204
    hostage situations
        210–212
    intruders 19
    shields 202, 236
    target areas 67, 231
    using your body 176,
        221, 227
    weapons improvisation
        50, 67, 70, 202–204,
        227, 234–237

sexting 95
sexual crime, date rape
    65–68
'shark watch' 58, 75
shelter
    building collapses 152
    earthquakes 112
    emergency kit 259, 265,
        273–274
    at home after disasters
        281–282
    improvisation 273, 274
    nuclear radiation 156,
        157, 197
    priority 278
    safety checks 279, 281
    storms 106, 108
    on the street 279,
        280–281
    train crashes 151
    war zones 185, 186
shipwrecks 130, 140–142
shock 243
shoelaces 273
shootings 52–53, 178–179,
    184–185, 233
shopping online 90–92
siege 206–213
signalling
    emergency kit 266,
        268–269
    methods 293–295
    phones 275
sleeping bags 259, 262,
    265, 273
smoke alarms 28
smoke for signalling 295
smoke inhalation 28,
    146, 151
    first aid 249
snow
    avalanches 100–105
    clothing 122
    driving 123–124
social media *see also*
    online security
    cyberbullying 94
    dangers 78–79
    getting home safely 68
    privacy settings 79
    statistics 78
    use in emergencies 153,
        157, 269–270
solar power phone
    chargers 261
splints *249*, 255, 273
sprains and strains 250

stars as navigation aid 291
statistics resources
    296–297
sterilizing water 260, 265,
    285–286
stings 128, 253
storms
    hurricanes 105–107
    tornadoes 107–108
    window protection
        106–107, 281
street safety *see also*
    travelling
    abroad 164
    on bikes 45–47
    by car 39–44
    emergency kit at night
        61
    on foot 31–39
    hit-and-runs 137, *138*
    hitchhiking 48–50
    on public transport
        47–48, 178
    riots 53–55
    robberies 51–52
    safe routes 32, 35, 48
    shootings 52–53, 233
    terrorism 194–195
stroke 242–243
suffocation 28, 104
suicide bombers 192–196
sun as navigation aid 290,
    292
sun protection 122, 126–127
survival essentials 10–11,
    257, 261
survival kit
    basic emergency kit 122,
        258–261
    in the car 123, 136, 139,
        261–263
    earthquakes 113
    first aid 260
    floods 118
    on foot 61
    travelling 184, 264–266
swimming 146–147, *148*

T
taste test 289
taxis 68, 70, 159, 170, 178
tear gas 54–55
terrorism
    biological or chemical
        attacks 198–199
    dirty bombs 196–197
    hijacking 200–205

identifying suspicious
    activity 189, 190–193
siege 206–213
suicide bombers
    192–196
timer switches 23
tinder 283
toilet facilities in
    emergencies 260, 265
tongue as stroke indicator
    243
tools
    improvisation 274–275
    multi-function in travel
        kit 266, 274
torches
    as self-defence 19, 128,
        235, 266, 269
    signalling 294
    specifications 269
    travel kit 143, 265, 266,
        269
tornadoes 107–108
traffic
    abroad 169
    keep your distance 41,
        46, 47, 124, 133
trail maps 292
trains
    abroad 170–171
    crashes 150–151
    safety 47–48
travelling see also street
    safety
    clothing 270–273
    first aid kit 264
    foreign travel advice
        160, 167, 177, 180, 182
    hand luggage 265,
        266, 275
    hijacking 200–205
    insurance 162
    kidnap 174–177
    language survival 264
    luggage security 163,
        171, 172–173
    night time 48, 68
    packing 265
    passports and visas
        161, 265
    planning journeys 169,
        171, 183
    public transport 47–48
    recording your journey
        49
    road accidents 168–169
    scams 160, 165–166

survival kit 162–163,
    264–266
telling others your
    plans 37, 48, 49, 68,
    70, 160, 180, 293
war zones 181–187
weapons improvisation
    235–236
trousers 142, 271
tsunamis 113, 114–115
Twitter see social media

U
UTAG ICE memory sticks
    161, 265

V
valuables
    abroad 163–164, 165,
        167
    in the car 39
    in the garden 26
    in the home 15, 17
    identification 20–21,
        26–27, 39
    on public transport 47
    on the street 34, 35, 68,
        165, 167
violence see also self-
    defence
    attacker's motivation
        219
    avoidance 216–219
    drug overdoses 63
    drunkenness 57
    gangs 31–34
    road rage 42–44
    shootings 52–53, 233
    statistics 34
volcanoes 116–117

W
walking
    avoid the dark 48
    confidence 32, 35, 36
    floods 119
war zones 181–187
warmth in emergencies
    see also fire lighting
    clothing 270
    emergency kit 259, 265,
        266, 273–274
    at home 281
watches 268
    as compass 290, 291
water see also drinks
    abroad 165

collection in
    emergencies 284–285
drowning first aid 245,
    252
emergency supplies
    122, 184, 259, 262, 263
escaping from
    submerged car
    137–140
floods 118–120
hangover prevention 72
plane crashes 146–148
shipwrecks 130, 140–142
sources 285
staying afloat 147–148
sterilization 260, 265,
    285–286
tsunamis 113, 114–115
water cannon 54
water spouts 108
weapons improvisation
    50, 67, 70, 202–204, 227,
    234–237, 235
weather hazards
    biking 46
    extreme cold 120–124
    heatwaves 125–127
websites 85, 96
whistles 268, 294
WiFi, public-access risks 90
wildlife
    avoiding attack 127–129
    earthquake predictors
        111
    tsunami predictors 114
windows
    burglary access points
        22
    confirming a break-in
        20–21
    earthquakes 112
    escaping from
        submerged car
        138–140
    fire escape plans 27
    heat protection 125–126
    storm protection 106–
        107, 281
    valuables on display 22
women
    clothing 50, 66
    date rape 65–68
    as drug mules 172
    drunkenness 59
    hitchhiking 50
    online dating 82
    stiletto weapons 70, 227

Dedicated to Chad Cain, RIP who treated me like a son and taught me so many important lessons about soldiering and life.

ACKNOWLEDGEMENTS

Thanks to Richard Milner, David North, Josh Ireland and all their colleagues at Quercus for buying into another of my ideas. To Annabel Merullo, my literary agent for being there again, to Digby Halsby, the publicist at Flint PR and to Damien Lewis, who wrote the original book proposal.

Special Thanks to Julie Davies for putting up with my lunacy and helping to make the project work. To Jack P for finding me a job which afforded me the time to do this, and Terrence the Turtle Royal Marine for washing up when I said I was busy writing (he loved it). To The Barrel (Jerusalem's finest bar) for putting up with my drunken antics whilst letting off steam, and to everyone I ever served with or worked alongside on the circuit – you have all contributed.

A big thank you to the NSPCC for their invaluable advice on how to protect our children in today's online world. To Nick, a very good friend and pilot for checking our section on airplane emergencies. The drinks are on me the next time I see you at The Royal Oak, Blean Common.

Finally, to everyone who has bought my books so far and helped keep me interested in pursuing my writing – thank you.

Quercus Editions Ltd
55 Baker Street
7th floor, South Block
London
W1U 8EW

First published in 2014

A catalogue record of this book is available from the British Library

ISBN 978 1 78206 852 5

Designed by Austin Taylor
Illustrations by Glyn Walton

Printed and bound in Portugal

10 9 8 7 6 5 4 3 2 1